"This book is elegant, subtle, and spacious honest. Therefore it can be extremely useful to those with serious aspirations to teach and those who already do teach mindfulness in the forms of mindfulness-based stress reduction (MBSR), mindfulness-based cognitive therapy (MBCT), and beyond. You can learn a lot about yourself by incorporating Brandsma's high-resolution perspective into your own meditation practice and attending carefully to what if offers, both inwardly, and in terms of your own teaching. You will find that it is your own emergent embodied learning from the process that does all the work, only then it is not exactly 'work,' or entirely a matter of 'doing.'"

—**Jon Kabat-Zinn**, founder of mindfulness-based stress reduction (MBSR) and author of *Full Catastrophe Living* and *Coming to Our Senses*

"This is a must-have book for anyone interested in teaching mindfulness! Brandsma shares his considerable knowledge of the ins and outs of teaching in a way that is incredibly helpful, including lots of concrete examples of esoteric practices like inquiry which make the process of teaching mindfulness much easier and straight-forward. I wish I'd had this book when I was first learning to teach."

—**Kristin Neff, PhD**, associate professor in the department of educational psychology at The University of Texas at Austin, and author of *Self-Compassion*

"This is an outstanding and welcome book! With clarity and insight based in extensive personal practice, and considerable experience teaching mindfulness, Rob Brandsma identifies essential skills and competencies, and provides in-depth examples, including scripts, citations, and historical context, to help the aspiring or experienced teacher grow, enrich, and deepen their mindfulness work with others."

—**Jeffrey Brantley, MD**, founder and director of the Mindfulness Based Stress Reduction program at Duke Integrative Medicine, author of *Calming Your Angry Mind*, and coauthor of *Daily Meditations for Calming Your Anxious Mind*

"Mindfulness transforms lives. Rob's warm but practical book will help you do this ever more effectively."

—**Danny Penman, PhD**, coauthor of the international bestseller, *Mindfulness*

"As someone who has been involved in the teaching of mindfulness since it was first brought to the United States, I found myself continually applauding *The Mindfulness Teaching Guide* for its accuracy (not easily attained), depth, and usefulness. It will carry forward the fields of mindfulness studies and application."

—**Sharon Salzberg**, cofounder of the Insight Meditation Society and author of *Lovingkindness* and *Real Happiness*

"Teaching mindfulness is as much an art as a science. It requires a firm understanding of how mindfulness can serve to reduce stress and alleviate suffering as much as the ability to make this understanding come alive, intuitively and intellectually, for others. This book is a wonderful gift. It goes far beyond what any manual can offer, and opens the reader's perspective to what might be referred to as the 'hidden curriculum.' It serves as a companion and wise teacher, providing answers and insights from the minute details of teaching to the broader view on the inner journey of becoming a teacher. Few people are as exceptionally well placed to serve as a guide on this journey as Rob Brandsma is, having taught and supported hundreds of teachers at his center in Amsterdam, Netherlands. This book will be treasured by anyone who is passionate about teaching mindfulness."

—**Thorsten Barnhofer, PhD**, associate professor at the University of Exeter, and coauthor of *Mindfulness and the Transformation of Despair*

"This how-to guide to teaching MBSR fills an important gap, and does so with great skill, discernment, and heart. Rob Brandsma's wealth of experience shines through as he explains the artistry and practical skills of MBSR teaching. He tackles some of the most important questions inviting teachers to be the very best teachers they can be in the service of their clients, but never losing sight of the heart as the compass for this work. It is a beautifully rich and practical contribution."

—**Willem Kuyken**, professor of clinical psychology in the department of psychiatry at the University of Oxford

"This book is the most comprehensive guide to teaching mindfulness to date. Rob Brandsma, who has taught mindfulness for many years, including at the Dutch Parliament, systematically unpacks and addresses the subtle details of the art. No question is left unanswered. Both seasoned and novice mindfulness teachers will want this book as a reference for years to come."

—**Christopher Germer, PhD**, clinical instructor at Harvard Medical School, and author of *The Mindful Path to Self-Compassion*

"This lovely book is full of the sort of wisdom and insight that comes from long and thoughtful experience. The author obviously teaches a lot, and pays attention to exactly what's happening. He understands the limits of words, yet offers clear explanations and nice examples of helpful ways to phrase things. Highly recommended."

—**Ruth Baer**, author of *The Practicing Happiness Workbook*

"This book is a great contribution. The subtleties and nuances of the subject come alive in the writing. It very beautifully articulates the essence of the mindfulness-based teaching process, and will be a great support to developing teachers (all of us!)."

—**Rebecca Crane, PhD**, director at the Centre for Mindfulness Research and Practice at Bangor University in the United Kingdom

"Rob is a dear colleague of mine and I have greatly enjoyed teaching together. I warmly recommend his book for both mindfulness teachers to be, and experienced mindfulness teachers. May it not only enhance their own mindfulness skills, but also that of their participants!"

—**Anne Speckens**, professor of psychiatry, and founder and director of the Radboud University Medical Centre for Mindfulness in Nijmegen, Netherlands

"As mindfulness training becomes ever more popular, more and more people are drawn to share their experience of it. Sadly, not all of these have taken the time to train appropriately. Rob Brandsma has a deep understanding of MBSR and other mindfulness-based approaches, and the wisdom he shares in this book will be a great help to anyone setting out on the path of teaching mindfulness to others."

—**Michael Chaskalson**, author of *Mindfulness in Eight Weeks*

"Based on years of experience, Rob Brandsma offers mindfulness teachers clear, step-by-step guidance for leading students through the often-challenging adventure of learning mindfulness practices. Filled with detailed, real-world examples, this book offers us a caring, balanced, seasoned mentor at our side as we strive to help our students live richer, more awakened lives."

—**Ronald D. Siegel, PsyD**, part-time assistant professor of psychology at Harvard Medical School, and author of *The Mindfulness Solution*

The
Mindfulness
TEACHING GUIDE

Essential Skills &
Competencies
for Teaching
Mindfulness-Based
Interventions

ROB BRANDSMA

New Harbinger Publications, Inc.

Cover design by Amy Shoup

Acquired by Jess O'Brien

Edited by Jasmine Star

Indexed by James Minkin

Library of Congress Cataloging-in-Publication Data on file

19   18   17

10   9   8   7   6   5   4   3   2   1   First Printing

A young meditation practitioner saw his teacher walking on the other side of the river. He yelled over to the teacher, "Wise one, can you tell me how to get to the other side?"

The teacher yelled back, "You are already on the other side."

—Zen proverb

Contents

Introduction

Mindfulness, the capacity to be with and in the constant flow of awareness, is an inherent ability that we all share: It's not so much a gift as a given. The real gift, then, is the teaching of mindfulness.

—Donald McCown, Diane Reibel, and Marc Micozzi

My Lord, why do I storm heaven for answers that are already in my heart? Every grace I need…has been given me… Oh lead me to the beyond within.

—Macrina Wiederkehr

Mindfulness training is the art of putting our splendid ability for self-awareness into practice. Mindfulness is about receiving the present moment, with all its nuances and depths, in an open and welcoming manner.

Mindfulness is something that can only be experienced by the individual, yet many people do try to write about it because mindfulness is something people can practice, and this practice can be facilitated through training. For training, a teacher is required. And teaching mindfulness is a task that must strike a balance between art and methodology, which is indeed something one can write a thing or two about.

Mindfulness training teaches people to deal in a more conscious way with the challenges that are part and parcel of life. It also increases the quality and intensity of people's daily life by helping them be more present. It is, in short, a training that teaches people to live more consciously.

The essence of mindfulness practices stems from Buddhist traditions, which aren't familiar to many people in the West. Yet now, halfway into the second decade of the twenty-first century, mindfulness has found its way into many sectors of Western society, from hospitals to therapeutic institutions, and from the financial world to leading Internet companies. People from many different walks of life are signing up for mindfulness training.

One key reason for this success is the solid evidence base that has been built through hundreds of scientific studies. Mindfulness works! This explains, in part, why it's been applied so widely and why it's taken off in such a big way in the West.

The Intention of This Book

In tandem with the spread of mindfulness in the West, there has been a huge increase in the number of scientific publications and books on the subject. However, publications and books about *teaching* mindfulness are largely conspicuous by their absence.[1] This book seeks to fill that void. It is the first book to systematically address the skills and competencies needed and is intended for anyone who is interested in teaching mindfulness.

Given that mindfulness is about being in the moment, mindfulness teaching also needs to have a strong link to the present moment. Mindfulness teaching is, therefore, more a way of being than a way of doing. Consequently, highly personal concepts such as competencies and embodiment are crucial in a teacher's development. This book deals with what is needed for that development—the way of doing *and* the way of being. To that end, it outlines the competencies and embodiment needed for mindfulness teachers to open up again and again to the most important question they face: What does this specific learning moment ask from me?

Mindfulness Takes Root in the West: MBSR

In the spring of 1979, Jon Kabat-Zinn (then a molecular biologist) was on a meditation retreat conducted by vipassana teachers Christopher Titmuss and Christina Feldman. On the afternoon of the tenth day, he had a sudden, ten-to-fifteen-second flash of insight that presented a fully formed idea on an issue that had been occupying him for considerable time: "The flash had to do with the question of how to take the heart of something as meaningful, as sacred if you will, as Buddha Dharma and bring it into the world in a way that doesn't dilute, profane, or distort it, but at the same time is not locked into a culturally and tradition-bound framework that would make it absolutely impenetrable to the vast majority of people, who are nevertheless suffering and who might find it extraordinarily useful and liberative" (Kabat-Zinn, 1999, pp. 226–227).

Like most meaningful insights, this one was simple at its core: "It struck me in that fleeting moment that afternoon at the Insight Meditation Society that it would be a worthy work to simply share the essence of meditation and yoga practices as I had been learning and practicing them…with those who would never… be able to hear it through the words and forms that were being used at meditation centers" (Kabat-Zinn, 2011, p. 287).[2] That is how the vision of a universal dhamma, as a formula for Buddhist practice in mainstream America, presented itself to him.[3]

When Jon Kabat-Zinn received that flash of insight, it was also immediately clear to him where he wanted to introduce this practice—in hospitals, based on his experiences working in that setting: "Hospitals…function as 'dukkha [suffering] magnets' in our society. So they are logical places in which to do Dharma work" (1999, p. 228).

And so the introduction of the dhamma in the Western world started in a clinical setting, forging a remarkable union of East and West. In 1979 Kabat-Zinn's flash of insight was transformed into a training program offered at the University of Massachusetts Medical Center, and in the early 1990s, this program was given the name mindfulness-based stress reduction (MBSR).

MBSR in Historical Perspective

Even though MBSR emerged through one person's flash of insight, its development occurred in a broader context. By the late 1970s, Eastern meditative and contemplative practices had gained a foothold in the West. At the same time, more and more limitations of medical science and the pathology-based psychiatric paradigm were coming to light. Kabat-Zinn turned that paradigm upside down. In his words, "The MBSR approach takes the medical/psychiatric model...and appears to turn it on its head, in the sense that we are working with people with a wide range of different kinds of problems, yet we offer them all more or less the same intervention. The only way that could possibly make any sense and be of any value is if we appeal to what is 'right' with them rather than focus on what is 'wrong' with them" (1999, p. 236).

This shift in focus also meant a shift of power from the other (the medical specialist who knows what's wrong) to patients themselves. Only the latter can tap into their sources of health and strength. This shift in focus implies empowerment, another aspect of that same paradigm shift in health care advocated by Kabat-Zinn, wherein "a core principle of the medicine of the future [is] that twenty-first century medicine will be fundamentally participatory" (1999, p. 236).

Revolutions rarely occur in isolation. It is no coincidence that, independently from Kabat-Zinn, others also began experimenting with mindfulness in the treatment of patients around the same time, including Steven Hayes, one of the developers of acceptance and commitment therapy (ACT; Hayes, Strosahl, & Wilson, 1999), and Marsha Linehan (1993), the creator of dialectical behavior therapy (DBT) for borderline personality disorder. This synchronicity shows that the time was ripe for developing alternatives to existing treatment methods, and for mindfulness to be used as an ingredient in these alternatives.

That the time was ripe is further evidenced by the relatively rapid spread of MBSR. Other hospitals soon started expressing an interest in MBSR, and Kabat-Zinn's meditations were included in many a hospital's television programming. Public awareness was raised by the publication of Kabat-Zinn's book *Full Catastrophe Living*, in 1990, and the broadcast of Bill Moyers's documentary *Healing from Within*, in 1993. The 1990s saw a huge influx of participants into mindfulness courses, the expansion of teacher training programs, and the application of mindfulness to many specific issues, particularly stress-related conditions such as psoriasis and fibromyalgia. However, mindfulness was still predominantly applied to somatic conditions. That began to change in the late 1990s, when Zindel Segal,

Mark Williams, and John Teasdale used the eight-week MBSR course as the basis for their mindfulness-based cognitive therapy (MBCT; Segal, Williams, & Teasdale, 2002), which addresses a psychological vulnerability: depression. After the turn of the century, different versions of MBSR for groups with specific vulnerabilities or challenges mushroomed, giving rise to numerous mindfulness-based interventions, or mindfulness-based applications. Now, in the second decade of this century, trainings that focus on the attitudinal aspect of mindfulness are beginning to emerge, such as Kristin Neff and Chris Germer's mindful self-compassion training (see Germer, 2009; and Neff, 2011).

This book applies to all of these approaches, as all forms of mindfulness-based training require teachers to have the same competencies. However, because I am primarily experienced with MBSR and MBCT, the examples in this book are largely drawn from these forms of training.

Defining MBSR: To Catch a Butterfly

To provide you with a solid understanding of the contents of mindfulness training, I'll describe the curriculum for MBSR, the most generic mindfulness-based application. But first, it's important that we regain awareness of the dhamma. Although it has found its place in MBSR, it is still essentially elusive.

The *dhamma* refers to all practices that aim at attaining liberating insight into our conditioned way of living. Insight can arise in wondrous ways. Insight isn't something you can "do," although it can be invited to rise, and MBSR amply extends this invitation. Perhaps even more so than the curriculum itself, the attitude of the teacher and the setting convey this invitation. The atmosphere of spaciousness, curiosity, rest, and silence not only leads to a new awareness of experiences, but also triggers reappraisal of experiences. These are qualities that cannot be captured in a curriculum. Trying to catch the effects of MBSR in a detailed and fixed curriculum is like actively trying to attain happiness, which has been described as follows: "Happiness is a butterfly, which, when pursued, is always just beyond your grasp; but which, if you will sit down quietly, may come and alight upon you" (Howe, 1885, p. 169).

With that orientation in mind, Kabat-Zinn and his Center for Mindfulness in Medicine, Health Care, and Society exercised restraint in regard to establishing a protocol for MBSR. Teaching from the moment is considered to be more important than following a strict curriculum, so if teachers have good reason to change the order of components, they can. Teachers are also encouraged to inject their own style into the program (for example, some teachers replace MBSR's usual yoga with aikido practices). In short, the embodiment of mindfulness is more important than an exact format. In fact, it could be said that there are as many forms of MBSR as there are teachers.

And yet there is a global MBSR program, with certain specifications, and if teachers don't include the established, fixed components, they are asked not to call their program MBSR. Later in this book, we'll explore the tension between fixed components and the freedom to work with whatever emerges.

The MBSR Program

Given that there is something magical about MBSR, and that it is fluid and multilayered, any set description would be too fixed and would fail to do the program justice. Therefore, consider the following description to be a rough outline, intended only to give you an idea of what the course entails. Actual insight into the program is acquired only by working with it.

MBSR is a group-based training. It is an eight-week program with weekly sessions that generally last two and a half hours. Participants receive daily home assignments and are encouraged to practice at home for around one hour per day. About two-thirds of the way through the training, usually between sessions 6 and 7, an entire day is devoted to group practice, generally in silence. The training is always preceded by an individual interview and sometimes concludes with an individual interview to wrap up. At the start of the training, participants receive a course workbook containing handouts with additional information on the course themes, poems, summaries of the homework assignments for each session, blank pages for keeping a diary during the course, and other ancillary materials as appropriate to the particular program.

The first group session begins, after an introduction, with an eating meditation that consists of exploring experiences triggered by slowly and attentively eating a raisin. These experiences are subsequently discussed in the group. Next is the body scan, a practice that lasts about forty-five minutes and involves checking in with each part of the body and asking participants to attend to their experience: What is there to be noticed? How do you tend to react to what you notice? Are you aware of your attention drifting, returning, zooming in, and zooming out? And are you aware of your reactions and responses to this process? Afterward, this practice is subjected to a group review, referred to as inquiry. The session concludes with assigning homework: doing the body scan with an audio recording to provide guidance, along with several informal exercises that are intended to help participants get familiar with the workings and effects of mindfulness in day-to-day life. (The term "practice" generally refers to meditative approaches, whereas "exercise" typically refers to didactic approaches. However, in teaching, and sometimes in this book, the terms are used interchangeably.) Informal practices are continued throughout the training.

The first session sets the tone for the rest of the training. The next session starts with the body scan, offering participants another invitation to be mindful of the body and the movement of awareness or attention. Next, homework assignments are discussed, again with the intention to help participants explore and learn to see their experiences and reactions, and the patterns therein, more clearly. The body scan continues to be a basic practice for several weeks, after which it is replaced with walking meditation, sitting meditation, and mindful stretches based on yoga. The yoga practice is basically a body scan in motion and invites participants to get in touch with how they usually relate to their physical body—in terms of both opportunities and boundaries. Walking meditation, introduced in the second half of the training, is a practice of being fully of aware the body in movement while walking at a slow pace.

Sitting meditation, which is gradually introduced over the first several weeks, is similar to meditation as practiced in various Buddhist traditions; however, in MBSR sitting meditation is built up gradually through all fields of sensory information, until, in session 4, the essence of vipassana meditation is reached: choiceless awareness, meditating without a preferred object or field of awareness. The full day of practice is intended to familiarize participants with longer practice and help them see how this can lead to a deeper experience. It's akin to a miniretreat.

During sessions 7 and 8, participants are asked to look back to the past and ahead to the future. Stressing the fact that mindful awareness requires continuing practice, toward the end of the program participants are asked to make a personal plan for including mindfulness practice in their lives.

Based on the principle of experiential learning, sessions usually start with a practice: a body scan, sitting meditation, or mindful yoga. (Shortly, I will provide an overview of meditations used in MBSR.) This opening practice is followed by a review of participants' experiences with that practice and then a debriefing of the homework assignments. Inquiry, the process of reviewing participants' experiences with the practice in the group setting, is oriented toward distilling insights that can ensue from doing the practice. Various teaching subjects, such as the importance of bodily awareness and the major impact of automatic reactive patterns in our lives, are woven into these inquiry sequences. Following the inquiry, the theme of the session is often addressed didactically, through an exercise, or both. After assigning home practices for the coming week, sessions usually conclude with another meditation practice.

To provide a more concrete overview of the program, here's a list setting forth the theme of each session (based on McCown, Reibel, & Micozzi, 2010). The all-day silent retreat isn't included in this overview:

Session 1: Understanding that there is more right with you than wrong with you

Session 2: Exploring perception and creative responding

Session 3: Discovering the pleasure and power of being present

Session 4: Understanding the impact of stress

Session 5: Finding the space for making choices

Session 6: Working with difficult situations

Session 7: Cultivating kindness toward self and others

Session 8: Embarking on the rest of your life

Here are the meditations practiced in MBSR, in the order in which they are presented. In MBSR, these meditations are often referred to as formal practices:

Eating meditation: Mindful eating (typically using a raisin); being aware of all of the sensations and shifts of attention, including loss of attention

Body scan: Lying meditation; checking in with individual body parts and being aware of all sensations and attention shifts, including loss of attention

Mindfulness of breathing: Sitting meditation; learning to work with attention by focusing on an object (one's breathing)

Sitting meditation: Sitting meditation; checking in with each object of attention (body, sound, thoughts, and feelings), then sitting with open (choiceless) awareness, as in vipassana meditation

Mindful yoga, lying postures: Yoga-based stretches; being aware of physical sensations, reactions to these sensations, boundaries, balance, and doing mode versus being mode of mind

Mindful yoga, standing postures: Similar to mindful yoga in lying poses, but utilizing standing postures

Walking meditation: Walking slowly while bringing awareness to the movement of the feet

Visualization meditation: Guided meditation involving visualization of an image (such as a mountain, lake, or tree); inviting a certain attitude, such as openness or firmness

***Metta* meditation:** Sitting meditation; cultivating the qualities of the heart

This book does not contain scripts of guided formal practices. Words set down on paper are a poor medium for learning to guide these practices. Hopefully your own mindfulness training will have included repeated practice with your own teacher guiding the meditations. In addition, there are many audio recordings available to purchase or download, including some by Jon Kabat-Zinn. All of that said, if you'd like to have scripts in written form, you can find them in the following books: *Mindfulness-Based Cognitive Therapy for Depression* (Segal, Williams, & Teasdale, 2002, 2013); *The Mindful Way Through Depression* (Williams et al., 2007); and *A Mindfulness-Based Stress Reduction Workbook* (Stahl & Goldstein, 2010).

Finally, here's a list of the informal practices and exercises typically used in MBSR, again in the order in which they are presented. Most of these are assigned as homework:

Nine dots exercise: A puzzle that can be solved only by thinking outside the box

Trompe l'oeil: An optical illusion in which a picture can be seen in two different ways (think of the face/vase illusion), inviting beholders to think outside the box

Mindfulness of routine activities: A daily practice of being mindful during one routine activity

Mindfulness of pleasant events: A daily practice of being mindful of a pleasant event and its effects on the mind-body system

Mindfulness of unpleasant events: A daily practice of being mindful of an unpleasant event and its effects on the mind-body system

Seeing or hearing exercise: Seeing or hearing experiences without interpreting them or while being mindful of interpretations

Awareness of stress reactions: Being aware of stressful events and their effects on the mind-body system

Mindfully responding to stress reactions: Exploring the possibility of consciously responding to stressful events instead of reacting in an uncontrolled way

Mindfulness of difficult communications: Being mindful of tension in interactions with others and mindful of the reactions (such as passivity or aggression) triggered by these difficulties

Awareness of clinging: Being aware of the degree to which we cling to our usual position and the degree to which this determines our perceptions and options in life

Awareness of what we take in: Being aware of what the mind-body system takes in, from food to information, and the effects thereof, and making conscious choices

The MBSR curriculum is held together by a sophisticated logic. Its many aspects are interlaced and organized in a way that optimizes the training of an average Western participant: the duration of sessions and practices; the scheduling of the all-day silent retreat; the sequence of components (starting with the body, then moving on to sitting meditation, which is itself gradually stepped up from short to long and from more focused, concentration-type meditation to mindfulness meditation); the alternation between sitting meditation and walking meditation and yoga; the ratio of time devoted to practice versus time allotted for group-based inquiry; the inclusion of mindfulness of daily activities (like eating) right from the start; and more.

Furthermore, the schedule of weekly sessions leaves enough time between sessions for participants to sufficiently work on the practices at home, yet it is frequent enough to provide optimal support from group sessions. Even the overall duration of eight weeks was carefully chosen: it's short enough to keep the program manageable and facilitate a substantial effort but long enough to have a lasting effect.

Experience has shown that the program's logic is effective: "It has an extremely powerful intuitive logic—it *feels right* to the teachers" (McCown, Reibel, & Micozzi, 2010, p. 139). This does not mean, however, that the MBSR curriculum is rigid. As Kabat-Zinn says, "There is a great deal of latitude and space built into the MBSR curriculum for the teacher to bring in himself or herself in critical ways, including, where appropriate, new information and practices. That latitude in creativity is essential for the curriculum to come alive" (2010, p. xv). He has also emphasized "that there are many different ways to structure and deliver mindfulness-based stress reduction programs. The optimal form of its delivery will depend critically on local factors" (1996, p. 165). So even though there are limits to variation, the program is also quite open.

Teaching Methods in Mindfulness Training

The main teaching methods used in mindfulness training are practice, inquiry, and didactic presentations.

Practice (mindfulness or meditation practice) creates situations that stimulate trainees to be consciously present more often. It requires that people step outside of their typical behavior, which is largely driven by habits and automatic reactions that leave little room for being aware of what's actually happening.

Inquiry consists of reviewing and exploring personal experiences that arise during practice, along with reactions to these experiences, patterns in these reactions, the broader context in which these patterns can be observed, and the implications of all of this. Inquiry invites participants to transcend their usual perspective and see their experiences and patterns of reacting in a new light.

Didactic presentations shift the focus from the context of specific, current personal or group experience to the general human context. They convey how things work in general.

These three teaching methods are mutually interactive and reinforcing; for example, you might include something you just presented didactically in a practice, use a meditation experience as the subject for inquiry, or offer a didactic presentation as an outgrowth of something that comes up during inquiry. Together, these teaching methods form the trinity that underpins the learning process in mindfulness training.

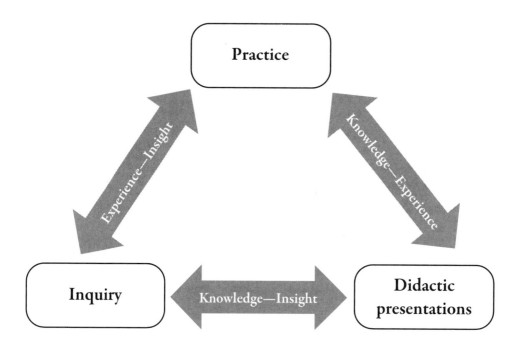

Figure 1. The mindfulness training trinity. Practice, inquiry, and didactic presentations are mutually interactive.

Mindfulness training isn't easy for participants. They're asked to practice for long periods of time. They're also asked to intensively look at the most difficult aspects of their being—aspects they'd often prefer to avoid—and to muster openness, curiosity, and flexibility in doing so. In addition, they're asked to experiment with new and unknown ways of dealing with experiences without the promise of a concrete result. Because of these challenges, an atmosphere of safety, support, and trust is essential. You can foster such an atmosphere by creating a setting characterized by tranquility, spaciousness, and acceptance, combined with a certain level of clarity. To a certain extent, you can accomplish this in the physical setting and by using a structured yet flexible program, but your attitude or presence will be equally if not more important. The latter is often referred to as embodiment of mindfulness, to underline that this fundamental attitude is embodied in the teacher's way of being present and cannot be captured in a technique or protocol.

This book addresses all of these components of effective mindfulness training: practice, inquiry, didactic presentations, and the teacher's attitude or presence.

Development of the Mindfulness Teacher

Mindfulness training typically offers many short-term benefits to participants. They receive a lot of attention from the teacher. They may also find some relaxation and learn to be a bit more focused at times. These factors alone may make them feel satisfied about the training. However, the power of mindfulness extends well beyond the temporary effects that may make people feel good. Ultimately, mindfulness training is about transforming lives.

This book will elucidate how you can make the most of that transformative potential. In this endeavor, it's well supported by the substantial developments now occurring in the world of teaching mindfulness. A growing number of peer networks, teacher training courses, and assessment tools are available to complement what you'll learn in these pages. In some senses, this book also contributes to consolidating current knowledge about teaching mindfulness.

In mindfulness training, the principle of teaching from the moment, and being present with all of your heart in that endeavor, takes precedence over the curriculum. A quality often referred to as heartfulness is the key element in teaching mindfulness, but this quality is applied against a particular backdrop of somewhat fixed elements, such as bringing rules to the setting, working with group dynamics, and utilizing certain conversation techniques. Of course, the training has a goal, along with particular directions and pathways for arriving there. If you keep this mapped out in the back of your head, you'll know where participants are in their development and how best to facilitate their learning process.

All of this is akin to the art of experienced musicians. They make playing music seem effortless, exuding a simplicity that may make you think, *I can do that*. But that ease is the result of extensive practice and in-depth study of techniques and theory. You can only perform a piece of music to its full potential if you've attained a grasp of the rules of harmony, practiced the arrangements, and studied the score. Only then will you be able to make the rendition your own while still conveying the essence of the piece. And even though experts—whether musicians or mindfulness teachers—navigate largely from intuition, they can always specify why they do what they do and why the moment called for it.

About This Book

In this book, I'll describe all of the qualities necessary in a mindfulness teacher, endeavoring to strike a balance between the form and the formless. I'll also try to describe training techniques and teaching competencies as dynamically as possible. My approach is descriptive, rather than prescriptive, offering options, not set instructions. Along the way, I'll describe the landscape of mindfulness teaching from the mountains, rivers, and roads down to the smallest of goat tracks. This maximizes your opportunity to develop your own way of teaching.

The downside to this approach is that you won't always find a conclusive answer to questions you may have. You may find signposts, but you won't find a fixed route.

As an author, rising to the challenge of describing mindfulness training as a landscape often felt like walking a slackline, balancing between forces pulling from different sides. I had to navigate between the forces of curriculum versus individualized interpretation, and between comprehensiveness and conciseness. Another issue is that the landscape to be described is vast. When teaching mindfulness, it is important to know something about group dynamics, conversation techniques, the learning process, psychology, psychopathology, and Eastern contemplative traditions. But each of these is fully-fledged science in its own right. Ultimately, it wasn't possible to convey the essence of these sciences without reflecting their depth, and I had to gloss over most them in preference to focusing on the core teaching issues.

Further, a sentence spoken in a live setting is so much richer than that same sentence on dry, crackly paper. On so many occasions I felt the need to rewrite, add nuance, or insert another possible approach. Often, I faced the ultimate question of whether that richness can even be captured on paper. Yet when printed on paper, words acquire an aura of truth. As you read this book, you might think, *This is how it is. This is the way.* To counteract this notion, bear in mind that this book was born out of my practical experience, and I am merely one person. Other approaches, practices, and options are possible. To that end, I tried my best to be careful about making firm statements and or conveying fixed concepts. I've tried to bring order to the information without claiming some sort of universal truth. In doing so, I deliberately chose not to interconnect concepts because I didn't want to form a hermetic whole. As a result, some of my statements and concepts may appear firm, only to open up again later, leaving room for other options or views.

As a reader, you may find this frustrating. You may feel that constructions along the lines of "on the one hand X, but on the other hand Y" force you to walk a slackline yourself. If so, know that my main aim is to keep you from stepping into the pitfall of taking the written word as absolute truth.

The Chapters

Chapter 1, "How People Learn During Mindfulness Training," breaks the learning process down from the angle of the learning moment: the moment when actual learning happens through insight—when "the penny drops." It includes a focus on individual characteristics, such as personal learning style. Following that, chapter 2, "Creating a Fertile Learning Setting," describes the qualities of a context that will support the learning process. Chapter 3, "Guiding Mindfulness Practices," presents a structure and key points for guiding formal exercises, especially meditations. Chapter 4, "Inquiry," systematically deals with all aspects of this special conversational format. Because inquiry can be one of the more challenging aspects of teaching mindfulness, chapter 4 is quite lengthy and detailed. In contrast, chapter 5, "Didactic Presentations," is short and succinct, given that this is such a straightforward aspect of the teaching. This short chapter is primarily focused on setting forth when this teaching tool is desirable and which themes can be covered in didactic presentations.

To conclude the book, chapter 6, "What the Teacher Brings to the Training," shifts the focus to the person of the teacher. In that final chapter, we'll look at how your style of training reflects who you are both as a teacher and as a human being. Remember, you, the teacher, have an immense bearing on whether the message comes across. You'll want to make a big investment in how you present the training, both as a teacher and as a human being, given that this cannot be captured in techniques.

The Reading Routes

This book basically follows the structure of the learning process, first looking into how people learn, and then into what kind of setting is the most fertile environment for learning. This is in keeping with general knowledge about the psychology of learning: teachers need to have a good grasp of how people learn in order to adequately guide the process. The subsequent chapters take an increasingly specific look at teaching mindfulness, from the development of particular skills (such as techniques to guide participants in practices and exercises) to competencies (the teacher's qualities). Therefore, one reading route is to proceed through the chapters sequentially, mirroring the topography of this natural learning process.

However, as emphasized, the stance from which you teach (heartfulness and embodiment) is more important that what you teach. So from this angle, the final chapter ("What the Teacher Brings to the Training") would be the foundation. Therefore, an equally good case could be made for starting with chapter 6 and reading the book in reverse, arriving finally at the more technical and general aspects of teaching mindfulness.

Then, there is a third way of reading this book: without a fixed plan. In this approach, you can let yourself be guided by your natural interests. Or, if you're already teaching, you can turn to whatever topics are coming up in your teaching right now.

A Book Cannot Equal Practice

Lawyers are often pictured in front of wall-to-wall bookshelves filled with hefty tomes. This may look impressive, but they obviously don't have all of that information memorized. Rather, they may occasionally consult a specific book that has a bearing on an upcoming court hearing or scour their shelves looking for an article or legal precedent to refer to in an appeal. When they step into the courtroom, they leave their books behind and surrender to the dynamics of the moment. Simply reading reference books won't allow them to argue a case well. In a similar way, you can't teach mindfulness well if you only read books about doing so.

In Edgar Allan Poe's short story "The Oval Portrait," an artist loves his wife so much that he wants to capture her essence in paint. When he finally feels that he has achieved a perfect depiction of her, he looks up from his canvas only to discover that his wife has died of exhaustion while sitting for the portrait.

No text can ever describe the living process of teaching mindfulness without some of that process dying in the attempt to render it. Reading is only a small part of teacher training, albeit an indispensable one. Just as participants have to rely on their personal experience during mindfulness training, so must the teacher.

CHAPTER 1

How People Learn During Mindfulness Training

Before I can tell my life what I want to do with it, I must listen to my life telling me who I am.

—Parker J. Palmer

In a time of drastic change it is the learners who inherit the future. The learned usually find themselves equipped to live in a world that no longer exists

—Eric Hoffer

In a monastery in the East, you sit down for meditation at 4 a.m. and keep at it—for an hour, a week, or a lifetime. In contrast, mindfulness training in the West typically involves creating a setting for systematic learning. A training course could be conceived of as a Western concept: a restricted process within which certain learning experiences are facilitated to the maximum degree possible in the hopes that this will lead to insight and change.[4] One of Jon Kabat-Zinn's unique contributions in bringing mindfulness to the West was to package the practice into a Western training format.[5] Development of insight through practice remains the central ingredient, but a specific structure was added, along with the supplementary training methods of inquiry and didactic presentation.

So, returning to the pragmatic basis of mindfulness training in the West, the salient question is how best to organize the way the material is presented. Even here, we run into difficulties, as "material" isn't a fitting term in the context of mindfulness training. Mindfulness practice is about being present and aware more often. In mindfulness training, the learning moment is one of "falling awake," so to speak. It's a moment of seeing clearly, of insight, and of receptivity to a deeper knowing, in combination with the ability to integrate this experience. Therefore, in the milieu of mindfulness, effective teaching also tends to revolve around qualities of the learner. Those qualities are the topic of this chapter. Then, in chapter 2, I'll turn to the setting and creating a learning environment that maximizes the potential for participants to gain these insights, before turning to specific teaching techniques in chapters 3 through 5.

Interactions Between Personal Attributes, Setting, and Teaching Methods

Everyone comes to mindfulness training with their own specific and highly individual characteristics. This set of personal attributes is made up of learning style, focus in learning, and receptivity to the moment, all of which are influenced by the person's pathway to the learning moment. These qualities interact with the setting and teaching methods in a dynamic mutual relationship, each influencing and being influenced by the others.[6]

An individual participant will adapt to the setting. The setting, in turn, is influenced by the participant. Teaching methods are carried by a setting but also have an impact on that setting, and around and around it goes. The dynamic interplay between personal attributes, setting, and method is depicted in figure 2.

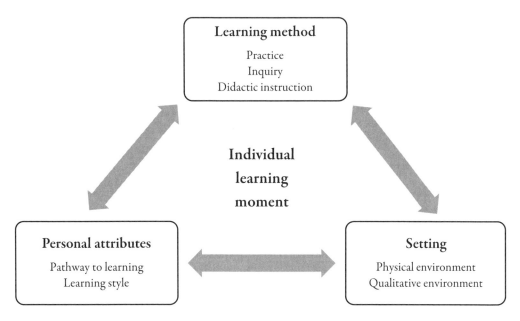

Figure 2. The dynamic relationship between personal attributes, setting, and method, which shapes the learning moment in mindfulness training.

You may wonder where the teacher is in figure 2. Choosing and implementing the learning methods is, of course, the teacher's job. The teacher does screening and preprogram interviews before the group starts, influencing the setting. In addition, the teacher organizes the physical environment and is the determining factor in the quality of the environment, largely through that intangible factor of embodiment. And finally, as discussed in the next section, the teacher must take participants' personal attributes into account and adjust both message and teaching style accordingly. The reason I've omitted the teacher from this figure is simple: the teacher is everywhere.

Personal Attributes

As mentioned, setting and methods will be addressed in later chapters, so let's turn to personal attributes. Given the interdependence of factors in the preceding model of the learning moment, you won't be able to get through to everyone equally effectively using the same method and setting. You'll need to consider participants' individual differences and how you can work with these differences.

Personal attributes are what each participant brings to mindfulness training. And as you now know, these attributes have an influence on other aspects of the learning moment. From the teacher's perspective, these personal attributes are the factors least amenable to influence. They also tend to be the least flexible. People's personal attributes are the result of a complex process of shaping by genes, culture, history, and, depending on your belief system, chance, fate, or maybe even karma.

Each participant's highly idiosyncratic mind-body system defines the person's patterns in attending to the moment and determines the filters through which experiences are perceived and hence which aspects of that experience come to the fore, and which don't. Personality also determines a participant's learning style in facing new experiences. All of this plays a role in participants' present-moment awareness and receptivity to the learning process.

The fact that these traits are so individualized means that mindfulness training will be a unique journey for each participant. And yet (and this may sound a little disrespectful), these individual attributes aren't of particular interest within the framework of this book. After all, these attributes are largely a given and difficult to change. Nevertheless, they do have a bearing on the learning process, so in the rest of the chapter I'll discuss four key qualities: the personal pathway to learning, learning style, focus in learning, and receptivity to the moment.

The Personal Pathway to Learning

You don't have to believe in karma to be able to acknowledge that experiences from the past partly define who you are today. Happiness, grief, trauma, family dynamics, illnesses, and many other experiences shape our preferences and aversions. They also have a bearing on why insight may be easier or harder to attain for a given individual. Disposition is also a determining factor in the ease or difficulty with which a person is able to reach insight. Some people are naturally more inclined toward somberness, restlessness, or dreaminess than others.

To some extent, personal history and general disposition define the hindrances and obstacles participants encounter during their learning process. All participants run into personal obstacles and hindrances on their learning pathway, and there is no way of predicting what these will be, how difficult they will be, or when they will arise. This is part of what makes mindfulness training a voyage of discovery.

As a teacher, your job is to exude faith in the process, and in participants' capacity for self-healing whenever they sigh that their progress seems so minimal in comparison to that of others. As long as a participant has sufficient commitment, the themes or obstacles that arise will be the right ones, precisely because they arise. The process of developing insight follows its own course, independently from the mind's expectations. Given that this is a self-regulating process, each and every participant's learning pathway will eventually lead to more mindfulness. How long that pathway is, how much it meanders, and how much of it is uphill or downhill is something that simply cannot be predicted.

Learning Style

Learning style refers to an individual's preferred way of learning. The word "style" already suggests that this is personal—a trait that differs from one person to the next. One example of a typical learning style is that of the theorist. A theorist will generally want to know the idea behind an exercise before surrendering to it.

In the early 1970s, US educational theorist David Kolb developed a theory of learning that was subsequently elaborated into four learning styles, or preferences, by Peter Honey and Alan Mumford (1982), which I summarize here. I don't offer these styles in an attempt to pigeonhole people, but rather to illustrate the differences in how various individuals may relate to the same learning setting and method. One consequence of this is that different people will have a preference for particular parts of the learning process. As a teacher, you can opt to cater to these preferences in order to facilitate a participant's access to the training. Needless to say, teachers must always strike a balance between the needs of the individual and the needs of the group (a topic I'll return to at the end of the chapter). When dealing with a theorist, for example, you could explain an exercise before conducting it. Although that would deviate from the typical modus operandi of first offering the experience and then reviewing it afterward, doing so can help get theorists to buy into doing the exercise.

Here, then, are the four primary learning styles as outlined by Honey and Mumford: the activist, the reflector, the theorist, and the pragmatist. If it seems that these descriptions are slanted toward the more problematic aspects of each learning style, that's because these challenges are precisely what the teacher needs to attend to and work with.

THE ACTIVIST

Activists' defining qualities are being active and concrete. Their strength is their ability to have tangible experiences. They experiment and are hands-on, and when a job's done, they want to dive right in to the next one. Activists will struggle to step back, stop, and take time for reflection to identify contexts and patterns. They need explicit prompting in that direction. An example of an activist is a police officer—always moving from one incident to the next, engrossed in the concrete situation that presents itself, without focusing on the underlying causes and patterns (and perhaps being unable to focus on these factors).

THE REFLECTOR

Reflectors' defining qualities are being concrete and reflective. They're very good at observing experiences—so much so that their eye for detail may cause them to have difficulty seeing the big picture. Precision in observations is sacred to reflectors, whereas they tend to be less interested in what they might do with their observations. Reflectors are like lab workers who take their time to establish and perfect observations with great precision. They require direction to let go of the details and open up to the bigger picture.

THE THEORIST

Theorists' defining qualities are being reflective and abstract. They prefer interpretation and conceptualization to actual experiences. They want to know the idea behind an experiment or exercise before undertaking it, and they tend to start analyzing and drawing conclusions before the experiment has been completed. The challenge they face is to surrender to the experiment without immediately conceptualizing their experiences. A lawyer is a typical theorist, seeking to assimilate certain events into a particular (legal) context.

THE PRAGMATIST

Pragmatists' defining qualities are being abstract and active. They want to learn as quickly as possible so they can put whatever they've learned into practice. They consequently have a tendency to not appreciate the benefits of the learning process itself. Working with pragmatists involves curbing their enthusiasm and inviting them to take another look before they charge ahead. They often say things like "I'm not interested in problems; I'm interested in solutions" or "What does this mean for next time?" Managers are typically pragmatists.

Focus in Learning

An attribute that's related to personal learning style is habits in attending to one's experience. One's attention follows one's natural interests, but it doesn't have free rein. Over the course of our lives, we develop habits and patterns in how we focus and what we focus on. Some people are more focused on problems, while others are drawn to solutions. Some veer toward effort, while others are inclined toward relaxation. Some are more aware of differences, while others are more aware of similarities. And some may bring more attention to color, while others attend to contour.

This personal style of paying attention determines one's focus, and therefore which dimensions of an overall experience the person does or does not behold. Focus allows us to see, but it also blinds us. It's somewhat like in the well-known parable of three blind people encountering an elephant: the person touching the elephant's tail thinks it's a piece of rope; the person touching one of the elephant's legs thinks it's a tree; and the person touching the trunk thinks it's a snake.

In this same vein, people have personal preferences in how they attend to their experiences. You're likely to notice this during the body scan: some participants will follow the journey through the body by visualizing body parts; others will do so by bringing awareness to bodily sensations; and yet others will engage the metaphor of spaciousness, opening to their experience and embracing it with their awareness. For some, instructions of a visual nature will be more effective, while others are more likely to benefit from instructions that appeal to other senses.

This kind of focus in learning is habitual and often bound to people's personality; therefore, in most cases it's only flexible to a limited degree. Again, it's up to the teacher to strike a balance between catering to individuals and aligning the training with the group average. In terms of the body scan, for example, this may mean alternating between visual, auditory, and proprioceptive orientations as you guide the practice.

Receptivity to the Moment

One element of personal attributes that is seemingly amenable to more influence is receptivity to the moment. The learning setting (described in chapter 2) can go a long way toward creating or supporting receptivity, particularly if it creates a sense of safety. Ultimately, receptivity can trump all of the preceding factors, for good or ill. Imagine that you could offer a learning moment that is perfectly tailored to an individual participant, suiting that person's pathway, learning style, and focus. This still wouldn't guarantee success. That particular participant could be zoned out at that moment, be distracted by the person sitting next to him, or still have his mind on a conflict at work. And even if that participant is present to the moment, he may doubt your authority or may simply have already absorbed so much information that he's saturated.

All of these factors, and more, determine participants' receptivity to the moment—in other words, their openness, willingness, and ability to let in new information in one particular learning moment. In this way, receptivity is perhaps the most fleeting of factors in determining whether the penny drops.

Balancing Between Personal and Group Needs

Individual needs are best served by a tailored approach. But that isn't always possible, particularly in group settings. The teacher's job is to strike a balance between meeting the needs of individuals and meeting the needs of the group overall. I'll return to this topic in chapter 2, and again in chapter 4. For now, I'll just mention that certain approaches can help you cater to individual needs.

For example, a preprogram interview provides an opportunity to prepare individuals for the group experience or, sometimes, to recognize that an individual isn't a good candidate for a group approach.[7] Another option for tailoring the approach is to engage with a participant outside of the group setting. (In chapter 4, I'll give more details on how to approach participants individually.)

At this point, it may seem as though the fact that there are few means of tailoring group mindfulness training to individual needs and styles is a limitation. However, people are social creatures, and as a result, a group setting is usually far more powerful than an individual learning setting, even if that individual setting is highly customized.

Ultimately, the most important conditions for a fertile learning setting are that participants feel seen, supported, and challenged in a way that suits them, and mindfulness training offers ample room for that. Besides, not fully meeting a participant's needs can have positive effects. Wherever personal attributes clash with the training method, there is also something to learn.

In fact, excessively trying to meet individuals' needs may diminish or threaten the learning process. If you feel overly responsible for how someone is developing while also lacking a clear view of that development, you might tend to intervene individually too soon. I remember a time when I approached a participant because I was concerned that she was being rather quiet, and I wondered whether she felt connected to the group process. After I mentioned my concern to her, I noticed that she seemed a bit embarrassed, as if she had to justify her natural way of attending. As she explained it, "I enjoy listening to others. I recognize a lot of myself in what people say, and I use that to my advantage. I'm learning a lot. I don't feel the need to contribute. I've found that everything I've experienced will come up sooner or later, anyway. As it is, I already do a lot of talking every day."

When leading a group, you may sometimes think, *I have no control whatsoever over whether or not understanding arises.* That's true. The learning moment is the result of complex dynamics, and the outcome is unpredictable. Yet the illustration of the learning moment in figure 2 may lead you to think, *There's a structure to this approach. When I follow that structure, I'll get somewhere.* That's also true. In the end, we can say something about the moments of insight—and we cannot. It can be structured—and it's elusive.

Having a structure, pattern, or map you can use to find your bearings is useful. It will help you know what to do and why to do it. It can also illuminate where you can effectively deploy your skills and what you might expect to result from your efforts. That said, how a flash of insight strikes remains a mystery. Mindfulness teachers never cease to be surprised by the moments when insights arise in participants and how these moments are always unpredictable. No one can provide a recipe for that. There is no blueprint that will tell you what to do to make the penny drop.

CHAPTER 2

Creating a Fertile Learning Setting

In the measurement world, you set a goal and strive for it. In the universe of possibility, you set the context and let life unfold.

—Rosamund Stone Zander and Benjamin Zander

There came a time when the risk to remain tight in the bud was more painful than the risk it took to blossom.

—Author unknown

We learn mindfulness by experience. In that regard, it can be compared to how children learn through play. Of course, when describing this kind of relationship with experience for adults, we usually don't use the term "play," but rather a word like "exploration" or "experiment." Still, think about how children explore. There is the suspense of the unknown, but also a sense that exploring is safe. There is a parent or, if need be, the floor to catch them. As you can see from this example, a fertile learning setting provides a stimulus to embark on something new and unknown, along with the feeling that it's okay to do so.

Learning requires the being mode of mind. Some of the qualities of being mode are safety, rest, nondoing, openness, and connectivity. Our conditioned, driven, doing mode of mind curbs the open and playful attitude needed to engage in experiential learning. We are conditioned to approach experiences with thought, seriousness, a preconception of complexity, and a focus on results. A fertile learning setting counterbalances this conditioning by offering invitations to stay present and oriented on the process (instead of the results), to sense (instead of think), and to approach experiences with lightness and simplicity. All of these qualities are associated with the being mode of mind.

This does not mean, however, that everything happens by itself and we never have to be alert. When a setting is too safe, we can fall asleep and miss potential moments of awakening. A setting that is too restful can make us inert. When nondoing dominates, practices won't provide enough incentive to open up to new experiences. Boundless openness can lead to vagueness, aimlessness, and eventually nonchalance and demoralization. Taking care of ourselves doesn't mean discipline will never be required. And when it comes to training as a learning process, as mindfulness teachers we need to work with what comes up in the moment but also proceed through a program. Further, although the not-knowing that's characteristic of openness is essential, this doesn't mean you aren't allowed to convey knowledge when knowledge would indeed be helpful for the learning process.

In short, for optimum learning, the being mode of mind must be integrated with the doing mode of mind. The being mode of mind offers a context within which we can open up, feeling safe and relaxed, while the doing mode of mind helps us engage with the challenges of the learning process. The balance between the two is what's crucial.

Balancing Doing Mode of Mind and Being Mode of Mind

The objective of mindfulness training is not to convert people from the doing mode of mind to the being mode of mind; rather, it is to help people learn to strike a balance between these modes. The teacher needs to be skilled in fostering the being mode of mind, but also in helping participants switch between these two modes as the situation requires. Basically, you should encourage the qualities of the doing mode of mind whenever that would be helpful to the learning process. At such times, it's good to call participants to alertness and action. This is also the time to explain how things are by conveying factual knowledge, and to provide direction, rather than options. This may also be a time to promise concrete things, even if only a promise to stop on time. The doing mode of mind serves as the Zen stick in the training setting, prodding participants back to alertness and focus.

Traditional learning settings (parent-child, master-apprentice, guru-disciple) are often characterized by a balance between a sense of security and alertness, between restfulness and action, and between openness and direction. There is a kind of playfulness and unconditionality that facilitates learning, yet there are also rules that keep the process on track. Ultimately, learning requires both attention and broad focus, both rest and action, both nondoing and effort, both feeling and thinking, both being oriented to the process and keeping an eye on the outcome, both experiencing lightness and being able to be serious, both restoring things to their simplicity and being able to recognize complexity.

That we mainly focus on the being mode in mindfulness training comes down to the fact that almost all participants need to get reacquainted with this old friend and be weaned from excessive dominance of the doing mode of mind—a potential helpmate who turns into a kind of Rasputin.

The majority of this chapter is devoted to an in-depth exploration of ten qualities of the being mode of mind and the corresponding qualities of the doing mode of mind. I'll address their role in mindfulness training and describe when each is called for. First, however, in the table that follows I'll summarize the functions of each pair of qualities and describe exaggerated, problematic versions of each. As mentioned, our Western conditioning has given us a tendency to gravitate toward the qualities of the doing mode of mind. The teacher's job is to compensate for that by engendering the qualities of the being mode of mind and then helping participants achieve a good balance between the two, stimulating either the being mode or the doing mode as needed. A fertile quality in the training setting results from the interplay of these opposing forces.

Functions and Exaggerations of the Qualities of the Doing Mode of Mind and the Being Mode of Mind in the Learning Setting

Exaggeration	Function	Being mode		Doing mode	Function	Exaggeration
Being sleepy, bored, or absentminded	Surrendering while retaining personal boundaries and attending to self-care	Safe	↕	Alert	Being awake, focused, stimulated, interested, and challenged	Feeling agitated, pushed, threatened, or stressed
Not devoting enough time to practice	Taking time to let new experiences in and process them	Restful	↕	Active	Stepping forward to engage in learning, have experiences, and complete exercises	Getting stuck in automated, driven, doing mode
Being idle and giving up	Letting things happen	Nondoing	↕	Effort	Practicing sufficiently and committing to engaging in the practices that are needed	Being stubbornly tenacious
Feeling aimless, nonchalant, disoriented, or that nothing matters	Allowing not-knowing, the unformed, and silence; being led by natural interests	Open and silent	↕	Structured	Providing structure (support and boundaries); facilitating knowing (being clear and precise); following the program	Being rigid or passive; giving up
Merging or disappearing into others or the group process	Being engrossed in others or the group process	Connected	↕	Independent	Being a separate, unique individual with the ability to navigate challenges that arise	Being isolated

(Excess)	Benefit	Pole		Pole	Benefit	(Excess)
Not having any attention span	Focusing on here-and-now experience, relaxation, and not having to achieve anything	**Process oriented**	↕	**Results oriented**	Taking stock, staying real, and getting satisfaction	Having an excessive focus on concrete, short-term results
Hanging on too long; going beyond personal boundaries; feeling exhaustion or boredom	Seeing experiences in their richness and depth and understanding their fleeting nature	**Staying present**	↕	**Varying**	Facilitating focus through rhythm and alertness; completing and starting anew	Avoiding, covering up, and seeking excitement
Floating along on waves of emotions and feeling aimless	Getting the physical or feeling sense of an experience and its direct, nonconceptual, nonpermanent, here-and-now nature	**Sensing**	↕	**Thinking**	Promoting cognitive integration and organization; perceiving patterns and implications	Overrating mental constructions and analysis
Being superficial or jumping over important experiences or topics	Having the ability to let go, put things into perspective, and see the bigger picture	**Light**	↕	**Serious**	Being able to stay focused and look at things in depth	Being preoccupied with problems; feeling heavy or negative
Oversimplifying or becoming numb	Clarifying by putting the illusionary complexity of thinking into perspective	**Simple**	↕	**Complex**	Being able to see complexity and subtlety	Philosophizing

31

Qualities of the Being Mode of Mind

In this section, I'll describe the ten key qualities of the being mode of mind: safe, restful, nondoing, open and silent, connected, process oriented, staying present, sensing, light, and simple. I'll also give examples of how you can promote these qualities in participants.

Safe

People learn best in a safe environment. Certain characteristics create this kind of environment: setting boundaries, providing a supportive and caring setting, facilitating self-care, and conveying a sense that things are okay, even when at first glance they don't appear to be.

SETTING BOUNDARIES

When people have a sense that the unknown they are venturing into won't overwhelm them, they feel a sense of safety. One thing you can do to provide that sense of safety is set boundaries. To that end, you can ask participants to see mindfulness training and its exercises as an experiment—an experiment that's set within a known and safe framework.

The process of setting boundaries starts even before the training does, as you clearly communicate the steps necessary for admission to the training and details about the course and its schedule. It continues as the program gets underway, when you establish rules about privacy, breaks, and how participants can interact. Similarly, you establish boundaries that help participants feel safe. Even discussing expectations has an element of setting boundaries to it, as you tell participants what they can and cannot expect.

Once the course and practices get underway, you can help participants feel safe by clearly describing the sequence of events, which provide another kind of boundary: "First, we're going to X, then Y, and finally Z." Then, as you guide participants in practices and inquiry afterward, you can support their sense of safety by telling them that they can set their own boundaries for practice and inquiry, using statements like these:

It's your foot on the gas.

When things get too difficult, you can stop doing the practice or change it to suit your needs.

You can also establish boundaries by creating a sense that the practices are small and manageable:

The limits of this practice provide a safe space to experiment with this feeling [e.g., anxiety]. *See whether you can, very carefully, tune in to that feeling, taking small steps at your own pace.*

Asking permission is another way of indicating that you have a sense of participants' boundaries and respect them:

Is it okay if I ask further questions about this?

Is it okay if we move on now?

All of that said, don't view these boundaries as a firm given. After all, learning will be curtailed if we always stay within the same boundaries. At a retreat for mindfulness trainers, I recall Florence Meleo-Meyer, senior MBSR teacher at the Center for Mindfulness, saying, "We are working at the limits of what we can do at any moment." In other words, the best learning occurs when people approach their boundaries, rather than shying away from them. So as you explore the boundaries with participants, challenge them to cross those boundaries. Just be sure to do so in a context of safety—a context that's guaranteed when participants are given space to set their own boundaries.

PROVIDING SUPPORT AND CARE

When you ask a stocker at a supermarket where you can find the sugar, she's likely to walk with you part of the way to the baking goods aisle. Providing this kind of guidance is part of the stocker's professional training; although her job is to stock shelves, the supermarket knows how important it is to accompany customers and show them the way when they're disoriented.

A proficient mindfulness teacher does something similar, making participants feel as if the teacher is walking by their side in the field of new experiences—a field that is unknown to them, where they can easily lose their bearings. The most important form of support and care you can offer participants is the sense that you recognize and appreciate their search process—that you know the field and can, if need be, take them by the hand part of the way.

Feeling seen is in itself an important form of support, especially when people are struggling. You can convey this simply:

I see that things are a bit difficult for you just now.

You can also make participants feel seen by meeting a specific need. This could be as concrete as getting a blanket for someone who's feeling cold. Or it could be more subtle; for example, if you know a participant has hearing problems or feels particularly vulnerable due to personal grief, you could invite that person to sit next to you.

Participants also draw support from sensing that they aren't alone in a particular struggle. Here, you can evoke support from the group at large, asking whether others are struggling with something similar and then pointing out this common experience:

Does anyone recognize this? [Other participants nod.] *See? You're not the only one!*

Giving compliments for intention and commitment is a very direct form of support:

You're doing well!

Meditation doesn't always have to feel good to be good. You brought your best intentions to the practice, and that's good.

Another way to provide support is by clearly making your presence felt:

I can't take your feelings away, but I can sit together with you and your feelings and explore them with you, as if I were holding your hand.

And finally, making informal contact prior to or during breaks can be highly supportive. These informal signs of support can be as simple as a nod of the head or a touch, or they could take the form of an affirmative remark.

EMPHASIZING SELF-CARE

Safety is also created by emphasizing the importance of self-care and being aware of participants' personal boundaries and needs. Physical unease provides a good avenue for exploring mindful self-care. For example, you might mention to participants that they can meditate while seated on a chair instead of a cushion, that they can do the body scan with their knees bent, or that they can sit down if a standing posture becomes uncomfortable. You can also convey that participants are free to organize their practice in a way that fits them by establishing that it's okay to be late if traffic is bad, that they can bring their own meditation bench or cushion, or that they can have a snack during class if need be.

In these ways, you partially hand over your role of managing the training, allowing participants to engage in self-management. This too offers safety, as it allows participants to explore and define their individual needs and boundaries. Here are some examples of how you can invite participants to attend to their self-care:

What do you need right now?

How could this work for you? What suits you?

Encouraging participants to go with whatever emerges is another way of offering space for self-care:

Perhaps you have nothing to say. That's okay too.

Just see what comes up.

CREATING A SENSE THAT THINGS ARE OKAY

In the way a parent has the back of her child, ready to catch him when he falls, the mindfulness teacher is on hand whenever participants hit a dead end. The teacher is also always there when participants are approaching their limits in terms of feeling safe or okay. The key here is to embody a deep trust in the process, with your very being conveying that there is a deeper sense of being okay or a broader perspective, even if a participant can't feel a connection with that in the moment. Here are some statements that can establish a large safety net:

So that was your experience. Can you be okay with that? Is it okay for the experience to be exactly as it is?

So that experience was unpleasant. But was it okay? I mean, could you in some way be with whatever was uncomfortable?

We can get so wrapped up in it, right? And then we notice our reactions and see how they work, and they fall away. We realize how small the situation actually is, seen from the perspective of everything else. From that perspective, we don't have a care in the world—or perhaps just a tiny one.

Here's a brief dialogue that exemplifies creating this sense that things are okay, even when they aren't—or at least it doesn't feel that they are.

Teacher:	And then?
Participant:	Then... I don't know. Then it stops... Then there's only black.
Teacher:	So there's only black?
Participant:	I don't know...
Teacher:	Is there only black now?
Participant:	No.
Teacher:	So it has changed?
Participant:	Well, eventually...
Teacher:	Anyhow, it passed. Experiences come and go. Knowing this, might it be possible to simply note, "only black," and leave it at that?

Restful

Going fast generally means being on autopilot and reacting reflexively, whereas slowing the pace extends the sense of spaciousness, allowing for a response rather than a reaction. Time is also necessary for processing learning experiences. The deeper the learning, the more time people need to let it sink in. Of course, people in Western cultures generally have a hurried, harried lifestyle. Our internal clock ticks so speedily and relentlessly that our moments get glued together. It's not easy for mindfulness to find an entry point into our days.

Aside from that, participants need time to become accustomed to some radically new perspectives. Chief among them is the invitation to look inward instead of outward. The things we learn from this inward view can be peculiar and sometimes alarming: how much we tend to function on autopilot, how wildly our thoughts wander, how deeply our experiences are grounded in the body. We discover, as UK psychology professor and MBCT-developer Mark Williams sometimes says, "parts of our minds we didn't know, we never explored, and nobody told us about."

Participants are ill at ease. They feel inadequate. Mindfulness is new, the training is extensive, and they don't yet have the tools and vocabulary to skillfully work with the experiences that come up. The process of familiarization also requires time, patience, and space. At a retreat for mindfulness teachers, Florence Meleo-Meyer once said, "If there is one thing I've learned in teaching, it is to put less in the program and to go more slowly." Slowness and restfulness are the compost in creating a fertile breeding ground for learning.

The primary way you can convey restfulness is by staying in touch with the effects of your pacing and how events unfold. Setting forth a clear structure will also aid you in embodying restfulness. You can do so using words:

We've got time.

Take some time to…

Bring the practice to a close in your own way. Take your time.

Haste is of no help to mindfulness.

Whenever the group as a whole accelerates into the doing mode of mind, perhaps after a digression on practicalities or a break with a lot of socializing, create a moment of rest and transition. There are many resources for doing so: mindfulness of breathing; ringing a bell; or, if you have the floor, falling silent for a few moments.

When an individual participant speeds up—for example, by losing himself in a narrative—you can simply point that out. This may have a confrontational effect, but it can also offer a learning opportunity. Here's an example of how that might play out.

Teacher: Can I interrupt you for a second there? You're very eloquent, and I hear how involved you are in the story, but I'm feeling my attention shift to my head and ending up in a fast-paced and mental atmosphere… Could you connect with your body, your contact with the floor, your breathing?… Yes, there's space now. Are you noticing it?

Participant: Yes.

Teacher: Me too.

Participant: So anyway, I was already late, and then the phone rang, and then I thought…

Teacher: Hello?… What's happening now?

Participant: What do you mean?

Teacher: Well, you're so wrapped up into your narrative…

Participant: Yes, as I was saying…

Teacher: But I asked you how it felt in your body.

Nondoing

Learning will happen spontaneously in a relaxed atmosphere. Interest is innately motivating for humans; we are simply attracted to insight and self-healing. We feel the wind at our backs, despite the obstacles. However, we Westerners have been conditioned to believe that we have to work to achieve something and therefore have a tendency to put in too much effort. Due to the tension and contracted focus of the driven doing mode of mind, we tend to lack the openness we need to let the learning process run its course.

Fortunately, participants already have a deep, if buried, understanding of the benefits of nondoing. Simply reminding them of it is enough. After all, recalling something you already know is one of the aspects of *sati*, the original Pali word for mindfulness. Here are some examples of how you can help participants connect with this deep knowing:

Seeing is enough. Let insight do its work. If you see something, you don't have to do anything else with it. Let it sink in. The mind knows how to use this insight.

Learning happens spontaneously. Decisions or "good intentions," such as "I have to remember this for next time," are not necessary here. They would bring all our ideas of good and bad back into the game, and those already bear the seeds of failure.

Stress that working at something is not necessary to achieve a result, as illustrated in the following dialogue.

Teacher: I wonder: Has this exploration given you any insights?

Participant: Yes.

Teacher: What do you notice?

Participant: I feel more space, more relaxation.

Teacher: And we didn't do anything. This is an important point to see. We didn't analyze or psychologize. We didn't look for causes or solutions. All we did was touch it with our mindful awareness, with consciousness. That alone brings a sense of space to the experience.

Open and Silent

Training in mindfulness is all about meeting the experience of the present moment. This requires receptivity, which in turn calls for two qualities: an open mind, free of assumptions and presumptions, and the silencing of concepts, comments, and stories—in other words, the usual verbal noise of the mind. Thus, in training sessions we seek to cultivate the qualities of openness and silence.

NOT-KNOWING, OPEN MIND

Openness is letting go of form and direction and embracing not-knowing and the not yet formed. A good learning environment opens entrenched old beliefs to new inquiry. It helps people regain access to the unprejudiced perspective of beginner's mind, free of preconceptions, allowing them to perceive each new experience as unique. This creates a sense of spaciousness that clears the path for ongoing exploration. And only when exploration keeps progressing can insight keep developing. An oft-quoted aphorism in hatha yoga is "Where there is space, there is growth." The same goes for the development of insight.

Answers close doors. In contrast, every time you convey not-knowing, you embody openness. If you are able to create a space in which questions are asked and remain open, both you and your participants can stay in the space of not-knowing.

Participant: Am I doing it right?

Teacher: There's more than one answer to that question. And it's an interesting question in itself. So let's take a closer look at it.

Mindfulness requires curiosity. In one of his talks, English vipassana teacher John Peacock said, "Mindfulness does not have a mantra. But if it did, it would be

'What is this?'" So as a teacher, exude curiosity. This can have the effect of reframing participants' experience and opening their eyes to other perspectives. A chief way to convey your openness and curiosity is to express your personal interest:

I find this hugely interesting.

What we are doing here is very special: having found a way to talk about this.

Interesting! This is what I like.

Those differences are special, right? Initially, we don't notice them. It's when we attend to the nuances that they come to the fore. Amazing.

SILENCE

Silence is the most widely used "form," or transmitter, of the unformed, of openness. As Florence Meleo-Meyer sometimes says in her trainings, "Silence is more spacious than words." Kabat-Zinn has gone so far as to claim that silence, stillness, and spaciousness are the most fundamental elements by which mindfulness is expressed. He warns of MBSR teachers' tendency to fill the nonconceptual parts of the training with extra "stuff": "Without the silence, the stillness, the spaciousness of the non-conceptual, it would merely become a cognitive exercise, no longer speaking to or cultivating the heart of mindfulness, which is practice" (2010, p. xv). He cautions that this tendency can loom particularly large when "we feel uncomfortable with extended silence or uncertain that the participants in the class are 'getting' what we want them to 'get'" (p. xv). So even though mindfulness training is a highly language-based training, silence is far more important. Words diminish the richness of experiences, reducing them to concepts the mind can grasp.

In effect, silence is what makes words powerful. It has an effect that far exceeds that of words, as so accurately described by spiritual teacher Eckhart Tolle in his book *Stillness Speaks* (2003). Silence also provides for containment of emotions. Perhaps every mindfulness teacher should take to heart the adage "Speak only if it improves upon the silence."

For mindfulness teachers, working with silence is perhaps the quality of being mode of mind that most appeals to intuition. In employing it, you are using something nonconceptual to express something. It is both an art and a challenge to use silence in this way, venturing out of the realm of cognition and language, and perhaps outside of your own comfort zone. (I'll revisit working with silence in chapter 4.)

Connected

A sense of connection within a group is essential for helping participants open up. It also provides an important source of support. In addition, participants will learn more from you if they feel a connection to you than if they're wary of you. However, it is not a given that participants will feel a sense of connection, including with you.

It is the teacher's job to establish a connection with each and every participant, insofar as this is possible. Ideally, the teacher would build relationships that stimulate each participant's learning process to the maximum degree. This isn't always easy, as the teacher is also the one who is leading, and people react to leaders in different ways. They may rebel against you, compete with you, seek your attention, try to please you, or try to stay invisible. Individuals' reactions to leadership are related to their personality and sometimes reflect patterns established in early childhood.

Although you may be a therapist, bear in mind that mindfulness training isn't intended to approach such reactions in a therapeutic way. Still, it's good to be aware of these patterns. In doing so, be alert to your own reactivity in this context and then, within appropriate boundaries, offer participants whatever they need to shape their relationship with you in ways that will facilitate their learning process.

This can be challenging. How do you offer a participant who competes with you what he needs without being dragged into the competition? How do you get through to someone who tends to withdraw without undermining her sense of security? The key is to strike a balance between allowing participants space and setting boundaries, between challenging and supporting, between taking initiative and exercising restraint, between making contact and keeping your distance. And you can only seek, and perhaps strike, this balance in each individual situation. Therefore, a preprogram interview is a crucial step in creating a relationship with participants. It is the first and possibly only one-on-one contact between teacher and student, and it is where the foundation for the relationship is laid.

Another aspect of connection is a participant's relationship to the group. At the start of the training, participants typically relate to others in the group as "they." It usually doesn't take long for that to change. As soon as participants get to know each other and interact a bit, "they" is transformed into "we." However, in a new group people may be on their guard at first. If so, you could initiate the process of connecting, perhaps by having everyone introduce themselves. Alternatively, you could employ basic, fundamental ways of establishing human connection. Nothing is as effective in defusing a tense situation as humor, and nothing is as effective in transforming "they" into "we" as getting participants to connect on a basic level by looking each other in the eye, using friendly gestures, doing a physical activity together, or sharing emotions. Simple action methods derived from psychodrama can also be useful,[8] though few teachers utilize this approach.

As the training progresses, a sense of connection will automatically develop, both among participants and between participants and the teacher. Meditating together reinforces that, and discussing intense personal experiences does so to an even greater extent. At the end of the training, it can be quite moving to hear how connected the participants feel to each other, how natural this connection feels to them, and how they miss this in other settings in their day-to-day lives.

Process Oriented

In mindfulness training, when we (teachers and students alike) focus on the process, we generally realize that we don't have to get somewhere—that we don't have to achieve something through willpower. As long as we don't turn away, we will see insights and solutions emerging. The antidote to the doing mode of mind, with its impatience to arrive at concrete results, solutions, and answers, is to focus on the process. You can foster this quality with comments along these lines:

We cannot control any results. We simply don't know what will happen. That's why the journey is one of discovery.

Just stick to the process and forget about the results. If you look after the process, the process will look after the results.

Staying Present

The quality of staying present helps people move beyond the point where they're inclined to quit. This allows them to travel into uncharted territory where they can make new discoveries. Here are a couple of statements that can promote this quality:

When exploring new things, you aren't always at ease, since you don't know what will come next. One way of giving new things a chance is to not immediately turn away when something feels uncomfortable or unpleasant.

Had you given in to your impulse to quit, you never would have discovered that there is actually fear behind this anger.

Sensing

Normally, the thinking mind predominates over people's awareness of their body and emotions. Mindfulness training aims to open people up to the dimension of sensing and teach them to appreciate this dimension. The body is a key, if often overlooked, place from which we can experience reality, offering a rich and spacious dimension.

You can invoke the realm of sensing by suggesting that participants explore what it means to take good care of themselves by, for example, making them aware of their posture during sitting meditation and reminding them to look after their basic needs, such as eating and drinking. It can also extend to encouraging participants to acknowledge and accept whatever emotions may be present, rather than trying to control them, as is so often the case in other social settings.

Sensing is therefore ideally addressed by the teacher's ongoing attention to the bodily aspect of an experience. For example, when guiding meditation, you might say, "First tune in to your physical posture." Then, during inquiry, you might say, "Where did you feel that in your body?" And at any time, you can direct attention to sensing through a question as simple as "What's happening for you now?" or "What are you experiencing inside?" These kinds of suggestions and questions will implicitly stress the importance of sensitization to the full breadth of participants' experiences, extending beyond words and thoughts to body and emotions. Perhaps it is needless to say, but this is a key part of mindfulness training.

Light

Problems can weigh people down and obstruct the learning process. It's often helpful to switch the focus to the body or the senses to break through this sense of heaviness. Taking some time to attend to the breath or do a bit of stretching is often a better way of wrapping up a heavy subject than any words you could come up with. Humor can also free the group from entrapment in the spiderweb of heavy thinking.

Another way of creating a lighter atmosphere is to focus attention on what has been achieved and what is possible, attending to the realm of yes rather than the realm of no. Here's a brief dialogue to illustrate this approach.

Participant: I was running around like crazy all day, trying to get things done, and I felt a headache coming on. I thought being so busy and stressed would only make it worse. So I sat down to meditate. I sat for half an hour but my headache didn't get any better.

Teacher: You did something very new. You didn't keep running. Instead, you stopped, and your headache didn't get worse. Wow! Congratulations!

Another cause of heaviness is a sense of personal responsibility, such as during the ups and downs of formal practice. People often take the tendency to be on autopilot personally, as if it stems from a conscious decision, and burden themselves with a sense of guilt and self-reproach. Yet this produces stress and tension and obstructs insight and learning. You can help participants who are experiencing this by exploring the process of identifying with automatic patterns, as demonstrated in the following dialogue.

Participant: I'm angry with myself for making this same mistake again.

Teacher: Would you have done things differently if you had been able to consciously choose your course?

Participant: Yes, of course I would have.

Teacher: So you didn't make a conscious choice to do it. It happened by itself. You didn't have any control over it. And now you see this.

Participant: But I really did make the wrong decision, even though I knew better.

Teacher: Really? It seems to me that in that moment you made the choice you thought was best. In that moment, you didn't know better. Now you can see it. Why make it personal?

Helping participants cast off a sense of guilt fosters lightness. This throws the tendencies of the mind to analyze past events overboard, which facilitates letting go and returning to beginner's mind.

Simple

Another consequence of the habit of letting the thinking mind prevail is a tendency to think reality is more complex than it actually is or to overly emphasize the complex aspects of experience. If you can help participants eliminate unnecessary complexity, they will experience lightness, spaciousness, and beginner's mind.

A common example is the dilemmas participants often feel around finding time for practice. The following dialogue provides an example of how you might address this difficulty.

> *Participant:* That's when I made a kind of schedule in my head: yoga, then my child's party, and then a few other things I needed or wanted to do. And I wondered whether it was really necessary to meditate so soon after our all-day silent retreat. It was a tough decision, so I kept thinking about it.
>
> *Teacher:* What if you had used that time you spent thinking about meditating to meditate?
>
> *Participant:* Well, I also want to watch the news. After all, you gotta keep up with what's going on in the world. It's difficult.
>
> *Teacher:* If you have time to watch TV, you've also got time to practice. I don't see what's so difficult.

We humans try to contain complexity through analysis, control, and evaluation. This takes us into the realm of the thinking mind and obstructs our present-moment awareness. An effective way of approaching such mental reactions is to qualify them as passing experiences, as illustrated in the following brief dialogue.

> *Participant:* And that's when I thought, "So this is how it's done. This is what it's about. I have to hold on to this."
>
> *Teacher:* So you were aware of thoughts. And then?

Developing the perspective that experiences are impermanent, always coming and going, can allow people to see their "problems" in new ways. Here's an example of how you might promote this perspective.

> *Participant:* And then, in the middle of the meditation, I'm busy solving this dispute with my friend. I'm also aware that I'm thinking, and I'm judging that, but I still can't get myself out of that train of thought… That's when I'm really lost and just don't know anymore.

Teacher: And then?

Participant: Then I hear your voice again and settle my awareness back on my breathing.

Teacher: We sometimes have the impression that we should "know" something before we can leave it behind, but that doesn't seem necessary. Just noticing there is a busy mind with a lot of thoughts oftentimes will do. Thoughts will go by themselves if we don't fuel them.

Sometimes participants may resist abandoning the illusion of complexity. We humans are so accustomed to falling back on our thinking that it can be disconcerting to intentionally sideline the mind. In addition, participants sometimes think, *Surely it can't be this simple.* As the teacher, you can bring a touch of playfulness and lightness to the experience to help ensure that the deconstruction of complexity creates space, rather than making participants defensive.

Qualities of the Doing Mode of Mind

When entering mindfulness training, people are usually in the doing mode of mind. This is our habitual mode, filled with thoughts such as *What do I have to do?* and *Am I doing it right?* and *What are the results?* Being mode of mind can feel alien and out of reach.

Relearning to enter the being mode of mind is quite a process, and it's central to the early stages of mindfulness training. Jon Kabat-Zinn compares it to meeting an old friend you haven't seen in years: "There may be some awkwardness in the beginning, not knowing who this person is anymore, not knowing quite how to be with him or her" (Kabat-Zinn, 1990, p. 60).

When the teacher then suddenly appeals to the doing mode of mind again at some stage, participants may get confused. Nonetheless, it is sometimes necessary to do so, given that the learning setting must strike a balance between the qualities of the doing mode of mind and the being mode of mind. The former, with its qualities of being alert, active, effortful, structured, independent, results oriented, varying, thinking, serious, and complex, makes its own essential contribution to the creation of a fertile learning setting.

Alert

When the atmosphere is too cozy and safe, participants may become drowsy and succumb to sleepiness. There may be a sense of flatness. There are various ways of introducing more alertness, including humor or doing a few mindful stretches. You could also share a personal anecdote, as the group will instantly wake up when the teacher shares something personal. Changing the subject, which I'll discuss later, is another effective method for increasing alertness.

Of course, speaking clearly and using targeted, pithy speech and actions can stimulate participants, keep them awake, and prevent drowsiness. Another option is to alternate between styles: between speaking loudly and softly, between speaking quickly and slowly, between addressing individuals and addressing the group, between taking an in-depth approach and widening the focus more broadly. You can accomplish something similar by responding to serious comments in a light-hearted way or making a provocative remark.

Participant: Stress is always a bad thing.

Teacher: I don't agree with you there! When I'm up against a deadline for an article, the adrenaline pumping through my body makes me very efficient and creative.

You can also break up a sense of monotony by saying something absurd.

Teacher: We're now going to do a sitting meditation.

Participant: How long will it take?

Teacher: Three hours.

Not letting participants know what's next in the program can also boost alertness because it creates anticipatory excitement. However, this approach shouldn't be taken at the expense of a sense of safety.

Whichever of these methods you employ, it's likely that alertness will resonate and spark within the group. It tends to be contagious.

Active

Being mode of mind typically rules in mindfulness training. The setting is characterized by slowness, periods of silence, and restfulness. We usually have plenty of time. After a few weeks, participants often start saying that entering the session room is like stepping into a warm bath. It helps them realize how hurried and tired they usually are, and how ease and rest are lacking in their lives. However, because they are not yet trained in managing the being mode of mind, they may have a tendency to indulge in it, which can lead to an atmosphere of lethargy and indolence.

The antidote to excessive dominance of restfulness is to engage in action. This can take the form of physical action, like doing some stretches, or it can involve activating the mind by asking an open question and seeking responses from the group. You can also use your authority to stimulate the group when it's too sluggish in responding to your call to action:

I'd like to continue. Will you join us again?

A subtle but important way of getting participants to act is to ensure that they realize the responsibility for doing so is theirs. When the dynamic excessively involves the trainer bringing the teaching to participants, rather than participants having to come to get it, the group will increasingly lean back into restfulness. So be careful when filling a void created by a group's inaction. If need be, you can counter with a stimulating remark without relinquishing the invitation to be active.

Teacher: Would any of you be willing to say something about your experiences?

Participants: [Resounding silence.]

Teacher: Were there no experiences?

This allows the invitation to share experiences to stand without creating tension. Eventually, the group will spring into action. (I'll provide specific techniques for stimulating an active quality of mind in chapter 4.)

Effortful

In many contemplative traditions, every meditation starts with renewing the meditator's intention, and for good reason: When people forget about their intentions and commitments, they lose an important connection to their motivation and resources for devoting effort to the endeavor. They may also lose their way, forgetting what really matters and falling back on the limited scope of their day-to-day to-do lists. When this quality dominates, people can easily fall prey to confusion and doubt: *I just can't make it happen. The automatic patterns are stronger than I am.*

Mindfulness practice can benefit immensely from a frequent renewal of intentions, and it's up to the teacher to bring this message to the fore time and again. An important way of doing that is to inspire participants by displaying your own energy, commitment, enthusiasm, and confidence. You can show this in the way you do things. If you visibly try to do your best, you'll set the tone for the group.

You can also explicitly solicit effort by reminding participants of their initial motivation for seeking mindfulness training. Good opportunities for doing so are during your introductory talk in session 1 or an interim progress review, at the beginning of a meditation, or when explaining the next home practice.

Another way of drawing attention to the importance of commitment is to bring attention to the time-limited nature of the training and communicate that you want to make the most of the time available to the group:

You may think eight weeks is a long time, but it will be over in a flash.

The impact of the digital world on our stress levels would make an interesting topic for discussion. In the scope of this training, however, we don't have time for that.

Another option is to use approaches derived from motivational interviewing:

You should only do what you yourself want to do. It's your choice.

For whom are you doing the home practices? For me?

Why are you here?

You can also share poems that might help participants reconnect with their initial motivation. The great thing about poems is that they appeal to deeper values in an open and positive way, without activating participants' guilty conscience. Poems I recommend for this purpose include "Enough," by David Whyte; "Autobiography in Five Short Chapters," by Portia Nelson; "Keeping Quiet," by Pablo Neruda; "Kindness," by Naomi Shihab Nye; "Love After Love," by Derek Walcott; "Now Is the Time," by Hafiz; and "Wild Geese," by Mary Oliver.

A somewhat subtle way of renewing intention is to call to mind how blessed and rich we are with everything we already have, especially in the West. Reminding participants not to take that for granted will activate a sense of gratitude that will give them renewed energy for working on what's truly important to them.

Structured

In discussing the qualities of the being mode of mind, I wrote that we need the qualities of openness and silence to free ourselves from the mind's preconceptions. Yet to prevent ourselves from getting lost in this openness, we need definition and form. I discuss key elements of this aspect of the doing mode of mind in the sections that follow.

OFFERING STRUCTURE AND KNOWLEDGE

Clear structure, clear frameworks, and clearly formulated knowledge provide essential support to the learning process, so don't get stuck in unnecessary formlessness. For participants, exploring and examining their own experience is an important quality of the setting, but this doesn't mean that there is nothing concrete for the teacher to say about anything or that you can't offer something for participants to hold on to.

You are the expert in mindfulness. You know a lot more about it than participants do, if only because you've gone through the learning process several times, with different perspectives. Don't fall prey to the common misconception wherein teachers mistake mindfulness for formlessness. That can lead to an exaggeration of an approach of "That's interesting; let's explore it" or "On the one hand…And on the other hand…" Such approaches send the message *I don't offer anything to hold on to* or even *I don't know anything*. (I'll address this pitfall in greater detail in chapter 6.)

Lack of structure can provoke a sense of insecurity and disorientation in participants, which isn't helpful in the learning process. True, you can explore everything, but that doesn't mean there are no concrete results; that there is no truth (even if it's relative); that there are no established methods; and that you, the teacher, can never make unequivocal statements. Don't be afraid to throw in snappy one-liners now and again. They can offer support and direction:

Don't worry about that. It isn't important.

That is exactly how it's supposed to be. Keep it up.

The teacher's firmness provides a needed source of support when participants are in the difficult and intensive process of self-exploration. It's a life jacket participants can wear when entering the unknown sea of new experiences. This firmness can take the form of resoluteness. In regard to mindfulness, it's common to say,

"Dare to not know." But for teachers, the opposite is sometimes more fitting: Dare to know! Knowledge and facts offer a framework that can temporarily support further exploration and learning.

For instance, you could set forth details on the differences between various meditations. As an example, imagine that a participant has said, "For the mindfulness of breathing meditation we had to stay present to something, and now we don't. So what am I supposed to do? What should I be focusing on?" From the perspective of openness, or not-knowing, you might reply, "That question—What should I be focusing on?—does that arise during the practice? And is it accompanied by a certain feeling?" In this case, it would probably be better to reply based on knowledge: "You're right. There is a difference between these meditations. They are basically two kinds of meditation, each with its own value. One is concentration meditation, and the other is insight meditation. Let me tell you a bit more about that…"

Likewise, you might address the importance of a good sitting posture during meditation. Imagine that a participant has said, "I can't sit with my legs crossed. I keep having to move a leg." From the perspective of not-knowing, you might say, "That feeling of having to move your leg—can you tell me a bit more about that?" But in this case, it may be just as good to take the knowing route: "Finding the right seated position can sometimes be an issue in the beginning. It's not about the form. There are also people who meditate while seated on a chair. But still, there are a few things to bear in mind…"

A different context in which it can also be helpful to embrace knowing is when participants have questions revolving around "why" that are prompted by doubt. For example, a participant might ask, "Why should we bother with meditation? What's the purpose?" If you were to take the not-knowing route, you might respond with a question of your own: "Good question! What do *you* think?" However, in this case it may be more helpful to make short work of the doubt by taking the knowing route and say something like this: "By sitting still, you're making a statement that doing is not everything. It's also an exercise in clear seeing. You learn to see patterns you'd otherwise overlook—patterns you follow automatically, without realizing it, and that control your life. While there may not be concrete results, meditation can still add great value to your life. At least, that's what I think."

That last line is important. It subtly emphasizes that you're stating your opinion, and not an absolute truth handed down by an authority. Yet at the same time, you're also taking a position, showing that you stand for something and have confidence in your insights. That can prove enormously supportive to participants.

After all, questions about purpose are often prompted by doubts that can undermine the person's practice.

MANAGING TIME EFFECTIVELY

Another aspect of structure or form is time management. This is the skill of being focused on the group, the content of the program, and yourself, while also keeping an eye on the context, including the time.

Many practices and inquiries be can shortened without compromising their quality. And while it's important to review all home practices, how much time you spend reviewing each one is less crucial. Similarly, it's important to lead the body scan during sessions when it's called for, but it's less important to note each body part.

I'll address tempo in greater detail in chapter 3. For now, I'll just say that tempo is so crucial to training that it's best to use the appropriate tempo and cut things short if need be. If any aspect of a session feels incomplete, just say, "We'll come back to that later," and then be sure to follow up.

Because you're working with such rich material, if you try to cover all the themes fully, you may have a feeling of being short on time. However, there is almost never a good reason to let a session run long. Time overruns are often caused by the teacher's desire to achieve a sense of completeness. This need limits the teacher's ability to strike a balance between form and spaciousness. Bear in mind that mindfulness training is a process in which none of the themes are ever finally and fully explored. That's a good thing. This open-ended nature allows participants to continue exploring mindfulness in their own way.

So keep an eye on your program and agenda for the session, and also on the time, and aim for a balance that respects the content, the needed tempo, and the schedule. Sometimes this may mean you'll want to adjust your program. Here are the three main reasons you may need to do so:

- There is emotional content that you don't want to gloss over.

- The group as a whole is developing faster or slower than anticipated.

- Opportunities for more in-depth understanding of the session's central theme arise.

Consciously adjusting the program during a session can be a skillful way of managing time. The key is that it be prompted by your understanding of and responsibility for the entire process, not because time is slipping away.

Independent

Experiencing a sense of connection and common humanity is an important quality of the group setting, increasing participants' capacity for learning, relaxation, trust, and healing. However, it's also essential to appeal to participants' sense of autonomy and commitment to engage in the program. After all, when they return to their day-to-day reality after the session, they'll need to be able to navigate their world with a sense of self that allows them to both open up and set boundaries. This ensures that they'll have the personal resources they need to meet challenges.

One way to foster independence is to appeal to each participant's sense of personal responsibility and ingenuity, approaching participants individually and tasking them with finding their own solutions to their challenges:

It's not about how someone else deals with this; it's about what best suits you.

Choose a comfortable position. Sit on a chair if that offers the best posture for you.

These kinds of statements make participants responsible for navigating their own obstacles. Besides challenging participants, this also shows respect for their independence, autonomy, and creativity. In this way, participants will feel that you've acknowledged their individuality.

Results Oriented

Participants usually have certain results in mind when they embark on mindfulness training. Therefore, it makes sense to sometimes focus on results. You might do so at the beginning of the training by simply asking, "What would you like to achieve through this training?" Then, at the end of training you might revisit this question and ask participants what they've learned and what they'll take home from the training.

Of course, there is also a sense in which the process *is* the result. You can elucidate this by confirming that experiencing a practice as calming is indeed a valuable result.

Participant: Simply remembering my breath already starts to calm me down.

Teacher: Good for you.

In the same way, developing a skill can also be considered a result. Here are two brief dialogues illustrating how the teacher might emphasize this.

Participant: I've gotten much better at being able to bring my mind back after wandering off.

Teacher: You're doing the same meditation and you keep coming back, yet it has become easier. That's a gain.

Participant: My thoughts still drift off as often as before, but I've stopped beating myself up over it.

Teacher: Great! That sounds like an improvement in quality, even as your experiences have stayed the same.

Results are legitimate and deserve acknowledgment—as long as the focus on results doesn't lead to a results-driven attitude that obstructs openness to unexpected experiences.

Varying

Mindfulness training consists of looking precisely, feeling precisely, experiencing physically, fathoming, contemplating the posture's effects on the mind, introspection, and letting go. This is a very intensive process. Group inquiry often takes half an hour or more, and the entire session usually lasts two and a half hours. You'll need to alternate between concentration and relaxation to tie in with people's natural rhythms of attention, varying between zooming in, letting go, shifting attention, and then zooming in and letting go again.

The moments of zooming out and relaxation do more than simply cater to people's attention spans; these tranquil interludes also allow them to process what they've seen and felt. It takes time for physical and emotional experiences, as well as insights, to sink in or settle. This assimilation is often more readily facilitated by something like walking meditation than through talking.

As the teacher, you decide when to alternate. You are the moderator. You dance to the rhythm of attention. You can alternate in various dimensions: between speech and silence, between practice and inquiry, between sitting and movement, between intensity and relaxation, between touching on a subject and letting it go again, or between didactic presentation and stimulating participants to explore their own experience. Even within a given teaching mode (guided practice, inquiry, or didactic presentation), you can alternate. For example, during inquiry you can vary between giving individuals a long turn and giving many brief turns, between following up or cutting the discussion short, or between setting the topic yourself or letting the group do so.

Of course, you can also vary your personal presentation: between being very serious and making a joke, between being warm and cooling down, between speeding up and slowing down, between speaking softly and speaking louder, or between lightening the mood and inserting gravitas. Other possibilities include alternating between zooming in on a participant and zooming out to the group, between exploring something in-depth and showing the bigger picture, or between coming back to a theme and letting it go. (In chapter 4, in the section "Auxiliary Conversation Techniques," you'll find many practical suggestions about how to dance this dance.)

Wherever possible, insert a transition before alternating, such as a brief break or allowing a moment of silence. Otherwise, simply intervene. For example, if a particular discussion is taking too long, you can interrupt—making an effort to do so in a gentle and flowing way:

Shall we pick up where we left off?

Let's conclude here.

I'd like to leave it at that. It's an interesting subject, and I'm sure we'll come back to it.

It's time for something else.

Shall we wrap up now? This discussion may feel unfinished, but it's quite a broad topic. We can come back to it later.

Thinking

Mindfulness training is not only about "right experiencing"; it's also about "right understanding." The latter objective draws, at least partly, on the thinking mind and its analytic ability. Mindfulness training courses include concepts, theories, explanations, and information, both in handouts and on a whiteboard or other display. Together, the subjects of didactic presentations and course workbooks comprise a brief course in the psychology of the human mind.

In addition, inquiry obviously draws on the mind, as it involves associating thoughts, feelings, reactions, and patterns and making new connections to arrive at insights. So participants' cognitive abilities are often invoked in the setting. This is fine; it's good to let the mind do what it's equipped to do.

Serious

Whenever lightness is exaggerated, commitment and focus may falter, leading to an inability to muster the required concentration and effort, and to avoidance of difficult things. The antidote is seriousness. Being serious comes easy to most of us; it tends to be the usual mode of mind. Therefore, all that's required to maintain some degree of seriousness is to keep humor, playfulness, and other such qualities in check. This is especially important when humor, irony, or making light of something is used as an avoidance technique.

Participant: Crying child, angry husband, and me running around with my cleaning stuff—it's as if I've got OCD. Obsessive cleaning disorder!

Teacher: You're making light of it now, but the underlying issue isn't light. Can you describe what's actually happening here?

Participant: Then I thought, "It is what it is," as we say in mindfulness!

Teacher: Hold on. Can we look into that a little further? When exactly did this thought, "It is what it is," come up?

Complex

Life is simple. By that, I mean the final causes and the biggest insights are simple. Much of the rest is complex. Great teachers can express the truth in a word or sentence but may spend the rest of their lives explaining the nuances of that statement.

Any given experience is simple and complex at the same time. That's the koan of life. Try describing the whole of a minor experience—something as simple as a color, a smell, or a passing emotion or thought. Only when we attempt to do that do we discover how many layers, nuances, and dynamics that minor experience holds. The description becomes endless. So as we guide participants to see reality for what it is, we cannot let them remain limited to its simplicity; they must also see and honor its complexity.

Teacher: You started out with something as simple as the experience of pain. And now, five minutes later, we've discovered that there are numerous sensations, thoughts, feelings, tendencies, and moods hovering around it, like moths around a flame. It reminds me of that simple raisin and the many nuances it had…

The Power of the Circle

Whenever people form a group, "something" happens. In mindfulness training, the group takes a very explicit form: a circle. We ask participants to sit down, facing each other, and invest their time and attention in mindfulness practice and exploring how they deal with what's difficult. Group members explore together, listen to each other, compare their individual experience to the others' experiences, and integrate what they hear. Practice turns into joint exploration, creating something special that transcends what typically occurs in a circle at a meeting or get-together.

The circle is an ancient form for gathering and learning. Over two thousand years ago, the Buddha and his contemporaries sat together to explore truth. Indeed, this practice dates back even further. In some pre-Hindu traditions, it was common to sit around the teacher and explore truth together. This is referred to as *satsang*: in Sanskrit, *sat* means "truth" and *sang* means "together," so *satsang* means "gathering together in truth." *Sang* is also the etymological source of the word *sangha*: a group of devotees who keep in touch with each other and nourish and support each other on their path toward insight, either guided by a teacher or not.

In the tradition of mindfulness, teachings are passed on horizontally, rather than vertically. The teacher, or perhaps more accurately the trainer, is someone who guides and practices together with the group, not someone who "knows." This, in combination with three specific qualities of the circle in mindfulness training, adds a great deal of value to the setting and makes it special. Those three specific qualities are resonance, group wisdom, and togetherness. "Resonance" means that one individual's experience directly links up with that of others. When group wisdom arises, participants' eyes are opened to the fact that there are many more possibilities than one could come up with individually. And togetherness teaches participants to feel that their difficulties and pain aren't personal; rather, they are part of the greater whole of universal human difficulties and pain. Together, these qualities add inestimable power to the setting of mindfulness training.

Resonance

Participants often say that practicing meditation is easier in the group than at home. In the group, the silence feels stronger and the insights deeper. At home, alone in a room, meditation can feel somewhat subdued, less powerful, and less rich. This is partly due to situational conditioning—the phenomenon wherein recognition of a situation triggers a neural network that revives associations with the situation. This happens, for example, when you visit a foreign country and notice that the language of that country, which you'd once been familiar with, comes back to you. Another example is keying in your PIN at an ATM without even thinking about it, whereas you might struggle to come up with the code in other situations. In the same way, participants' associations with previous sessions come back to them as soon as they set foot in the meditation room.

But there's more. In his book *Primal Leadership* (2002), Daniel Goleman presents the concept of an "open-loop" system of emotions. By comparison, blood circulation is a closed system: its parameters are all held within our bodies. Our system of emotion regulation, however, is open: we externalize emotions, receive them back from others, and then reinternalize them. Emotions are a key way of getting people on the same page, and early in human evolution they served as a primitive communication system between group members. You've probably experienced how emotions allow you to feel any tension directly—without words or without even exchanging a glance—when entering a room full of people. (Besides facilitating communication, aligning emotions also has a strong binding effect. This may be why song and rhythmic rituals were so prominent in early cultures.)

We also align ourselves with others in neurological terms. When you see someone perform an action, the same neurons you would use to perform that action are activated in your brain. Jon Kabat-Zinn calls this kind of neural mirroring intersubjective resonance (2010, p. xviii). And Daniel Siegel (2007) describes how this resonance is invoked not only on a social, interpersonal level, but also on an intrapersonal level, such as when a certain posture or way of breathing invokes resonance with previous situations in which the same posture or way of breathing occurred. Clearly, this phenomenon is reminiscent of situational learning and could be used as a way of tuning in at the start of a meditation. (For more information about learning through mirroring, see Iacoboni, 2008.)

Neural mirroring is sometimes referred to as resonance, coherence, attunement, or, in the case of meditation, self-attunement. Resonance can also be invoked by imagining yourself doing what you aspire to do. Musicians sometimes practice by imagining physically performing a piece. In sports, this type of imagery is believed to improve athletes' performance and significantly speed recovery after injury.

When we put all of this information on resonance and mirroring together with the fact that we learn through activating (firing) neurons and doing so repeatedly (causing connections between neurons to become stronger), something remarkable emerges: people can learn by observing someone demonstrating something, just as if they were doing it themselves. And this isn't limited to observing outward behavior. Meditating together is more effective because group members resonate with each other's silence. (For that matter, perhaps this kind of subtle resonance plays a role in direct transmission through the physical presence of the teacher, which is a prominent method in some traditions.) Again, there is an open loop, with the intrasubjective circuit linking up with the intersubjective resonance circuit.

The miraculous power of resonance is illustrated nicely by the Vedic myth of Indra's net. Over the palace of the Vedic god Indra hangs a net with a diamond at each knot. The facets of the diamonds reflect each other. As soon as one diamond starts to sparkle, all of the other diamonds reflect some of that sparkle. The entire net resonates and shines thanks to that first spot of light.

Group Wisdom

Shared interests can also strengthen the group bond. While sitting together focused on the same exploration, group members' individual observations and reflections merge: searching, observing, being silent, letting the experience sink in, confirming, inquiring, and supplementing one another's experience. One person may be convinced of something only to have that conviction blown out of the water by another person's opposite experience. This, in turn, could lead to a profound insight for a third person. Information whirls around within the group and is verified or adjusted. For some individuals, information that they forgot they knew comes back to the surface, triggered by an unexpected word or flash of insight from someone else. In this way, group exploration can reach entirely new levels. It's like hooking devices up in a network. A group of people forms a network that knows more than the sum of its parts.

Group-based exploration is a constantly evolving process of coming together and breaking apart, settling on temporary denominators, and leaving questions open. Clarity emerges, becomes obscured, and reemerges in a new form. Things arise, transform, recede, and arise again. The wisdom of the group involves recognition and inquiry, and it's a living thing that cannot be pinned down. Meanwhile, on the individual level, lasting insight arises—almost coincidentally, as a by-product. Putting these individual insights and experiences together is like pushing smoldering logs of wood closer. They feed off each other to form a rich and powerful fire that will flare up again and again in unexpected places.

The process of group exploration can take many forms. That's where the wisdom is. One person's firm assertion may be refined by another's experience. One person's view may be reversed by another's perspective. Yet it is all possible, given that even contradictions are relative. This brings to mind a line from Walt Whitman's *Song of Myself*: "I am large… I contain multitudes" (1855, p. 55). The same goes for group wisdom. When everyone seeks their own truth, each person's insight is equally valid. After all, there are as many realities as there are participants. It is precisely the multidimensional nature of joint exploration that reveals insight in its full richness.

The synergy among participants' insights breeds a kind of group wisdom that borders on universal truth. This is not to be mistaken for unequivocal truth; rather, it is a multifaceted diamond in which individual insights are mere glimpses of the whole, regardless of whether the individual has been engaging in practice for years or is just beginning. By joining together in a group, we connect these individual insights. It's like assembling a giant jigsaw puzzle together. Once joined, the pieces of the puzzle make up the map of deep human knowing, charting the path of the dhamma—the way out of suffering.

Togetherness

In times of grief, stress, and illness, people tend to isolate themselves. Their original pain is then compounded by the hurt caused by the idea that they are on their own. It can feel like the rest of the world moves on, as if nothing has happened, and is indifferent to their suffering. This can activate a tendency to take one's suffering personally and feel guilty about it.

The best way to ease suffering is through awareness that it is part of the shared human experience. None of us are alone in our pain. We are not different when we suffer. We are all part of a greater suffering. This is part of being human, and there is no personal fault involved. Only when we experience that can we focus on forging an accepting relationship with what is difficult.

This is beautifully illustrated by the Indian parable of Kisa Gotami. Heartbroken after the loss of her son, she turned to the Buddha and asked him to relieve her of her suffering.

"Bring me white mustard seeds from different houses," the Buddha told her, "but only from homes of families who have not lost any family members." The woman set off in good spirits. Every home she visited had mustard seeds in the kitchen, but when Kisa asked whether the family had ever mourned the loss of one of its members, the answer was always yes. She often stayed to listen, touched by the pain and grief of the people she met. After a few days, she returned to the Buddha. Although she hadn't gathered a single mustard seed, learning that all people live with grief and sharing that experience with them had changed something in her. She told the Buddha, "My loss and grief have been soothed because I've consoled others and seen that my loss is the loss of all people, and my grief is the grief of all people."

Recognizing our shared suffering offers invaluable support and greatly eases that suffering. We truly are all in the same boat. Our separateness is merely an illusion, according to Jon Kabat-Zinn (1990), and glimpses of unity bring us healing. Vietnamese Zen master Thich Nhat Hanh speaks to this with his concept of "interbeing" (1987), and Kristin Neff points out that a sense of common humanity is one of the crucial elements of self-compassion (2011).

When we recognize we are all connected, the heart jumps up and says, "Yes!" In group mindfulness training, we share this experience by turning toward our hardships together, letting ourselves be struck by them, and sitting among the fragments—together. (I'll discuss this further in chapter 4, in the section "Working with the Causes of Suffering.")

CHAPTER 3

Guiding Mindfulness Practices

Meditation is the only intentional, systematic human activity which at bottom is about *not* trying to improve yourself or get anywhere else, but simply to realize where you already are.

—Jon Kabat-Zinn

Meditation is hugely important. It yields a microcosmic view of our relationship with our most important companions in life: our mind, our thinking, our emotions, our body.

—Christina Feldman

Mindfulness training is often equated with doing formal meditation practices, but there is much more to it. Informal practices help participants bring more mindfulness into their day-to-day life and are equally important. The group setting offers an opportunity to experience being mode of mind (as an alternative to doing mode of mind) and allows participants to become more familiar with this mode of mind. In addition, inquiry is a powerful tool for acquiring insight. All of these are important aspects of mindfulness training.

That said, meditation still predominates both during sessions and in home practice. Further, the experience of meditation provides a large chunk of the raw material from which insight arises. The meditative practices also serve as a kind of container in which everything that is touched, opened, and learned can settle and be processed. And ultimately, meditation is the core of the program's self-healing power. In mindfulness training, the aphorism "Trust the program" basically means "Trust the practice."

In short, mindfulness practices create situations that invite us to be more mindful. And that's what the training is about.

In this chapter, I'll discuss key focal points when guiding these practices. Although I generally use sitting meditation as the context, all of the material is equally valid for guiding other kinds of meditation. I'll begin by detailing how you, the person guiding the practices, can work with your own attention during meditations. Next, I'll delve into the structure of guided instructions. I'll also address some technical aspects of guiding meditation, such as wording, qualities of voice, and tempo.

As you read this chapter, bear in mind that the expressive power of words is limited. Words are, in themselves, already metaphors. When guiding meditation, we often give them additional metaphoric meanings to designate inner experiences. However, inner experiences have a reality of their own that cannot be adequately captured by words. So words will always fall short as a tool for guiding meditation. Unfortunately, words are all we have. And they're certainly better than nothing for pointing people down the learning pathway they must travel. By providing references, tips, reminders, and cues, words can serve as signposts along this pathway.

Dividing Attention While Guiding Meditation

There are three fields of information over which teachers have to divide their attention during guided meditation: the group, word-for-word meditation (the script, or spoken guidance), and the teacher's own meditative consciousness. As depicted in figure 3, these three fields mutually influence each other, and focusing too much attention on one field results in too little attention left for the other fields. In this section, I'll first describe each field, and then I'll turn to the art of spreading attention evenly over all three of them.

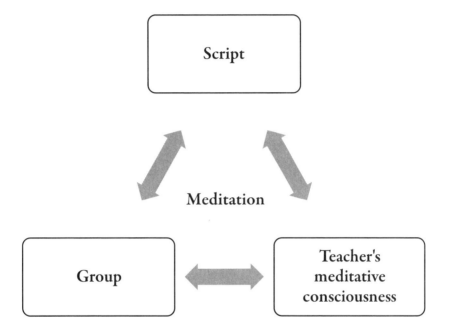

Figure 3. The teacher's attention during meditation, divided between the group, the script, and the teacher's own meditative consciousness.

Attention to the Group

During formal practice, participants close themselves off from the group. You, however, as the teacher, stay tuned in to the group. After all, you are responsible for the group and therefore need to know what's going on so you can respond appropriately. Noticing how participants are experiencing the meditation can inform your choices as you proceed with a practice, as well as the inquiry afterward and later in the course.

Sometimes you'll sense that the group is tired or that their awareness is waning. Should you cut the meditation short? Or perhaps you'll notice that a participant is crying. Should you adjust your words or say something about it? There aren't concrete rules to guide such choices. Trust your intuition and experience. If you're unsure how to proceed, you can follow the general guidance to trust the program. Here, trusting the program means trusting the planned meditation, including its scheduled duration, and understanding that it isn't a problem if challenges arise for participants. Obstacles are part and parcel of meditation. So when in doubt, just stick to the program.

Also be aware that your impression of the group or a participant may be subjective. Perhaps you're feeling impatient, insecure, or mistrustful and project that attitude onto the group. Exercise restraint in adapting the meditation to what you perceive as the needs of the group.

Another consideration is that trying too hard to please participants can deprive them of valuable learning moments. Don't be overly fearful of certain situations doing damage. Meditation isn't open-heart surgery. It won't be a disaster if someone dozes off for a bit, if part of the meditation doesn't register, or if a participant becomes emotional. In fact, these and other challenges can provide fertile practice material.

To remain in contact with the group, you have three antennas at your disposal: your eyes, your ears, and your gut. By looking around, you can see how participants are doing physically. By tuning in with your ears, you'll receive another source of information: breathing, fidgeting, rearranging clothes, coughing. Information received through the gut is harder to describe. What I can say is that the gut is a sensitive organ that constantly supplies information, albeit in a very subtle manner, about one's environment—a capacity that's tied to our ability to resonate with one another, as discussed in chapter 2. It's easier to stay present to your own meditative consciousness when you're guided by the inner and more subtle antenna of the gut.

The general rule is that the more difficult the group, the more you need to direct your attention outward, to seeing and hearing. The easier the group, the more you can be guided by your gut.

You might think of gut feelings as a kind of pilot light that keeps burning at minimum level when the group requires little attention. The more you can let your perception of the group flow along at this minimum level, the more you can focus your attention on your own meditative consciousness. This is beneficial for allowing you to embody the guidance. But sometimes the pilot light flares up and ignites your attention. Your alertness increases, and you attend to what you hear and possibly to what you see in the group. In other words, in your gut you may sense restlessness in the group. Then you can focus on sounds. If you hear restlessness, you can open your eyes.

In addition to engaging in this kind of intuitive process, also consciously focus your attention outward several times during every meditation by listening or taking a quick look around. Your gut feelings are a rich source of information, but you can't rely on them exclusively.

Attention to the Script

The script (the words spoken as you guide a formal practice) has important functions and is part of the program for a reason. The words, the rhythm, and the silences are all carefully chosen. The script is a foundation stone you can rely on.

Still, excessive focus on following the script may lead to guidance that's rigid, rather than individualized or contextual. I've already mentioned a few reasons why you might want to deviate from the script (dozing off, restlessness, expressions of emotion). Other common reasons are if the script doesn't unfold smoothly during the presentation or if you haven't memorized it sufficiently. Beware of the latter. If you deviate for this reason, you're compromising the quality of the meditation. You might be tempted to read the script to the group, but this isn't an ideal solution, as the cognitive effort required to read it will generally block your own access to your meditative consciousness. To skillfully deliver a meditation, you need to master its script. I'll come back to this later in the chapter.

Attention to Your Own Meditative Consciousness

Although you may be good at telling stories or reading them to people, guiding meditation requires something beyond verbal skills: it requires that you contact your own meditative consciousness. Participants experience the meditative consciousness of the person guiding the meditation through direct transmission. Whereas participants often don't take notice of an incorrect sentence or a missing word, when the person guiding the meditation isn't in touch with her meditative consciousness, participants will immediately pick up on it. This might introduce tension or even insecurity into participants' meditation. So your embodiment of a meditation is more important than using the right words.

That said, you cannot fully surrender to your meditative consciousness. You also need to stay in touch with your pragmatic consciousness, using your cognitive skills to weigh and balance information to deal with specific situations. Your pragmatic consciousness can assess the effects of your meditative consciousness in regard to fulfilling the intentions of the meditation and meeting the needs of the current situation. In essence, as the teacher, part of you will be wrapped up in the inner experience of the meditation, another part will deliver the program and words of the meditation (the script), while yet another part will be attending to the outside world, with its occurrences and possible needs to be met. Maintaining a balance between these three fields of attention is a skill that requires some practice.

Because you are the link between your own meditation and your guiding of the practice, you might include elements of your personal experience in your guidance, whether directly or indirectly. That said, this must be done in a measured, intentional way. For example, during a meditation you might experience silence, a deepening insight, or a flash of inspiration. No matter how good this moment feels to you, that doesn't mean it's fitting to share it with the group. The group or the script may require that you offer something quite different than your meditative experience of the moment.

Balancing the Three Fields of Information: Qualities and Exaggerations

You need your pragmatic consciousness to assess and balance the input from the three key fields of information: the group, the script, and your own meditation. In this way, your pragmatic consciousness is a moderator—a levelheaded judge who weighs and filters the information you're receiving. To provide your pragmatic consciousness with some guidance on what to watch out for, here's an overview of the ideal qualities of each form of information, along with descriptions of how a disproportionately strong focus on one of the fields of information affects the meditation.

Attention to the Group

Qualities: Being sensitive to the setting and the needs of the group

Results of exaggerated focus: Adapting meditations excessively, not allowing helpful friction, or offering too few exercises or not offering challenging exercises

Attention to the Script

Qualities: Using the right words and sequences, including silences

Results of exaggerated focus: Being overly mechanical and insufficiently lively and not making sensory contact with the group

Attention to Your Own Meditative Consciousness

Qualities: Providing guidance based on lived experience and embodying the meditation

Results of exaggerated focus: Tuning out the group and not attending to the contents of the script

Note that there can be benefits to emphasizing a specific focus. Sometimes the situation calls for it. Again, it's a matter of striking a balance while considering what the group needs in a given learning moment. For example, during the first body scan it's important to follow the script as closely as possible to facilitate participants' home practice with an audio recording. Following the script precisely will be less important in later sessions, when you might sometimes choose to express something that arose spontaneously in your own meditation at the expense of the script. Likewise, you might want to adjust the script in response to an issue or feeling that's arisen in the group. For example, if there's a heavy feeling after a recent inquiry, you could add words that bring a lighter, more gentle tone to the script. The key in varying from the script is that your choices be led by the intent of the training, not by something that's important to you personally, such as sharing an interesting meditation experience of your own, attempting to please the group, or trying to combat a sense of restlessness.

You can maintain the balance between the three fields of information by staying gently tuned in to your pragmatic consciousness and using its moderating capacity. From time to time, ask yourself, "What's attracting my attention, and what would be a skillful response to that?" This is more a matter of weighing information than thinking about it. You may simply become aware of the fact that you're too focused on the script, too fixated on how the group is doing, or overly absorbed in your own meditation. These are all moments to open your attention to all three fields and rebalance your approach. You can work on this skill by observing your choices when reviewing recorded sessions later, on your own or with a coteacher or peer consultation group. As you observe, consider whether other choices might have been more balanced or appropriate to the moment.

Becoming aware of where your attention has gone, coming back to the moment, and responding—guiding meditation is clearly a mindfulness practice in its own right.

The Structure of Meditation Guidance

Mindfulness practice is made up of two primary components: attention and attitude. This is reflected in the script: not only do you say what participants could do (what to do), but you also speak to the attitude with which they might do it (how to do it). After that, with a third component—remaining silent—you offer participants time to put these instructions into practice Any guided meditation thus contains the three components depicted in figure 4.

"What to do" relates to the attention component: what to be mindful of, what participants are to do when they notice that their attention has drifted off, and so on. These instructions are of a technical nature. First you stress the concentration element and coming back when attention has wandered. Over time, you open the group's focus to various fields of experience, such as sounds and physical and mental experiences. At a more advanced level, you give them additional tools, such as noting, and elaborate on specific meditation themes.

"How to do it" relates to the attitude component. You address this with remarks inserted between practical instructions, reminding participants that meditation is not just about following instructions, but also about the way in which they do so. Such remarks address the style of meditation, so to speak. So reminding participants about drifting off is an instruction that relates to the attention component, whereas reminding them that it's okay to drift off is guidance that relates to the attitude component.

Finally, "time to do it" relates to the silence component. Time without instructions gives participants a chance to put all of your instructions into practice.

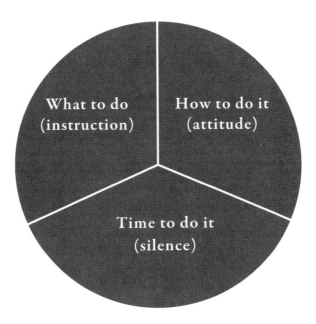

Figure 4. The basic structure of meditation guidance; the sizes of the segments aren't representative, as the proportions of the three components may vary substantially depending on the meditation and the group.

The proportion of time you'll devote to these three parts will differ from meditation to meditation. A body scan is filled with instructions about what to do, along with lots of suggestions about how to do it, and involves relatively little silence. A long sitting meditation session will have a great deal of silence, punctuated with occasional instructional remarks and observations about attitude.

The proportions of these constituent parts changes as the training progresses. When dealing with beginners, the emphasis will be on what to do. What is attention, what can you do with it, and what does attention do automatically? For advanced students, guided meditation includes more remarks on attitude, with instructions on what to do tending to focus more on hindrances or on subtle objects of mindfulness, such as moods. As the group advances in the training, spoken guidance will diminish and silence will increase.

Clearly, the ratios of these three constituents isn't rigid; rather, it's the result of a dynamic balance between the script, the group, and your meditative consciousness. You'll notice that your mental state influences the prominence of certain types of instructions. If you're feeling restless, you may be inclined to give more "what to do" instructions. If you've just been on a retreat, you may provide a lot of guidance on attitude or insert many silences.

Guidance for Working with Attention

Instructions about what to do with attention are standard statements that you repeat time and again, and they tend to be very straightforward:

Bring your attention to…

Being aware of…

Reminding participants about what to do when attention wanes also falls into this category: "And every time you notice that your attention has drifted off, you just come back." You can also provide "what" instructions in the form of an invitation. For example, you might say, "Opening to another field of experience, the field of sounds." Because instructions about what to do are generally so standardized, I won't delve into them further.

Guidance for Working with Attitude

Meditation instructions can lead to a perceived contradiction between how things are and how they should be. After all, every instruction suggests something participants could be aware of or something they could do—in short, something that's "good": less drifting, more noting, more awareness. This creates a risk of turning meditation into something that puts people at odds with the nature of the experiences they're already having, instead of helping them be at peace with their experiences. For this reason, I prefer the word "suggestion" to "instruction," even though there's still a touch of "this is how it should be" to a suggestion.

Guidance on attitude, or "how to do it," is intended to lend the right tone to instructions about what to do. But again, this gives rise to a contradiction: participants receive an instruction to do something while simultaneously being told it's okay if something else occurs. The Western emphasis on the doing mode of mind gives rise to that contradiction. The being mode of mind shows us the way out of it.

Fortunately, the teacher's tone and attitude in providing guidance convey a lot more of the actual message than the words and their explicit meanings. The most important guidance regarding attitude isn't given explicitly, but rather by presenting your message in a fitting way, using tone, intonation, volume, sound, and tempo, as well as silence, because these qualities have such a huge bearing on attitude. Even imperative statements, such as "Now get back up again," can come across as gentle when you use a tone of voice that's inviting and gives participants space.

Equally important is the context in which your words are spoken. For example, prior to giving an instruction, you might say something that gives participants space or puts things into perspective, or insert a silence. This can create an atmosphere that facilitates reception of the words that follow.

Most Westerners need a maintenance dose of guidance on attitude. "What" instructions tend to put us in the familiar, habitual doing mode of mind. Some people continue to use guided audio recordings, even after many years of practice, because they feel they need the guidance to remind them not to give in to the tendency to fall into doing mode of mind. Guidance on attitude is at least equally essential as instructions regarding attention, in large part because they are focused on the most important thing being practiced: gentleness and acceptance.

Clearly, guidance on attitude is crucial for balance. It is also much less straightforward than instructions on what to do and more dependent on contextual factors. Finally, it tends to be less explicitly addressed in scripts. For all of these reasons, in the sections that follow I provide many pointers on how to speak about attitude.

OPENING AND CREATING SPACE

Guidance about attitude is marked by its open and space-giving quality. For example, you might say, "See how this suggestion works for you," and then add, "And if you find that it isn't helpful, simply do it in a way that fits you. That's fine." This kind of guidance empowers participants to work with the practice and your instructions in their own way.

You can also suggest space by making your formulation conditional:

Perhaps you could...

Whenever you're ready...

If it feels good to you...

You can also provide completely open-ended guidance:

See if you can...

You might consider...

If you want, you can...

Explore for yourself how you can work with this.

Find a position that's comfortable for you.

See for yourself when it's a good moment to come back.

And if you prefer to do it in a different way, that's okay too.

Yet another way to convey openness and give participants space is by providing several options:

Sit on a cushion, or on a chair if that suits you better.

Know that you always have some resources available: tuning in to your breath, the experience of your physical posture, noting your experiences...

Sometimes you may want to emphasize the relative nature of your instructions. For example, you might say, "These instructions are suggestions. They are intended to help you practice working with your attention and attitude. So see for yourself whether or not they are helpful. If not, you can just let them pass by."

BALANCING GUIDANCE ON ATTITUDE AND ATTENTION BY ALTERNATING

Guidance on attitude can make instruction about attention (the "what" instructions) feel softer and more flexible. Conversely, instructions regarding attention provide boundaries in regard to attitude and help participants refocus on clear seeing.

The two types of instructions sometimes alternate rapidly. If you listen closely during a body scan or breathing meditation, you'll notice that an instruction about attention is often immediately followed by guidance on attitude. For example, after providing an instruction about attention, such as, "And every time you notice that your mind has wandered, you come back," you might say, "No problem. Wandering just happens."

Often, there's even alternation between the two types of instructions within a single remark: "Wherever you were, simply noticing it with a smile and coming back to the breath." When the alternation is smooth, the meditator won't experience the change in the nature of the guidance.

HELPING PARTICIPANTS ACCESS RESOURCES OF RELAXATION AND EASE

When giving instructions about meditation posture, it may be helpful to pepper them with words that help participants relax:

Whenever your mind has wandered, see whether you can bring it back to the breath, as relaxed as you can.

This posture is one of ease.

Note that these instructions are not really geared toward physical relaxation but instead are used to invoke an association with the being mode of mind. Some participants may notice that holding their posture is not easy at all and start to fight with that. This calls for taking a nuanced approach, qualifying the instructions with phrases like "as well as you can." Also, do be aware that associations with words such as "ease" can lead to loss of alertness. Sooner or later, this is likely to call for balancing with other types of instructions.

REMINDING PARTICIPANTS THAT WHATEVER THEY EXPERIENCE IS OKAY

From time to time, the doing mode of mind will kick in during meditation, accompanied by a sense that the person should try harder in order to more effectively achieve something. This creates a sense that the experience of the moment isn't good enough—that something is off and needs to be fixed. Yet meditation is a practice of being okay with whatever the individual experiences. You can get this across in a variety of ways:

There is no wrong way of doing this.

When you practice, you're allowing yourself to make mistakes. Mistakes are part of the process.

And sometimes you may have thoughts containing judgments. Being aware of those, too, acknowledging them, and letting them be as they are is also part of the practice.

If you have unpleasant experiences, you may ask yourself, "Is it okay to have these? Boredom, irritation, impatience, or fear—can it just be there, exactly in the way I'm feeling it now? Can I be at peace with unpleasant experiences?"

CONVEYING NONJUDGING AND KINDNESS

Constant judging is another habit of mind. It arises from the striving quality of the doing mode of mind: *This is what I want, and this is what I don't want.* Refraining from judgment has the immediate effect of allowing us to approach our experiences in a more open, friendly way. Here are a couple of examples of how you can convey nonjudging and kindness:

And sometimes, with the noticing, a feeling might come along. Perhaps a feeling of irritation or blame. Or a thought: "Jeez, I've drifted off again. I really should try harder." If that happens, see if you can just leave it at that: an emotion, a judgment. You are being aware of it. This noticing in itself creates a kind of distance and can bring some softness to this sharp feeling or thought.

See if you can bring some kindness to the way you pay attention. Instead of perhaps judging your experiences, see if you can bring a kind and gentle manner to seeing the experiences as they are and letting them be.

FOSTERING A PROCESS-ORIENTED ATTITUDE

Participants can often benefit from a reminder to focus on the process of meditation rather than its results. Here are some examples of how you might formulate such reminders:

There's nowhere we have to go. There's nothing we have to achieve.

Sometimes you'll find yourself wondering whether you're doing it right. In those moments, you're thinking about the practice instead of doing it. That too is something you can be aware of, after which you simply come back to the primary object of this meditation: This breath. This moment.

If you look after the process, the process will look after the results.

We are generally so focused on getting somewhere that we forget about being somewhere. With meditation we practice being in the present moment. So now, being with the experiences of this moment...

How can we be in the here and now more often? As soon as you're aware of the fact that you were elsewhere, you've already done most of the work—you're already back in the present moment. That's all you have to do.

ENCOURAGING LIGHTNESS

Concentrating means sustaining attention. Being mindful means touching experience lightly with our attention. Mindfulness meditation combines some concentration with a lot of mindfulness. Dutch vipassana teacher Frits Koster addressed this in an article (2010), and I've loosely translated his explanation here:

> For people who are practicing meditation, it often turns out to be a kind of liberation when they are told that they don't have to concentrate heavily, and that they don't have to go to great effort to fully, with their undivided attention, delve into and stay present to their foot, belly, or some action they perform—that it's enough to simply be aware of these experiences, noting them lightly. Needless to say, this also goes for being aware of unease, sounds, and so forth. Thai vipassana teacher Mettavihari once smilingly put it as follows: "Mindfulness is very superficial. You don't need to sink deeply into your belly and into your feelings. But you can be aware." Paradoxically, not letting awareness sink deep into the object of focus actually turns out to produce greater insight.

Incorporating this touch of lightness into meditation is an exercise in itself, and it's important to point this out from the start of the training. That's why instructions for the body scan contain numerous suggestions to that effect.[9] Unfortunately, remarks about lightness are often the ones that are least likely to register and most likely to be forgotten. Often it is only much later, for example, during a follow-up training, that participants have the liberating insight that they can practice mindfulness with more ease and a lighter touch. This is yet another indication of the tenacity of the doing mode of mind, with its illusion that we have to reach our goals using force. So reiterate the message that participants have to do less than they may think necessary:

Being mindful is enough. The rest will happen by itself.

When meditating, you have to do far less than we normally associate with the term "practicing." You note what you experience. That's all. You don't have to do anything with what you note.

You'll see what happens next when it presents itself. Experiences come and go. This happens by itself.

It's about being aware, not about changing. Basically, you are saying to yourself, "This is the experience, and I'm aware of it, but I don't have to do anything with it." This is something we aren't used to, this concept of not having to do anything with the experience. Still, it has a liberating effect. Try it!

Being mindful is very light. It doesn't require a great deal of effort.

ALLEVIATING GUILT ABOUT MIND WANDERING

All participants will, at one point or another, feel some self-reproach or a sense of guilt after realizing that their mind has wandered. This feeling can be strong and yet still stay unnoticed, thus hindering the practice. Therefore, it can be very liberating for participants to hear you pointing at these kinds of feelings and saying that they're a normal part of the process. Here are a few ways you might address this:

We are inclined to judge ourselves as soon as we notice that we've drifted off. But you could just as well congratulate yourself, because once you've noticed that you've drifted off, you've seen it. You're back!

We are so quick to feel guilt when we have the sense that we've failed again, like a child caught with her hand in the cookie jar. In those moments, remember that noticing and coming back is the practice, and that's exactly what you're doing.

Enjoy this waking up. Take a calm look around. Take the time to observe the landscape you've ended up in…the train of thought, the mood, or the preoccupation. You can now look at it. Take the time to say good-bye to it. And only then come back to your breathing.

AVOIDING PITFALLS IN GUIDANCE ON ATTITUDE

One pitfall when providing guidance on attitude is that participants may hear this as technical instructions and attempt to comply via the doing mode of mind. Then, rather than leading participants to the more accepting state characteristic of the being mode of mind, the guidance is interpreted as giving them additional things to do, increasing the likelihood that they'll fall back into judgments and evaluations of "right" versus "wrong."

In this way, invitations to practice gentleness can have an effect opposite to that intended if they increase participants' sense of self-reproach. This can lead to reactivity:

And I have to be mild and friendly, on top of everything else!

I find that boring, and then you tell me I don't need to judge, and I think, "I stink at this."

Such reactions can be a sign telling you that you need to deliver your message more subtly. That said, they can also arise when participants are overly reactive.

Refining Your Instructions

Just as meditation experiences can have endless subtle variations, we could also endlessly refine our meditation instructions. During retreats, teachers often increase the subtlety of their instructions step-by-step, over time. This kind of successive refinement also occurs in mindfulness training. For example, in sitting meditation we gradually introduce different fields of experience and then move on to noting all types of experience as they come and go.

In this section, I'll give pointers on providing more refined instructions. Still, it's important to be aware of the relative value of technical instructions. Ultimately, the right attitude is far more important than the refinement of any particular technique. When refining your meditation instructions, another key guideline is to not overestimate the pace at which participants develop meditation skills. In mindfulness training, development that, according to some traditions, takes years of monastic devotion is condensed into a few hours a week amidst a lifestyle typically full of distraction, busyness, and stress.

Another consideration is that when one particular technique is overly stressed, participants may get caught up in doing it correctly, and thus become dominated by the doing mode of mind. This is why refined instructions are coupled with statements that highlight the relative importance of refinement versus attitude. Putting all of these points together, a general rule of thumb for refining instructions is to not introduce too much too fast.

Noting

Registering experiences is trickier than it sounds. During meditation, this is particularly difficult when no specific field of information to dwell upon is offered, such as during so-called choiceless awareness. Mentally noting experiences can help participants see them more clearly. A second effect of noting is that it creates some distance—some space between the meditator and the experience. It helps separate the observer from the observed. Identification with one's experience decreases, and bringing attention back becomes easier. (In the following discussion of noting, I'm indebted to the wisdom of my vipassana teachers, Frits Koster, Joost van den Heuvel-Rijnders, and Jotika Hermsen.)

Mentally noting is about naming an experience, putting a label on it. It leads to a sense of coming home. Your attention was captured by something. Noting that "something" enables you to step back, observe it, and detach yourself from it. Noting is effective when it fulfills the following three criteria:

Clear: Seeing what's there and finding the right word for it

In the moment: Not holding on to what you see, allowing you to be open to the next moment

Unbiased: Not being biased by the content of the experience—noting a painful experience equally impartially as a joyful one

Within mindfulness practice, noting brings a sense of completion and mitigates the captivating power of passing experiences. It's as if it breaks the spell of experiences, including feelings and streams of thoughts. During meditation, a feeling of irritation, envy, or sorrow can have a hold on participants for a prolonged period of time without them realizing it. The moment they become aware of it and note it ("Ah…There's irritation"), it's as though the feeling is checked off and its effect starts to wane. Sometimes it even disappears.

The more precise the noting, the more the spell is broken. That said, noting does initially require a fair amount of mental effort, so it isn't advisable to strive for perfect descriptions of experiences. In fact, global labels such as "thinking" and "feeling" serve the purpose of noting better than more detailed or refined labels because they don't go into the content of a thought or a feeling. As people practice, their skills will develop and finding the right label will become easier.

Noting doesn't require a follow-up step. The next moment will naturally present itself. The experience first noted may have become different. It may be further away and smaller. Or perhaps something else will already have entered the foreground. If so, that's the next thing to note. Or perhaps the same experience has remained in the forefront or has become even more prominent. If so, that's the next thing to note. Or perhaps the noted experience has disappeared from the forefront and nothing else has arisen. That too can be noted as simply "nothing" or "not much."

In eight-week MBSR courses, many teachers include guidance on mental noting with their instructions for sitting practice. Some participants immediately find their way with this guidance, while others feel hampered by it. Unfortunately, the duration of the training is too short to go into this type of advanced technique with the group in great detail. Therefore, it is offered as optional. If participants find that it benefits them, they can use it. If not, they can let it go. Make sure you and your groups don't get bogged down in struggling with this technique. Instead, introduce it as a resource.

Teacher: What can prove helpful is to note your experiences, simply naming whatever is in the forefront of your mind. Noting recognizes and acknowledges the experience. At the same time, you're creating some distance. You realize that you are not the experience. That's all you have to do: note the experience, then wait to see what's in the forefront in the next moment.

With refined instructions, it can be especially important to follow up with guidance on attitude.

Teacher: Noting is a resource. Explore for yourself how you can work with it. Initially, you may not find a way of fitting it in. Just experiment. When you notice that you're starting to think about it or that it creates tension, just let it go. That's when it overshoots the mark. If that happens, simply continue in your own way.

You'll want to provide some direction on the level of noting, but in a way that emphasizes ease.

Teacher: Note what's in the forefront of your mind. Simply note a trembling sensation in your leg as "trembling," a sensation of heat as "heat," a sound as "sound," a thought as "thought." If you want, you can be more specific, noting a remembered thought as "memory," or a thought about how you'll do something in the future as "plan." If the right label doesn't pop into your head, keep it general. When you have to choose between noting precisely or more broadly, do so broadly. That's easier and just as good.

You can also specify a basic level participants can always return to in noting.

Teacher:　　You can always revert to the movement of the breath, and if you want to, you can note that, using "in-breath" and "out-breath" or, for sensations in the belly, "rising" and "falling."

Walking meditation lends itself particularly well to noting. This kind of meditation entails regular repetition of brief and clear experiences: the parts of the movement that constitute each step. Therefore, in MBSR, it's good to reintroduce noting while guiding walking meditation. During informal mindfulness practices, it is not common to provide instructions to engage in mental noting.

Techniques such as counting in-breaths and out-breaths, which are used in concentration meditation and Zen traditions, are different than noting. Whereas noting is intended to foster clear seeing of experiences, counting and similar techniques are simple but intentional mental activities used to refocus attention and curtail the mind's tendency to jump from thought to thought and drift off; counting and the like creates calmness. In mindfulness meditation, we don't add anything to our experience; we just note it. That said, some degree of concentration is needed in mindfulness meditation, which is why mindfulness of breathing is the initial focus when teaching sitting mediation.

Going Along with the Natural Flow of Experiences

Another somewhat advanced technique for teaching mindfulness involves seeing oneself as an observer, watching the natural coming and going of experiences as they present themselves without assuming oneself to be the creator of these experiences. One way to present this is as though the experiences themselves choose to come and go. In MBSR, we use Rumi's poem "The Guesthouse" to hint at this as early as session 2: "This being human is a guest house. Every morning a new arrival" (2005, p. 109).

Metaphors can be useful for describing the natural coming and going of experiences. Common images involve a movie screen or stage, clouds in the sky, or passing trains or ships:

It's as if you're sinking into a comfy theater seat and watching the film of your experiences. No matter how the film pans out, you just watch.

Experiences are like clouds in the sky. Clouds come and go. The sky doesn't change.

Such metaphors imply that a sense of "I" as an acting agent need not be involved in meditation. This is a powerful suggestion that invokes the perception of not-self (*anatta*) and emphasizes surrender and acceptance. In one of her retreats, Dutch vipassana teacher Jotika Hermsen encapsulated the essence of this stance in the question "Can you just let things be just the way they want to be?'

During inquiry, participants sometimes come back to this aspect—not being an "I" or the doer. This can provide an opportunity to expand on the idea behind such an image:

So if you are not the changing clouds, what is there that stays unmoved?

When dealing with participants who greatly identify with a self and the feeling of control that comes with that, the suggestion to simply observe the coming and going of experience, essentially without a center, may be disconcerting. If so, it might be wise to not explore the subject further, since it may cause too much unrest and exceed the scope of the training.

Promoting Right Concentration

Participants initially approach meditation in the same way they approach all tasks in life. And given that most are steeped in Western culture, this typically involves asking, "How do I do it?" "What do I aim for?" and "When am I doing it right?" As a result, they often deploy too much concentration. According to Dutch vipassana teacher Frits Koster (2010), 90 percent of all Westerners who meditate tend to overexert themselves in the beginning and focus far more than necessary.

The dominance of the doing mode of mind in approaching exercises is so deep-rooted that, in the early stages of training, it may be best not to try to counter the doing mode overly stringently, as this can confuse participants. Once they've gotten accustomed to meditating, which typically occurs toward the end of the training, it may be useful to draw attention to this tendency more specifically.

One method of doing so lies in how people direct their gaze. This can serve as a physical metaphor for the difference between observing in a concentrated versus relaxed way. Everyone is familiar with the experience of peering intently at something and can sense how that differs from a broad, open gaze. Further, a focused gaze can feel like interfering with the subject, whereas an open gaze leaves the subject alone. You can demonstrate this by moving a finger in front of your eyes from left to right, following the movement with concentration, and then moving it in front of your eyes a second time without following it at all, and instead just letting it move through your field of vision. You can also invite participants to try this for themselves or guide them in this instructive little exercise. The second time they're likely to experience that they still notice their finger moving from left to right, but that they do so in a lighter way, with far less effort.

The sensory differences between looking and seeing, or between seeking and receiving, can provide insight into what constitutes right concentration within mindfulness meditation. Koster (2010) adds that people shouldn't worry about whether or not they're concentrating sufficiently, observing that at the moment when we simply realize that whatever presents itself to or in us is there, we already have the right kind of concentration.

Balancing Fluctuations of Attention

The intensity and focus of attention tend to fluctuate naturally. It can be helpful to point this out to participants so they won't beat themselves up over something that's a natural phenomenon. At the same time, they can, paradoxically, still exert influence over the balance between alertness and drifting of attention.

In the previous section, I described the tendency to concentrate excessively while practicing mindfulness. Yet it isn't ideal to be too relaxed, either. After all, that can lead to being swept away by daydreams, moods, confusion, or analysis. The aspect of remembering to be aware and bringing attention back again and again would be lost, dissolving any distinction between meditation and just doing nothing.

Meditation is a dance of effort and relaxation, of letting go and recalling. Holding a light and measured intention to maintain balance in the practice is crucial. During the training, continuously stress this equilibrium between not too much and not too little. If the group is somewhat advanced, you might consider addressing this as a theme, perhaps using the metaphor of a horse-drawn carriage from the Buddhist tradition, which I present here in an adapted and simplified form.

Teacher: Meditating is like traveling in a horse-drawn carriage. The horses pulling the carriage are named Concentration, on the left, and Ease, on the right. When Concentration works too hard, the carriage veers to the left, and when Ease takes over, the carriage veers to the right. Either way, the carriage can career off the road. When you concentrate too much, you're working too hard and get tense. Your attention is dominated by the doing mode of mind, so you approach experiences as if you have to do something with them. Of course, you can also be too relaxed. When your attention isn't alert, you doze off and your vision gets clouded. If you want to keep the carriage on the road during meditation, strike a balance between concentration and ease.

You can use mindfulness to strike that balance. Mindfulness is the driver. Every time one of the horses becomes overeager—or doesn't do its share—the driver uses the reins to balance them, gently but surely, nudging the course of the carriage a little to the left or a little to the right. In this way, mindfulness can balance trying too hard and tensing up, on the one hand, and taking it too easy and becoming lazy, on the other. Mindfulness will bring you back to the middle of the road.

Working with Mindfulness of Internal Experiences

It is relatively easy to be mindful of external experiences. This is why, in MBSR, the teaching of sitting meditation starts with mindfulness of the breath and then moves on to sensory experiences, such as sounds. On the one hand, these objects of focus seem more tangible and concrete, and hence a bit removed from ourselves. A thought or a mood, on the other hand, often seems to converge with one's sense of self, and participants may feel at one with these kinds of experiences. It can be difficult to be mindful of something that's so close. People tend to overlook these experiences. It is like the decor in your living room: you're so close to it that you may fail to register it. However, internal experiences tend to be the ones that have the greatest impact on people.

As you guide meditations, you might occasionally bring participants' attention to phenomena such as thoughts and moods. Initially, invite them to notice the nature of such experiences.

Teacher: Some experiences are harder to be aware of because they're less clearly demarcated—a mood, for example, or perhaps boredom, vanity, pride, haste, or slight irritation. You might register such experiences as a subtle filter that colors all other observations. Also consider emotions, whether happiness, restfulness, grief, fear, or anger. Sometimes you may suddenly notice that a bit of an emotion is present. These internal experiences affect our other experiences without having a form themselves...until you become aware of them.

You can follow up by addressing what participants can do with these experiences once they're aware of them.

Teacher: Mental noting may be of help here: "Ah, now I can see it. There's irritation...or fear...or impatience." Being aware of internal experiences in this way will reduce the degree to which you're swept along with them. They will have less of a hold on you. Being mindful is enough.

Promoting Mindfulness of Under-the-Radar Experiences

There's another type of experience that's easily overlooked. Sometimes when meditating, people suddenly become aware of an undercurrent of thoughts that had been there for some time but that they hadn't consciously noticed. These thoughts are the running commentary that tends to provide subtitles to the practice: *You dummy, you're drifting off again*, or *Keep it up, you're doing great*, or *I'm such a dope; I'll never learn*. Typically, people haven't picked up these thoughts with their mindfulness radar because they felt such thoughts didn't belong in their meditation.

As long as participants consider such thoughts to be outside of the meditation, they won't be able to recognize them as thoughts. Rather, they are considered to be observations of some kind of objective truth or reality. It's important to include this undercurrent as an object of the meditation; otherwise these experiences and their influence will remain unnoticed and unexamined.

These kinds of under-the-radar experiences can be among the hardest experiences to recognize, even though they often have the greatest influence. People tend to identify with these thoughts, and they can impact almost every aspect of a person's experience. This is especially problematic for people who are prone to depression and its heavy and compelling thought patterns.

Even an innocent thought such as *I'm meditating now*—a typical under-the-radar thought—can have a major impact. For example, it often leads to a sense of

"I have to do this right. I have to get something out of it." So as you provide guidance, consider highlighting these under-the-radar thoughts and their effects as one of the experiences encompassed by the meditation.

> *Teacher:* Sometimes you'll find that you have thoughts you've had for a while, but that have remained hidden from the radar of your awareness—thoughts about meditation, for example. Perhaps you had the idea these thoughts weren't part of your meditation—that they were just observations of reality. And now they turn out to be thoughts. As soon as you become aware of this, these thoughts can become part of the meditation and you can treat them like any other meditation experience.

Fixed Structure at the Beginning and the End

Whether you're guiding sitting, walking, or lying meditation, and whether you follow a script or improvise, each meditation should begin and end with certain set steps. These steps offer participants the opportunity to switch from externally oriented everyday consciousness to internally oriented meditative consciousness, and then back again. Maintaining a fixed structure for these steps will help participants make these transitions more smoothly. It will also create a context in which participants can readily enter the being mode of mind and a state of meditation. This puts the power of conditioning to use in a positive way. So, given that there's good reason to approach the beginning and end of formal practices in the same way, there's no need to struggle with attempts to add variation.

Fixed Beginning

In the initial stage of the training, set forth the first steps specifically and in detail every time. This is akin to how a music teacher initially keeps reiterating how to hold the instrument. Setting forth the steps in this way will help participants become familiarized with the instrument of attention. Here are the typical first steps for most meditation:

1. Assuming the physical posture for the meditation

2. Closing one's eyes or keeping them lowered

3. Bringing awareness to whatever is in the forefront at that moment, physically, emotionally, or mentally

4. Turning awareness to the body and the senses

5. Turning awareness to breathing

6. Recalling a few general instructions, such as being aware of any tendencies to drift off or strive

7. Attending to basic instructions for the upcoming practice; for example, "The body scan is like a voyage of discovery through the body…"

For the body scan, you may need as long as ten minutes to complete these first steps, whereas they may take only three to five minutes for other formal practices. Don't worry about the time these steps take. This time will repay itself.

As the training proceeds, participants will increasingly develop more skills. Toward the end of the training, instructions about how to start will have become largely unnecessary, as participants will have developed their own way of starting a meditation with which they are comfortable. At this stage, all you need to do as the teacher is use reminders to refresh participants' memory about the first steps. This will make the meditation quieter and less technical:

You've all become familiar with the steps we take when starting each meditation. Let's go over them quickly: finding your posture, closing your eyes, seeing what's in the forefront of your attention…

We'll start by going through the usual steps, the ones we begin each meditation with to help us switch from our regular thinking to a meditative state of being. You're familiar with them at this point. Just go over them for yourself and in your own way. Take your time.

Fixed Ending

Just as it's best to start each meditation with certain fixed steps, it's also helpful to end meditations in a particular way. These concluding steps are important for gently transitioning from a meditative state of consciousness and make it easier to carry some of its qualities over to whatever is next on the agenda, while also teaching participants that slow and careful completion is important for each meditation. Here are the typical closing steps for most meditations:

1. Announcing that the practice is about to conclude, which you can do by sounding a bell if you wish

2. Instructing participants to make various physical changes, such as opening the eyes

3. Guiding participants to reestablish contact with the physical environment and the group

4. Attending to what individuals need in the moment, such as changing their seated posture, stretching, getting a drink of water, or using the restroom

To touch on every aspect outlined above, you might say something along these lines.

Teacher: We will be concluding the practice shortly… You can slowly begin to open your eyes. When you do, see whether you can keep your eyes relaxed for a bit longer. There's no need to immediately start looking around… Now bring attention to what your body might need right now, perhaps to stretch or wrap yourself in a warm blanket. Perhaps you feel a need to yawn or drink something. When you're ready, bring your attention back to the group. Then we'll continue with the program.

But again, as the training progresses, you'll need to devote increasingly fewer words to these steps.

Teacher: At the sound of the bell, we will conclude this practice. See if there's anything you need before we continue.

Technical Aspects

When you guide mindfulness practices, various technical aspects of your delivery can have a major impact on how your message comes across: wording, voice, tempo and timing, lightness and gravity, and whether you avoid or approach potentially painful areas. In this section, I'll discuss all of these aspects to heighten your awareness of them so you can work with them consciously. I'll also discuss memorizing meditation scripts and whether that is useful.

Wording

Wording can obviously have a huge influence on how participants receive your guidance and your message. There are a number of specific considerations and conventions in regard to the script that I discuss in the sections that follow.

TAKING THE "YOU" OUT

The more personal you make your instructions, the more you are referring to the sense of a personal "I" (or in this case, "you") and, in doing so, conveying the idea of a "self" who can do the meditation. However, meditation is being with what is, so the idea that meditators personally direct their experiences isn't helpful. Instead, by taking the "you" out of meditation instructions, the teacher provides a more impersonal format that is far more effective. There are two key ways to take the "you" out: using gerunds, and using imperatives.

The English language is blessed with the gerund, a verb form that has an expansive feel because it expresses a generalized action and is not limited by person or number. While gerunds typically function as verbal nouns, in mindfulness teaching they are often used as verbs without subjects. Although this may not be grammatically correct, it is quite effective:

Allowing the body to sink in the floor.

Opening to the sensations…

USING THE IMPERATIVE MOOD

Another option for getting the "you" out is to use the imperative mood, which doesn't require a subject. The downside of the imperative mood is that it is akin to a command. You can, however, soften this through intonation or by adding a clause indicating the optional nature of the command: "If it feels good to you, bring your awareness to…" You can also compensate for the compulsory nature of the imperative mood by choosing your verbs carefully. For example, you might use verbs that inherently offer space, such as "see" or "try":

See whether you can…

Try to find your own way with this.

When using the imperative, avoid constructions that remind participants of other instructional situations, such as a gym or classroom. Using imperatives in regard to breathing, movements, or other concrete physical actions is highly likely to evoke such associations, and to invoke the doing mode of mind. For example, if you simply say, "Breathe in... Breathe out," this may trigger associations with breathing therapy or sports. So use the imperative mood with care.

That said, there isn't a strictly right way or wrong way to use imperative statements. In most cases, intonation will outweigh the construction and determine its impact. For example, the instruction "Bring your attention to your left foot" can come across in very different ways depending on the teacher's intonation.

Another option is to simply eliminate the subject from the sentence: "Aware of the sensations." This creates a staccato rhythm, but that's okay as long as such sentences are interlaced with other kinds of phrasing to vary the rhythm and pacing.

In essence, the most effective instructions will be more impersonal. If you're new to this way of speaking, here are a few tips that will help you get familiar with impersonal language:

- Listen to how your peers guide meditations and employ impersonal language. You can also listen to audio recordings of guided meditations.

- Get peer feedback on your own delivery of instructions.

- Keep paying attention to impersonal language, as used by both yourself and others. You'll eventually master this new linguistic form. Allow yourself time to learn.

- Don't strain to get it "right." It's better to sound natural than to adhere to any formula.

- Make sure your instructions don't sound labored or convoluted.

- Beware of inarticulateness.

MAKING METAPHORICAL USE OF WORDS FOR THE PHYSICAL SENSES

Apart from a few somewhat cold and technical terms, such as "notice," "note," and "register," Western languages tend to lack a vocabulary for denoting inner observations. Therefore, in mindfulness instruction we borrow words that speak to our capacities for external observation, such as "seeing," "feeling," and "hearing."

Bear in mind that these are metaphors, and as such, they have a downside: participants may take them literally and believe that you're referring to their external senses. For example, if you say, "Looking at your experiences. Zoom in, zoom out, details, background," participants might not know where they're supposed to look. In this case, it would be better to word the instruction as "Being aware of all the experiences. Zoom in, zoom out, details, background."

Likewise, during the body scan, you might say, "Feel what you can notice in the belly," employing a metaphor of the sense of touch. But because the English language also uses "feel" for experiencing emotions, this instruction could lead participants to observe their emotions, rather than registering a physical experience in their belly. Therefore, the word "feel" is a tricky one to use as a metaphor for noticing.

Sight tends to be the sense most often used in a metaphorical way:

See what sensations there are.

Simply seeing what is present.

However, the auditory sense can also be used: "Listen to the experiences in that area." And sometimes even taste is invoked: "Tasting every experience… Savoring each one like a fine wine."

You may feel inclined to stick with one sense due to your own personal preference. However, it's best to vary the senses you use in instructions, as participants will differ in their sensory orientation. Some people are auditory types, others are visual, and yet others are tactile.

USE OF METAPHORICAL SPEECH IN GENERAL

More broadly, however, use metaphors sparingly and make sure that they're clear. The basic rule is that brief everyday metaphors are helpful:

…like the waves of the ocean

…a symphony of sounds

Long metaphors that aren't instantly understandable will only be a distraction:

A thought is like a frog—a frog that crawls out of the ditch to sit on the lily pad of your consciousness. It sticks its neck out and has a good stretch in the sunshine of your attention. And suddenly, it leaps off the lily pad to disappear into the water of your unconsciousness.

Also, be aware that metaphors won't get through to everyone. So when using one, you may wish to add a remark that provides space for participants to receive it—or not, if it doesn't work for them:

See whether you can work with this.

This metaphor may help you. If not, just let it go by.

USING THE CONCRETE TO ACCESS THE TRANSCENDENT

At a teacher training, I once heard Mark Williams say, "It's the concrete that delivers the message." That may sound contradictory because mindfulness involves practicing the nonconcrete: awareness, acceptance, trust, compassion… These are effects that flow from transcendent insight, rather than being founded on concrete experiences. Still, even transcendent insights depend on concrete experiences. Trust, for example, is based on a transcendent interpretation of concrete experiences.

The point here is that the path from the concrete to the cosmic is one we must all travel on our own. Mindfulness training provides a process that can stimulate participants to gradually glean transcendent insights from concrete experiences. As a teacher, your role is to offer concrete experience. As long as you offer both experience and a process that facilitates the development of insight, participants can arrive at a transcendent experience on their own.

It's best to limit words that attempt to steer participants toward experiences such as trust, acceptance, patience, or insight. Such words are likely to feel hollow if a participant's experience doesn't resonate with them. Plus, words that refer to the cosmic are conceptual, whereas in mindfulness the focus is on practicing bringing one's attention to the here and now. Concepts point away from the here and now.

Perhaps you have a rich spiritual life yourself and would like to transmit that. Bear in mind that mindfulness training has a different orientation: it offers participants the opportunity to build and extend their own transcendence. In addition, if you mix your instructions with your own personal cosmic awareness, this may lead participants away from the essence of mindfulness training. It can also create distance or even alienation between you and group members.

This can manifest in ways that may seem quite subtle. For example, an often heard expression like "trust emergence" can feel hollow to participants who don't feel any connection with trust. Or consider an instruction like "Feel the soles of your feet on the floor. Make contact with Mother Earth." As innocuous as that may sound, it would be much better to simply say, "Feel the soles of your feet on the floor. Make contact with the earth." The same goes for references to sophisticated concepts from meditation traditions, Eastern contemplative wisdom, and so on.

"YOUR BODY" OR "THE BODY"?

At the beginning of this section, I mentioned the benefits of getting the "you" out—avoiding the use of personal pronouns. In the same vein, there's also something to be said for limiting the use of possessive pronouns. There is a difference between "Bring *your* attention to *your* left arm," "Bring *your* attention to *the* left arm," and "Bring *the* attention to *the* left arm." Likewise, there's a difference between "Perhaps *you* can perceive something, in *your* chest, of the beating of *your* heart," "Perhaps *you* can perceive something, in *the* chest, of the beating of *the* heart," "Perhaps *there is*, in *the* chest, the experience of the beating of *the* heart."

In each case, the first version is more personal—with the downside that participants will therefore tend to include the notion of a self in their observations: "What am I feeling there? What does that say about me?"

The other options suggest a more detached self. From this perspective, there isn't a self who is doing the perceiving; there is only the function of perception. As vipassana teacher Frits Koster often says in his trainings, "It's mindfulness that's being mindful." So use instructions that are less self-oriented to offer a more open invitation to mindfulness: "In this moment, what are the experiences in that area?" This type of wording doesn't attribute awareness to a "self" that is aware, allowing mental activity to sooner be noticed for exactly what it is: simply mental activity.

On the whole, the impersonal option is the preferred one. But there are arguments to be made for mixed use of both. For one thing, people are accustomed to feeling their body and thinking and talking about it from a personal perspective. Using only articles, rather than possessive pronouns, may create a sense of alienation from the body. It can also feel artificial, especially when the teacher seems to be trying too hard. Participants will sense that artificiality and be distracted by it. Perhaps most importantly, some participants may have never fully owned their body, perhaps due to an early trauma or an autism spectrum disorder. For them, impersonal language may be unsafe. People can only experience healthy detachment from an earlier healthy attachment.

Voice

To be able to make the best use of your voice, you need to strike a balance between your pragmatic consciousness and meditative consciousness (discussed earlier in this chapter). This isn't easy, especially in the beginning, because guiding a group meditation while following a script can create tension. You may also be hampered by the idea that you need to create some certain atmosphere associated with meditation. Given the fact that while meditating we are working with our attention and awareness in a special way, it's natural to assume that the guiding voice also has to be special, and that a kind of solemnity is called for. For these reasons, meditation instructions are sometimes recited slowly and monotonously. If, in addition, the volume is low, participants are likely fall asleep, or at least become less alert.

Another common pitfall is trying too hard to employ a tone that implicitly conveys attitude instructions. This can result in an overly smooth, friendly voice that has a feeble impact. You don't have to use a special tone of voice. If you've found the right balance within yourself, the tone of your voice will follow automatically.

Effective meditation instructions are clear and vivid. You could even emulate the style of a public radio announcer: calm, fresh, and clear, with good volume, pleasant intonation, and even melody. Remember, you're are asking participants to be present and curious, so it's a good idea to reflect that invitation in your voice.

Reciting meditation instructions is a skill. And as with most other skills, anyone can learn it. All that's required is investing some time and effort in the learning process. Here are some tips on how to cultivate your voice:

- Listen to examples.

- Record yourself and listen to yourself. Although listening to your own voice may feel a bit awkward at first, technically evaluating your delivery is part of your professional practice.

- Have peers review your delivery. You can also ask friends and colleagues for feedback. However, don't ask participants for feedback; their critical remarks may arise from their learning process, rather than your delivery.

- Continue to work on developing this skill. It will probably take at least two years to master it. However, early on you'll improve quickly—your fifth meditation will be a lot more fluent and feel much easier than your first.

Tempo and Timing

Timing is the inner clock that makes a meditation fit within the overall program. Tempo relates to the pace at which you work within the time available to you. As mentioned earlier, the general rule is that timing should never dictate the tempo. If the tempo isn't right, you'll lose your feeling for the meditation. Whether you rush through it or leave overly long gaps, both you and the group will lose that essential balance between alertness and relaxation. The best way to maintain a sense of the right tempo is to make sure you're comfortable with the time available for the meditation within the program. Then, remember that tempo trumps the number of words in a meditation and even the specific parts of a meditation. A sitting meditation can be presented in five minutes, a body scan in fifteen. It's better to deviate from the script than to fall into an unnatural tempo.

Lightness and Gravity

Gravity can serve a purpose: it makes people serious. This can promote concentration, intention, determination, and even rest. However, meditation instructions tend to overly veer toward gravity. Teachers' voices often drop in register as soon as they start guiding a meditation. A sense of gravity can also be communicated through an excessive emphasis on problems and obstacles, with the many pleasant aspects of meditation not being highlighted.

This kind of gravity and emphasis on challenges can create an association with work, which may lead participants to believe that they have to achieve something difficult through great effort. This isn't helpful. After all, meditation is the practice of shifting attention (which is, in itself, light in nature), letting go of identification, experiencing the comfort this brings, and developing insight while doing so. Therefore, whenever you have the choice, opt for lightness over gravity. Consider it a compliment when participants say they found meditating easier than they thought it would be.

Here are a few pointers on how you can maintain lightness as you guide meditations:

- Ensure that your voice is sufficiently loud and imbued with vitality, and try to talk in a register that is slightly higher than the one you typically use when speaking from your meditative consciousness. As you experiment with these approaches, seek feedback, especially from your peers.

- Concrete, everyday things give a sense of grounding, which feels lighter than lofty concepts or words. So refer to concrete, everyday events in your meditation instructions, such as the lingering flavor of the raisin participants may still experience, the sound of raindrops falling on the window, or coughing in the group.

- Make occasional remarks to lighten the mood. That said, do be careful with humor—a topic I'll address further in chapter 4.

- Incorporate your own common humanity into your meditation guidance. Own up to any mistakes you make and correct them using everyday language.

Avoiding or Approaching Potentially Painful Areas

You may wonder about the extent to which your meditation guidance should factor in participants' vulnerabilities. You want to leave the door open to challenges that can provide practice material but not frustrate participants. So where do you draw the line between confronting and supporting?

Generally, try to maximize the challenge. After all, no pain, no gain. Although discomfort confronts, it also informs. There simply isn't a path to deepening insight that circumnavigates obstructions and difficulties. At the same time, however, you don't want to ask too much of your participants. When people are overwhelmed, they stop exploring, and therefore stop learning.

If you're working with a group that shares a specific challenge or vulnerability, the balance between challenge and support will be different than when working with a generic group. With a generic group, you're bound to an average. With a specific group, participants' shared vulnerabilities are a common denominator and therefore very present in the training. In this case, your job is to offer insight and care geared toward their shared vulnerabilities. A group with shared difficulties requires greater consideration for participants' limitations, while also allowing you to offer them a more targeted challenge. For example, when dealing with a group of participants who suffer from chronic headaches, during the body scan you can show special consideration for the head. Or if you're training a group of people with ADHD, you can initially offer greater support when guiding them into silence and emptiness. Then, slowly and with consideration, you can reduce this support, enabling the group to practice working with this specific vulnerability.

As mentioned, with a generic group, you'll chart a course based on the group average. Participants know that, even if they come to the training with a specific vulnerability. They don't expect special consideration for their particular condition, and often they don't want it. For example, a participant who's had a mastectomy might feel awkward if she notices that you avoid the breasts during the body scan, whereas the audio recording she uses for home practice does mention the breasts. So be aware of your own discomfort with specific vulnerability and endeavor to make choices that are based on creating ideal learning opportunities for participants.

A specific vulnerability can be acute or chronic. On the one hand, if it's acute, you know the participant's struggle with it is temporary. A chronic vulnerability, on the other hand, offers little prospect for recovery, so you know that the participant is in a process of acceptance. Someone who's recovering after a first episode of depression requires a different kind of consideration than someone with a chronic mood disorder. When you know that someone is struggling with something temporarily, make sure the person knows that you know, perhaps even during a meditation. You can do so by interjecting a supporting remark without changing anything in the practice:

And it may be that you're not following the meditation instructions, perhaps as a result of emotions being touched by some of the words of this meditation. If this happens, see whether you can be mindful of that and take care of those emotions. Let that be your meditation.

In short, with a generic group, pay attention to acute but not chronic vulnerabilities. In a specific group, your focus will be on the shared difficulties that all group members face, regardless of whether they are chronic or acute.

Recognizing Your Personal Bias

Your own biases can, of course, influence your delivery of meditation instructions in countless ways. However, there are two recurring issues that are especially worthwhile to consider: a sense of repetition, and your expectations, particularly in regard to the effectiveness of your words.

Working with a Sense of Repetition

What makes meditation guidance effective is not so much varying your words but choosing the right words. Given the fact that you will guide many of the same meditations time and time again, repetition is an inevitable part of teaching mindfulness.

Sometimes you may feel that you're repeating yourself too much. This can be a natural result of your experience. Though you may have said essentially the same thing to a previous group, the current group wasn't part of that. Besides, participants will be accustomed to repetition: the audio tracks they use for home practice are not only exactly the same from practice to practice but also repeat certain phrases frequently.

Also, consider whether you're actually repeating yourself. It's likely that, to some degree, you always adapt the script to the group, and to your own state of mind, perhaps without even noticing it. For example, you may start to sense that an experienced group needs fewer prompts to enter a meditative state, whereas with a group of beginners, you stay closer to the script. Each guided meditation is therefore different. In short, a feeling of monotony is generally the teacher's subjective experience. Bear this in mind whenever you feel that you're repeating yourself. Don't start varying your words due to a personal sense of boredom.

That said, don't be afraid to vary your words. You don't want to get stuck in a rut with worn-out phrases. The key is to be aware of your variations. Generally, the time to vary your words is when you feel that doing so will improve the quality of the meditation.

The scripts your own meditation teachers used contain a great deal of experience and wisdom. If you use them, don't change them just for the sake of variation. If you do, you may be decreasing their effectiveness, perhaps based on nothing more than personal bias. The best rule of thumb is to choose your scripts consciously and not change them without good reason.

Working with Your Expectations

Sometimes you'll find that a meditation really hits the mark. The group goes silent and is touched, and during inquiry, they recall the words that you considered to be particularly salient. Of course, this isn't always the case. And no matter how skillful your guidance is, the effects sometimes won't be what you hoped for. What you experience as the right word at the right moment simply may not register, or it could even trigger aversion.

This makes sense. After all, to participants, your voice during a meditation is just one of many fields of experience, along with personal thoughts, emotions, physical experiences, sounds produced by a neighbor, and so on. In addition, participants' moods will often differ from yours, as will their level of alertness and understanding. In this respect, meditation is a lot like communication: you may feel that you're making yourself clear, but if that assessment is based on your own perspective, others may be drawing very different messages from your words. Sender and recipient are each in their own world. Furthermore, you can't predict what certain words will trigger in participants. For example, a colleague of mine once found that the word "anchor" served as an obstacle for a participant who was deeply afraid of water.

The potency of your meditation guidance isn't something you can guarantee. Your instructions are basically invitations that you've crafted and compiled to the best of your ability. Whether they hit the mark and participants pick them up isn't in your hands. It can be helpful to share this awareness with participants:

Use whatever is helpful for your meditation and don't worry about the rest. Simply let go of the phrases that don't appeal to you and work with those that do.

As a teacher, part of your practice is to experience that your intentions aren't always received or reciprocated, even when you've put everything you have into your guided meditation. Remember that this isn't personal. Also realize that, on a subliminal level, participants often internalize more of the teacher's guidance and intent than they realize.

Guidance During Special Meditations

Apart from mindfulness meditations, MBSR provides some special meditations, such as the Mountain Meditation, which is a meditation with imagery, and *metta*, or loving-kindness meditation. These are not mindfulness meditations in that they invite participants to invoke a particular experience, rather than being with whatever arises. Always give participants advance notice when you'll be presenting a different type of meditation. Also note that in imagery or *metta* meditations, precision of the script is more important than it is during awareness of breathing or other forms of mindfulness meditation. When offering a physical experience, an image, or an emotional state, such as loving-kindness, the wording must be accurate, especially when you're inviting participants to invoke something that's difficult or may make them feel vulnerable. If you use a word or example that's off, participants could experience something quite different from what you're attempting to create. For that reason, reading the meditation could be an acceptable option during special meditations.

CHAPTER 4

Inquiry

We are exploring together. We are cultivating a garden together, backs to the sun. The question is a hoe in our hands and we are digging beneath the hard and crusty surface to the rich humus of our lives.

—Parker J. Palmer

The other person is the expert in their own experience.

—Melissa Blacker, Bob Stahl, and Florence Meleo-Meyer

Inquiry can be described as exploration of personal practice experiences through a group discussion, including reactions to these experiences, patterns in these reactions, the broader context in which these patterns can be observed, and the implications thereof. Inquiry starts where individual meditation ends. Exploring practice experiences jointly as a group gives participants access to richer meaning and insight than would be possible through personal perception alone. Inquiry adds to individual practice experiences through recalling, deepening, and broadening, creating a framework that supports and extends what individuals perceived, often latently, during the meditation. In the MBSR standards of practice, the intentions of inquiry are extended to exploring perceptions and mental and behavioral habits and patterns "that may be inhibiting learning, growth, and healing" (Santorelli, 2014, p. 4).

Inquiry is an indispensable and powerful element of mindfulness training. In this chapter, I'll first describe what inquiry is—and what it is not. Next I'll look at why inquiry is such a difficult part of the training for the teacher and explain how it relates to the other two teaching methods (meditation guidance and didactic presentations). Then I'll take a step back and consider the steps involved in inquiry, first in light of David Kolb's model of experiential learning, and then in light of the five hindrances, which in Buddhist traditions are considered to be the causes of reactivity, and therefore of our suffering. I'll describe the challenges of inquiry for both the group and the teacher, including when working with trauma. Finally, the chapter concludes with an elaboration of helpful conversation techniques.

Inquiry: What It Is and Is Not

I've just described inquiry as the exploration of personal practice. While this is correct, it doesn't describe the term completely. Just like the term "mindfulness," the word "inquiry" contains many layers. In this section, I'll expand upon these layers a bit. Inquiry can take just a minute, or it can consume an hour. It generally focuses on meditation experiences, but experiences in daily life or in the present moment can also be the subject. And although inquiry may stay with the initial experience, it can also extend to a greater context, such as a lifelong issue or the suffering of all human beings.

There is no fixed structure to inquiry. The process follows the experiences of participants and the development of insight into these experiences. Work with whatever arises as a current issue or thread, because that's where the actual learning moment is. Kolb's cycle of experiential learning, discussed later in this chapter, can provide a map of the context—one that is suitable for orientation but not to chart a fixed route. And while the conversational methods described at the end of this chapter provide some resources for structuring, don't cling to them. Although the process of inquiry can be informed by a general understanding of the learning process, it must be based on exploring, rather than seeking to change, and on trusting that insight, rather than action. Approaching inquiry in this manner is the best way to achieve beneficial changes in reactive patterns.

The Constituent Concepts

For our purposes, I'll define "inquiry" as follows: "A conversation method aimed at exploring a personal practice experience—and reactions to that experience—by inviting participants to transcend their usual way of looking in order to assume a different perspective, one through which participants can acquire insight into unconscious patterns, enabling them to be less reactive in dealing with life's challenges." Let's unpack the constituent concepts in that definition:

Conversation method. Inquiry is a conversation technique, a tool made up of words and dialogue. But it's a special kind of conversation technique because it interrupts the associative threads of normal conversation to return to the texture of the experience itself and the reactions to this experience.

Exploring. Exploring an experience means delving into it by searching for the right words to describe it precisely and in great detail, possibly placing it in a broader context. In mindfulness training, we sometimes use the verb "examine," though that suggests a more technical and targeted action and seems less open and free than "explore."

Personal experience. Inquiry begins with a participant's experience. This is a key feature of inquiry: it's about a participant's concrete experience and how the person dealt with that experience. The next step may be to elucidate common threads across a participant's experience, but that's not where it begins. This foundation in direct personal experience is what makes inquiry captivating: it's about the individual and about the here and now. In this way, inquiry has the spark of being a live show, not one that's prerecorded.

Different perspective. Inquiry reveals different ways of looking at, thinking about, and acting on experiences and offers these as alternatives. Whether the participant resonates with these alternatives is an individual matter, as is examining whether they are workable. In that sense, inquiry is like taking a somewhat random approach. It offers many possibilities for seeing differently, and these alternatives are communicated in numerous forms: using different words, different levels of abstraction, examples (whether imaginary, from others, or from the teacher), and metaphors.

Less reactive. Reactivity is the tendency to react after an experience in order to control or change it. It usually takes the form of attempts to push something away (aversion) or hold on to something (clinging). Reactions are generally the outcome of profound conditioning aimed at controlling a situation; however, reacting often isn't the most effective strategy for preventing suffering.

Because aversive reactivity is, in a sense, the target of inquiry, here are a few examples of how this might show up in participants during meditation:

I try to sit still, but the restlessness just keeps growing, and I'm thinking, "This is pointless."

I tried, but I couldn't do it. I didn't get anything out of it.

My mind is all over the place. That exercise doesn't work for me. I decided to do something else instead.

A reactive response can also be described as the opposite of one of the seven attitudinal factors that serve as the foundation of mindfulness practice, as set forth by Jon Kabat-Zinn in *Full Catastrophe Living* (1990):

Nonreactive Response	*Reactive Response*
Nonjudging	"Good!" "Not good!"
Patience	"It has to change."
Beginner's mind	"I've heard that before."
Trust	"Help! I have nothing to hold on to."
Nonstriving	"Do something!"
Acceptance	"Not this!"
Letting go	"I must keep going."

How Inquiry Differs from Other Forms of Conversation

Inquiry can also be defined by looking at how it differs from common conversation. Everyday conversations have a wide range of complex social and psychological functions. We talk to each other to get messages across, solve problems, process experiences, channel emotions, or get attention, recognition, or approval. As we talk, we follow mental associations—those threads that interconnect our thoughts. In fact, everyday dialogues often sound a lot like the confluence of two freely associating minds that hardly ever achieve genuine connection. Management coach Fred Kofman refers to these kinds of conversations as "overlapping monologues" (2006, p. 135). Such conversations tend to stay within the dimensions of each speaker's mind and are therefore predictable. When we start to chat, it's often as if we're putting on a record. The needle drops into a groove of existing associations that together form a story. Although this may sound undesirable, it takes nothing away from the important social purposes of conversation. Humans are narrative beings. We live in stories, and these stories serve an important purpose.

Inquiry, however, isn't about the everyday associations of the mind. Rather, it looks into participants' raw experience—its composition, how they relate to it, and their reactions to it. Therefore, inquiry usually begins with questions like these: *What was your experience? Can you describe it in greater detail? What happened next? How did you deal with that?*

Inquiry is also quite distinct from therapeutic conversations. Although therapy interrupts the patterns of everyday conversations, it does so mainly to reveal connections with deeper and less conscious associations, with the aim of gaining a better understanding of the client's feelings and behavior. In short, both everyday conversations and therapeutic conversations follow associative connections. Inquiry works the other way around: it works back from associations with an experience and explores the elements of the experience as well as reactions to it.

There are several other differences between these three types of conversation, summarized in brief in the following table.

Differences Between Inquiry, Day-to-Day Conversation, and Therapeutic Conversation

Themes	Inquiry	Day-to-day conversation	Therapeutic conversation
Length	Short	Short or long	Long
Nature	Descriptive	Descriptive, explanatory, or both	Explanatory
Focus	Looking at experiences	Being identified with experiences	Looking at experiences
Objective	Exploration	Exchange	Interpretation
Role of personal story	Of little importance	Holds a central position	Provides material for analysis
Conclusion	Open-ended	Wrapping up	Wrapping up
Role of outcome	Not important	Important	Important

Being Informed by the Practice

Meditation practice leads to clear seeing of what is actually going on in the moment: *Ah, now I see that I had drifted off.* It reveals the movement of awareness that just occurred: *My awareness had settled on my breathing, and all of a sudden I was thinking about something that happened earlier today.* This is followed by returning awareness to the object of attention: *Back to the breathing.* Meditation usually doesn't involve contemplating the event that just happened or its implications. We simply bring our attention back, in this case to the breath.

While meditating, participants are mindful of what they're doing and experience insight into the movement of awareness or any reactions to mind wandering, after which they return to the object of the meditation or to open awareness, depending on the meditation. Given that part of this process is insight, mindfulness meditation is a kind of self-inquiry. As Belgian mindfulness teacher Edel Maex puts it, "The first place to learn about inquiry is our own meditation practice. To sit or lie down non-judgmentally and with kindness, attending to what presents itself, is a powerful training. Exactly the same is what happens in inquiry" (2011, pp. 167–168).

The insight acquired through meditation is of an instantaneous nature. The basic instruction of meditation is "As soon as you are aware of mind wandering or reacting, bring your attention back." However, to attain deeper insight into patterns associated with this process, further exploration is needed. Inquiry picks up where meditation left off, and in this way, meditation and inquiry dovetail with each other. They also build on each other as insights acquired through inquiry are used in subsequent meditations.

Here are some of the key differences between meditation and inquiry as paths toward insight. (Some of the terms describing inquiry, such as "context" and "implication," will be covered later in this chapter, in the section on Kolb's learning cycle.)

Differences Between Meditation and Inquiry as Paths Toward Insight

	Meditation	Inquiry
Context	Intrapersonal	Interpersonal
Guidance	Internal, in the form of meditation instructions	External, in the form of guidance from the teacher, and internal, in the form of whatever arises
Exploration of experiences	No	Yes
Processing of insights	Letting insights go and returning to present-moment experience	Letting insights sink in and possibly connecting them to a broader personal or interpersonal context
Practice material	Current personal experiences	Personal experiences from previous practice, current personal experiences during inquiry, and resonance with experiences of other participants
Scope of insights	Momentary, regarding present-moment experience	Present-moment experience; the past; and, through implication, the future

Building on Interest

Inquiry always begins with a participant's experience. You cannot conduct an inquiry focusing on the experience of a third person. Of course, the participant must be willing to explore his experience and be interested in doing so. Another requirement is that inquiry must raise curiosity. When a topic doesn't arouse any interest or curiosity, exploration of that topic will feel like an academic exercise. If inquiry is a flame, interest is the oxygen that fuels the flame. If there is no interest, the flame will die out. Willingness to explore the experience is similar, and entirely necessary for the process to unfold. In principle, any experience of any participant that elicits interest or curiosity can be used for inquiry, whether it arises during formal practice within a session, during formal or informal home practice, or during inquiry itself.

Providing a Way out of Identification with Experiences

Describing an experience presupposes an ability to observe that experience, which is difficult when we are immersed in our experiences. When we identify with an experience, we converge with it. This is especially likely to happen with thoughts and with strong emotions, such as fear, anger, or irritation.

When people strongly identify with an experience, their speech will be heavily impregnated with that experience. Instead of saying, "There is fear," they equate themselves with the experience: "I'm afraid." In a sense, they *are* fear, and their words will reflect this. Helping participants label their experience is therefore the first step. As soon as they are able to observe and label their experience, they'll gain some degree of distance from it. Any questions that ask participants to identify and describe their experiences can help achieve this:

Can you describe your experiences?

What's in the foreground now?

Can you make a connection with the emotion?

Can you look at it?

Can you also bring your attention to something else, such as your body?

Horizontal Versus Deep Inquiry

Inquiry involves examining an experience, which suggests delving into it. But it's also possible to briefly note experiences, address them, and leave it at that. This is sometimes referred to as horizontal inquiry. Giving the experience a name highlights it, separates it from other experiences and the person who experienced it, and aids in sharing the experience. By helping participants describe the experience, you're utilizing the basics of experiential learning as conceptualized in Kolb's learning cycle, described later in this chapter. You can support participants in this process by confirming their experiences.

Teacher: Try to tell me, using a single word or short phrase, what experience was in the foreground for you during the last practice.

Participant 1: Pain.

Teacher: Where was this pain?

Participant 1: In my lower back.

Teacher: Okay, pain in the lower back.

Participant 2: Silence.

Teacher: Silence.

Participant 3: Boredom.

Teacher: And was there anything else?

Participant 3: Thoughts of being anywhere but here.

Teacher: Boredom and thoughts of being anywhere but here. Okay. Someone else?

The benefit of soliciting brief descriptions is that it doesn't take up much time, so all group members can have a chance to share. Many experiences can be mentioned—and seconded. Responses tend to be expressions of moods, feelings, and physical sensations. Horizontal inquiry is sometimes referred to as "popcorn" because of the way the group's contributions pop up.

Horizontal inquiry is a tool you might use in big groups or when only limited time is available. It produces more variety in tempo and makes everyone feel involved. Given that horizontal inquiry is a simple technique, I won't describe it further in this book and will instead devote the rest of this chapter to deep inquiry; however, that doesn't mean horizontal inquiry doesn't have important functions.

Deep inquiry zooms in on the experience of one participant. As a result, sometimes other group members won't feel equally involved in the conversation. This is something you can't prevent, but you can make sure that themes covered during deep inquiry aren't too exceptional. You can also broaden the scope from time to time to cover something that most or all group members will recognize. And during deep inquiry, it's important to keep dividing your attention between the person whose experience you are exploring and the rest of the group. One way to do this is by looking around the group and making eye contact. This will help you stay in tune with the effects of the inquiry on the rest of the group. Ultimately, the way in which you zoom your attention in on one person will have a far greater effect on whether the group stays with you than any particular words or subjects of deep inquiry.

Marking the Transition into Inquiry

Like any other social activity, teaching mindfulness is surrounded by everyday conversations. When a participant walks in and you ask her how she's doing and she says "Fine," you wouldn't ask her what she means by that. Asking an inquiry question at random moments in casual conversation is simply unnatural. It can also create a sense of insecurity, leading participants to feel that they might be questioned at any point in time.

As soon as you launch an inquiry, you change the social code and the rules of the game. The questions you ask are different from those you ask in normal conversation. You leave longer silences, your intentions are different, and so on. To ensure that the group understands this switch, mark the transition, either explicitly or in a subtle and implicit way.

The routines of the training are one source of markers. In short order, participants will understand that meditation is immediately followed by inquiry. Your own attitude, silence, or change in tempo, or simply using the same opening line, can also mark the switch to inquiry. You can also describe inquiry as an activity, but do avoid using jargon, including the word "inquiry." Use familiar terms—for example, "Let's spend some time sharing about the experiences with this practice."

(In the same vein, it's also useful to signal the switch from inquiry to didactic presentation, something I'll touch upon in chapter 5.)

Why Inquiry Is Difficult for the Teacher

Often, what would be good for a given participant seems so clear, and we're so eager to help. But given that only participants themselves can discover what's good for them, in many cases the best help we can give them is to not try to control the situation with our answers or reactions. More than any other aspect of the training, inquiry requires that the teacher trust the self-healing effects of meditation and exploration. This may make inquiry difficult for teachers, given that our Western social conditioning can drive us toward reactivity, and toward seeking control and answers.

No Reactivity

The mindfulness teacher's core task is to keep inviting participants to take a broader perspective and find a way out of their reactivity. To accomplish this task, mindfulness teachers need to have a profound understanding of their own tendencies to react and the ability to skillfully navigate those tendencies. If you're impeded by the blind spots created by your own reactivity, how can you guide others from the entrance to the exit?

No Control

Another challenging aspect of inquiry is that it isn't something you "do." Inquiry is being open to whatever arises, and you never know what that will be. There is no protocol you can rely on, and no role or formula to hide behind. More than any other part of mindfulness training, inquiry involves working with the moment. And what arises in the moment is the product of the combined experiences and background of everyone in the group, you included. Your responses to what arises are educated guesses and therefore far from random, and yet every inquiry is an unfamiliar dance. The only way to dance this dance is to surrender to it, based on trust that you'll bring yourself to the moment, along with everything you've learned and experienced thus far. In that moment, you must trust that a response will arise in you…or not—and that even if it doesn't, you can be confident of a good outcome.

An experienced teacher can guide a meditation with great ease, playing with the script and catering to the group all at once. Inquiry is a different kettle of fish. It will never become routine. You never know what the situation will bring, and you never know what responses will arise. You need to be alert and open, allowing all of the layers of your consciousness, and all sources of wisdom, to resonate with the moment. In essence, inquiry involves viewing the moment from the being mode of mind.

No Answer

Inquiry empowers participants to discover insights themselves. Therefore, on the teacher's part, a question is often more important than an answer. In fact, during inquiry it's often best not to answer questions. Your insight very well may not be a participant's insight. Our best intentions often lead us to answer, but what is an answer worth when, although "correct" in theory, it isn't reflected in the other's personal lived experience and therefore may curtail exploration of that experience?

Be on your guard against any tendency to fill in the not-knowing. This is often triggered by tension, for example, in the reaction to a thought like *Help! I don't have an answer to this!* or *It's not going the way I want it to go!* In such cases, you're likely to be inclined to speed up, fill any gaps, or otherwise "save" the situation. It's important to be aware of this inclination and, if possible, to create some space for yourself. Tune in to your breathing, keep still, and say that you don't have an answer. You don't need to control the process as much as you might be inclined to—and quite frankly, you can't.

In short, the best answer is often no answer. Honoring that dictum requires dedication, courage, and surrender...time and time again.

Kolb's Experiential Learning Model

Learning is the process that allows an experience to influence future behavior. To learn, people need to be interested. Something they aren't interested in won't attract their attention, and therefore it won't get through sufficiently.[10] There are two ways of learning: conceptual learning, which starts with a concept, and experiential learning, which starts with an experience. The Buddhist approach of "come and see what is true from your own experience" takes the latter as the starting point. Mindfulness training also leans heavily on experiential learning. After all, the training kicks off with eating a raisin, and not with an explanation.

In this section, I'll elaborate on the experiential learning model developed by educational theorist David Kolb (1984), which is widely used in adult education and can be quite helpful in mindfulness training, especially to give teachers some bearings to follow during inquiry.[11] Kolb's model is made up of four stages, with the last step leading back to the first one, creating a cycle.

Imitation-Based Learning and Exploration-Based Learning

Although most Western educational systems are focused on learning from systematically organized theories and concepts, this is hardly how we learn most things in life. After all, from the moment we're born, we mainly learn through observation and imitation, play, and exploration.[12] Experiential learning is characterized by enlarging one's insight through experiments or the integration of new experiences. It taps into intuitive learning processes, as can be readily observed in children.[13] Experiential learning has a much greater impact than learning through theory because it involves not just processing information cognitively, but experiencing it with the entire mind-body system—the senses, muscles, emotions, and nervous system.

In experiential learning, all past experiences serve as lessons, exercises, or experiments. Experiences leave traces that play a role in how people deal with the present moment. The basic sequence of experiential learning is experience, followed by evaluation, and then by implementation. David Kolb developed his experiential learning model in the early 1970s.[14] It revolves around the idea that the learning process starts with immersion in experience, with personal experiences providing the best learning material. After all, such experiences are reliable, known, and anchored in the individual's mind-body system. Insight and behavior change are subsequently produced through evaluation of the personal experience, rather than imparted concepts.

The Cycle of Experiential Learning

Kolb's model also sets itself apart from learning from theory by its cyclical nature. In contrast to a circle, a cycle can have a higher or lower starting point each time, which can create a spiral-like upward or downward movement as the cycles progress. In this view, the conclusion of each new learning experience marks the start of another learning experience, leading to a dynamic and ongoing learning process. In Kolb's model, this cycle has four sequential stages, as depicted in figure 5. Note that I've revised the descriptions of these stages to reflect the context of mindfulness training:

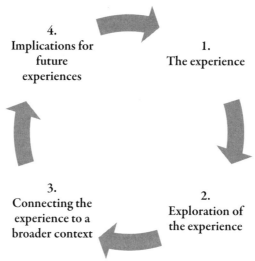

Figure 5. Kolb's learning cycle.

Stage 1: The Experience

All learning begins with an experience. This is the first stage. When this experience is consciously organized ahead of time, we call it an experiment, practice, or exercise. In mindfulness training, this first stage is the practice experience that forms the basis for the inquiry. Although it isn't part of the inquiry, it is the first stage in the experiential learning cycle and therefore the first step toward insight.

Stage 2: Exploration of the Experience

The second stage in the learning process is to explore this experience, examining it beyond its face value. We tend to quickly categorize our experiences, looking for familiar shapes we can fit into familiar holes. Yet in doing so, we're selling short the exceptional quality of individual experiences, ignoring their uniqueness. When we don't delve into our experiences, we can't really learn from them. We need to look at each experience as new and fresh.

We use words to describe our experiences, but words are abstractions or concepts. In mindfulness training, stage 2 ideally involves describing the experience in direct, concrete terms, using as basic a wording as possible.

REMOVING CONCEPTS

When something happens to us, whether pleasant or unpleasant, there is an immediate reaction from the mind as it tries to interpret the experience. We seek to correlate it with experiences that seem familiar, look for a concept that goes with it, and strap this concept to the experience, prompting associations with the concept. That's why we so often end up at an old story: attention moves from the unique experience and its novelty and possibilities to existing categories and concepts. A concept closes off further exploration of the experience, like a lid seals a jar shut. The idea of the second stage of the learning cycle is to remove the lid from the jar.

In inquiry, we look for a way back to the experience as it presented itself. We unravel the story, dismantling it. We go back to the primary sensations, the fibers of raw material that made up the experience. We strip the veils from it, removing the layers of concepts, associations, and memories that thinking had wrapped around the experience. This overall dynamic—automatically applying concepts to experience and the route back, removing them through inquiry—is depicted in figure 6.

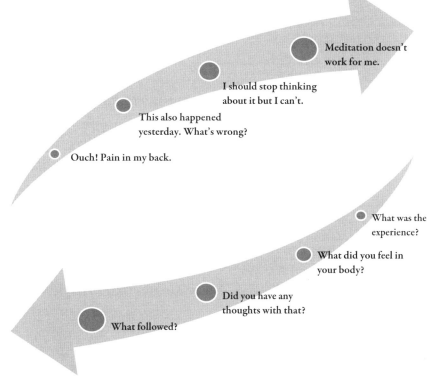

Figure 6. Movements away from and back to the experience.

QUESTIONS TO FACILITATE STAGE 2

There are numerous questions you can ask to lead participants back to the original experience. Here are just a few possibilities:

What happened at that moment?

What did you feel in your body?

Did you have any thoughts with that?

So it starts with…

How exactly does that happen?

How did you recognize it?

Can you tell me a bit more about that?

And how does it develop further?

Can you take us through that sequence step-by-step?

Let's go back to what exactly happened…

HOMING IN ON THE BARE EXPERIENCE

As you remove the veils from the experience, bear in mind that every practice experience can be traced back to a stimulus that has reached a person's physical, sensory, emotional, or mental perception—the original, bare experience. The process of unveiling is easier when an experience is recent and relatively simple. When asked about their emotions and moods, participants often describe and digress, hovering around the experience rather than moving quickly and directly to the essence of the experience.

You can curtail this tendency, in yourself as well as in participants, by asking about specifics. So steer clear of vague questions, such as "How did you feel about that?" They can yield answers that are overly vague or only indirectly related to the experience: "It reminded me of when I used to visit my aunt. It was positive. I felt like a small child who's happy with a piece of candy." Aim for targeted questions, such as "What emotions came with that?" This will invite the participant to describe the experience: "Pleasure. Joy. I felt a happy, tingling sensation in my belly."

Here's a more extended example, focused on the fairly common experience of boredom during practice.

Participant: I was bored. I was just lying there and thinking about everything but the exercise. It didn't work. And it took a long time.

Teacher: Would it be okay to take a closer look at that boredom? What did that experience consist of?

Participant: I don't know…restlessness…just irritated, really. And then I started thinking, "What on earth am I doing here?" I was also thinking that I wasn't doing it right, and that's when I tensed up.

Teacher: Restlessness, irritation…Where did you feel that in your body?

Participant: A need to move. Difficulty lying still. Twitching muscles. My skin heated up. It was actually more a thought.

Teacher: What kind of thought?

Participant: The thought "I want to move."

Teacher: Can you identify which came first, the physical need or the thought?

Participant: No. They happened at the same time, I think.

Teacher: Okay. So there's that thought and that physical sensation. And together they make up the experience you call "boredom."

Participant: Yes.

The preceding dialogue is fairly typical. Of course, experiences are never truly isolated. Experiences and reactions typically flow along in rapid succession. In fact, this development of experiences over time is also an excellent subject for inquiry, as illustrated in the following dialogue, which picks up where the previous one left off.

Teacher: And how does the boredom develop?

Participant: I start thinking, "This is no fun. Will it take much longer? What's the purpose of this?"

Teacher: Right, there are thoughts about the practice. And then?

Participant: Then I think I'm not getting the hang of it, that I can't do this—that I'd better quit the training.

Teacher: Wow! It starts with a thought and a physical sensation, followed by the experience you call boredom, followed by thoughts about how much longer it will take and what good it will do you. Then, finally, there's doubt about a much larger process: the training. And all of that within a time span of only a few seconds. Isn't it interesting to see how that works?

When a participant starts listing numerous experiences or multiple, complex components of an experience, guide the discussion to one concrete experience by selecting one part. Don't worry about the experiences you are omitting.

Participant: I'm actually still avoiding the pain of the loss of my father. I was always fighting with him, and with my brothers too. That's turned me into a loner. And suddenly he was dead. I didn't care, or so I always thought. But during the meditation, when you talked about avoiding pain, I thought of him.

Teacher: Did you feel pain?

Participant: It was more of a thought.

Teacher: Was there a physical reaction with that thought?

Participant: No.

Teacher: And what came after that thought?

Participant: I found myself thinking of someone completely different—a coworker.

Teacher: Okay, thank you.

When experiences are too complex to pick out a single element, when they're too old and no longer vivid, or when they're about someone other than the speaker, don't inquire further.

Participant: My daughter and I meditate together. Sometimes meditating gives her a headache. When that happens, I just don't know what to say.

Teacher: Neither do I.

Another difficulty that sometimes arises is that participants aren't willing or able to explore an experience. In such cases, it's pointless to keep attempting to solicit descriptions. The better bet is to stimulate greater interest, perhaps with an invitation.

Teacher: So there was a lot of restlessness. Can you describe this restlessness in greater detail? What was it made up of?

Participant: You know, just restlessness.

Teacher: Perhaps it might be interesting to explore that restlessness.

Alternatively, sometimes participants readily arrive at in-depth insight:

I now suddenly see how I always get angry with my children, and that it's a reaction to this sense of powerlessness.

Sure, I'm standing there and everybody's applauding, but now I see that in that moment I'm basically an attention-seeking little kid again.

When this happens, the experiential learning cycle is complete. Just facilitate the landing of the insight and leave it at that. There's no need to invert the cycle by asking how the participant gained that insight.

OPENING THE DOOR TO ALTERNATIVES

The essence of stage 2, exploring the experience, is to peel away all of the concepts participants affix to their experiences until the only thing that remains is the bare experience: thought as thought (a mental energy), emotion as emotion (a composite mental and physical state), and physical experience as physical experience (a vibration, movement, or sensation of warmth, cold, or pressure). Often a reaction to the experience then arises from the mind-body system, and that reaction itself constitutes another experience, with mental, emotional, and physical components.

Through the process of unraveling, you restore the experience to its elementary core and therefore to something that is more concrete, objective, and neutral. Peeling away the conceptual layers has a liberating effect: "This, and no more than this, is the bare essence." Participants can see that they add all of those other layers. This allows them to access an important perspective: once they see the difference between the actual experience and what they add to it, they can choose to add something different—or nothing at all.

In short, going back to the bare experience offers insight into patterns of reactivity and opens the door to alternative responses. It is the basic arc of inquiry.

Stage 3: Connecting the Experience to a Broader Context

The third stage in the experiential learning cycle is to link the experience to what we already know. We compare the experience to previous experiences that bear a resemblance to it, and also, through association, to experiences that don't resemble it but do show a likeness to some particular quality of it. For example, the experience of heart palpitations during a practice would probably be a difficult moment. It could be associated with previous experiences of heart palpitations, but it could also be associated with other difficult moments during previous practices, in which case the associative link would be the quality "difficult." In this way, present-moment experiences get connected to multiple contexts, gaining significance in the process. When a group of previous experiences is activated, this can reveal key mechanisms or principles. This is insight. An insight might be that heart palpitations are associated with anxious thoughts and seem to invoke them.

So the third stage in Kolb's cycle contextualizes the unique experience. We learn to see our reactions in the context of established patterns of reacting. These reactive pattern don't exist in isolation. They are the product of multiple contexts: the personal context, the context of the group, and the context of what Kristin Neff (2011) calls *common humanity*.

THE PERSONAL CONTEXT

The patterns participants recognize on a small scale (for example, in meditation or regarding everyday behavior) will also pertain to situations of greater importance. Although the impact is different, the pattern is the same. This is one of the principles that makes mindfulness training and formal practice so powerful: that which people practice on a small scale can be applied on a larger scale. For example, gaining insight about a tendency to avoid feelings of emptiness during meditation can grow into insight about not being able to fully engage in and enjoy life.

Participant: I experienced emptiness during the meditation. This was followed by racing thoughts and physical restlessness.

Teacher: Do you recognize that in yourself in other parts of your life?

Participant: Whenever I have an empty moment, I fill it with action. This leaves me unable to enjoy everyday events and causes me to make rash decisions. I run through my life.

THE CONTEXT OF THE GROUP

Another way of extending the context is to widen the scope to the group overall: Do others recognize this pattern in themselves? This kind of recognition within the group is a powerful way of helping individual participants see that they aren't alone in struggling with this difficulty. Broadening the scope in this way also gets the other participants involved and creates a learning experience for them, as well.

People often feel that they are somehow uniquely inept in dealing with their difficult emotions and experiences. This tends to lead to self-reproach and a sense of isolation. When participants discover that they aren't alone in these difficulties, it can be a great relief and can even help them see the nuances and a lighter side of it. This helps them view themselves differently and also opens them up to learning.

You can highlight this kind of shared experience by simply using the word "we": "That's how we try to keep the unpleasant out. It's an automatic reaction that can be triggered instantly, but it isn't always helpful to us. Is that recognizable to others in the room?" Or you can just move directly to asking whether other group members have experienced something similar: "Has anyone else had a similar experience?" Assuming other group members concur, you could then say, "So this happens to many of us: as soon as we notice mental 'emptiness,' the void is filled by a thought again."

One caveat with this approach: Be sure to use it only with fairly common types of experiences, difficulties, and reactions. If you solicit group recognition when you suspect that the participant's experience could be unique, the effect may be the opposite, emphasizing differences, inviting comparisons, and creating a sense of isolation.

Also note that when dealing with suffering or difficult feelings, linking with the experiences of other group members will be trickier. Suffering and difficult feelings are often shrouded in various kinds of individual reactivity, so the common aspects may not be easy to recognize. In such cases, it would probably be better to link the individual's experience with the general nature of suffering, as discussed in the next section.

That said, broadening the context to the group often happens spontaneously as participants resonate with each other's experiences.

Participant 1: I experienced a moment of complete silence for a second.

Teacher: And what happened?

Participant 1: When I noticed that, I thought, "Hey, that's nice." And then I realized that I was thinking about it.

Participant 2: Yes, I have that too. Silly, huh? Finally there's silence, and then you start thinking about that silence. That's so irritating!

COMMON HUMANITY

There's a very human tendency to take our individual obstacles and struggles as personal failings: *I can't do this, It's not for me, The others are way ahead of me,* and so on. Experiencing our obstacles as general difficulties that most people face helps us realize that we're actually "normal," not somehow uniquely flawed. It is because of our struggles, not despite them, that we have a sense of common humanity—of being in the same boat. The experience of being part of a greater whole is a source of comfort, offering the support and peace of mind that gives us the courage to continue, in life in general, and in mindfulness practice.

Here are a few examples of how you can help participants gain a sense of their common humanity.

Participant: It's happened to me so many times before. I thought I'd learned my lesson by now. And then I do the same thing again. It's just so discouraging.

Teacher: That's what being human is like: thinking we know what to do and then making the same mistakes again—and then feeling disappointed about that. That's how it goes for all of us.

Participant: I feel so abandoned, so alone.

Teacher: At least you're not alone in being alone. Millions of people are having the same experience right now, at this very moment. That's part of what connects us. Many of us share this large, painful feeling of feeling alone.

Teacher: The mind wanders. That's the nature of the human mind. That's how it works—for everyone.

When inquiry arrives at a basic, common human reaction or mechanism, you might consider broadening the context to society at large. Feel free to make space for this, providing examples or reading something to the group that highlights this aspect of common humanity. Given the fact that the group's current experience will have infused the topic with relevance, you can count on lively interest. This broadening will help the group see that they're working with themes that are somewhat universal. In addition, taking a moment for a more didactic approach will provide a bit of rest—a moment in which participants can quietly absorb information or ideas amidst the otherwise active process of inquiry.

Teacher: And what goes for this group also goes for the world around us. We all maintain the illusion that time is money and has to be spent usefully. Everything that brings quantity and speed is considered positive. But what does that mean for the quality of our lives? Take modern means of communication, for example. They're enabling us to consume more information and respond faster, but does that actually make us any happier?

However, this approach does have some pitfalls. One is that participants may project feelings of malaise onto the broader context of society's ills. Then the responsibility for working with that malaise can easily be externalized to others.

Participant: Yes, everyone is stuck to a computer screen these days. You're expected to reply to e-mails within thirty minutes, and a face-to-face chat is a thing of the past. People don't have personal contact anymore, and everything goes so fast…And you have to keep up, otherwise you're out. No wonder we get sick.

This type of dialogue diverges from the path to insight. Don't let inquiry turn into a social debate.

Stage 4: Implications for Future Experiences

The fourth stage of Kolb's learning cycle involves applying the lessons learned in stages 2 and 3 to future situations. Applying mindfulness to the future may sound like a contradiction. After all, mindfulness deals with here-and-now experiences, not with future applications. However, insight is most valuable when it has implications for the future. And just because these implications are noticed, that doesn't necessarily mean they must lead to concrete plans or a strategy, which would activate the doing mode of mind.

After insight has been acquired, learning automatically follows. The aim of stage 4 is to clarify and confirm the insight—anchoring it, so to speak, to increase the likelihood of it being available for future use. We humans have a natural tendency to embrace things that help us along. Therefore, as the teacher, you don't have to offer specific strategies. Indeed, that could be perceived as imposing solutions from the outside, which might trigger resistance while also undermining participants in learning to trust their own insight. Typically, participants independently figure out that an insight could lead to an alternative response to an experience. This process is depicted in figure 7.

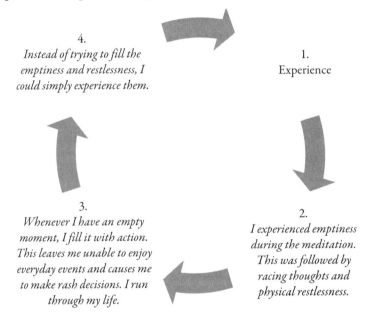

4.
Instead of trying to fill the emptiness and restlessness, I could simply experience them.

1.
Experience

3.
Whenever I have an empty moment, I fill it with action. This leaves me unable to enjoy everyday events and causes me to make rash decisions. I run through my life.

2.
I experienced emptiness during the meditation. This was followed by racing thoughts and physical restlessness.

Figure 7. Insight can lead to an alternative response to an experience.

During stage 4, you're coasting. You're working with the insights participants already have. All you have to do is clarify and confirm:

There's a feeling of restlessness. There's an impulse to move. Once you're aware of that, you can observe it, and then the restlessness may diminish rapidly without you having to act on that impulse. So now you have another option: to stay present. You know that now.

So, all of a sudden you feel your mood has changed and you don't know why. And then, looking back, you see there was a negative thought you hadn't noticed before. It crept in just before that mood change. It's good to be able to see that, isn't it?

By putting what participants have learned in the spotlight, you're confirming the importance of their insights. This can be immensely helpful, given that the lessons learned through mindfulness are often so simple that they're hard to believe. For example, consider the insight that the best response to many difficulties may be to not do anything. This is so deceptively straightforward that participants are likely to devalue it. It can be hard to believe that there's such an easy way out of some issue they've been struggling with. The mind thinks it's been fooled: *Surely it can't be that simple!* The human inclination toward complexity and analyzing leads people to dismiss simple truths.

Furthermore, it can be difficult for people to accept that a "problem" they've been fretting about for so long doesn't actually need to be solved. Here's how you might address this type of situation.

So this is how it goes: irritation, followed by thoughts, then by judging those thoughts, and then feeling bad about yourself. It piles up, and before you know it, there seems to be a lot wrong with you. The moment you become aware of all of this, you also realize that it's all unfounded—a bubble. There is really nothing to do.

Sometimes just one simple remark will suffice: "So now you see how this works."

You can also expand a bit on this kind of brief remark by pointing participants toward being alert to future situations where the insight might prove beneficial. Here are some examples:

Now you can see that the old strategy doesn't help you. This insight is enough. Next time you may remember this and choose a different course.

Next time, when the same situation occurs again, a warning light may come on: "No, not that way!"

The next time you're aware of that feeling of boredom, maybe you'll see whether you can explore it further: how it feels and the thoughts that go with it. Then maybe you'll realize, "Yes, I know this. This is boredom." Instead of reacting, you simply recognize it as one of the experiences that occur.

You now know that this is treacherous territory, with potent triggers, and that staying focused is hard. Take a look at that next time you're in this territory.

The Cycle Is Not the Be-All, End-All

When reviewing a meditation that has just ended, you are talking about experiences that, although still fresh, are past experiences nonetheless. These experiences are invoked during inquiry, but they are no longer the same experiences they were during the meditation. At best, the experience is relived or is a fresh and vivid memory, so there's always some kind of processing going on—processing that leads to thoughts, feelings, and physical reactions. This raises the question of whether it's better to go back to the original experience as much as possible or to work with the processed version of the experience.

One type of situation in which it's generally a good idea to go back to the original experience is when the processing seems to cover or veil the practice experience and decrease its intensity and richness. In these cases, directing attention back to the meditation experience is a way of inviting participants to turn toward something they may be avoiding.

Participant: It's over already. I'm seeing it from a different angle now.

Teacher: What's over already? Can you be more specific? Try to describe the feeling you had at that moment.

Participant: Oh yes, it's a bit of a shock for a second. It comes and goes.

Teacher: Tell me a little more about that shock you felt. What happened exactly?

Participant: Then I settle back on my breathing and the feeling goes. That works well.

Teacher: The feeling that went away with your breathing—what was so difficult about it?

Alternatively, relating the experience may bring the theme beneath it to life more vividly than what the participant experienced during the meditation. When that happens, work with the more lively, processed experience. In this case, the meditation experience serves as an entry point into inquiry about something that appears to be highly salient.

Participant: When you said, "This is time for self-care," I suddenly thought that I've been depriving myself in that respect.

Teacher: You realized that you don't take enough time for self-care…

Participant: Yes. *(Starts crying.)* Sorry…

Teacher: A major issue…

Participant: *(Sobs.)* It just suddenly came over me…Unexpected…

Teacher: *(Remains silent.)*

Participant: I know this…

Teacher: *(Remains silent.)*

Participant: Normally, I never cry. Others always come to me to cry. Okay, let's just continue.

Teacher: Instead of continuing, you could also stay present a bit more to what you're feeling right now, since it's here now anyway.

Sometimes a participant may describe a thought he had during a meditation, with it rapidly becoming clear that the content of this thought touches on a major personal issue. If you stick with the meditation experience, you might inadvertently prevent the participant from working with that thought.

Teacher: So you had a thought. And what came after that thought?

Participant: I noted it as a thought and then it floated by on the horizon. Then I settled my attention back on my breathing.

Furthermore, exploring a thought that touches on a major personal issue may lead to a major insight, so don't be rigid about going back to the meditation experience. Inquiry begins with that experience and circles around it, but don't lose sight of participants' here-and-now processing. If you do, inquiry will become a purely academic exercise. Ultimately, the meditation experience is the object of the inquiry, not the objective. The objective is insight.

Insight is what we leave the practice experience for and why we start looking for broader contexts. Every time you help participants make that step—stage 3 in the experiential learning cycle—you're basically moving away from the meditation experience anyway. As you go from stage 2 to stage 3—from the experience itself to a pattern—the discussion will assume a more general nature. One potential pitfall here is that inquiry can then drift too far from the lived experience, causing participants to end up in a narrative about their patterns.

Participant: That's when I thought, "I don't feel like doing this." So I quit.

Teacher: Do you recognize that in yourself?

Participant: Yes, it's the story of my life. I start all kinds of things but never finish anything. I've got a complete photography setup at home. I bought the works but lost interest after a few months. The same with gym memberships: I'm always getting them, but I never go to the gym. I'm hopeless in that respect. It's cost me so much money! But hey, what can you do about it, right? It's really a pattern. I've told myself on so many occasions that this time I was going to persevere, but I always end up quitting. My boyfriend tells me...

Somewhere along the way, as the narrative gets rolling, the needle drops into a groove. The person starts to speak faster and more monotonously, inserts digressions and anecdotes, draws conclusions, and repeats certain phrases. It turns into talking about the experience instead of talking from it. That's when you have to intervene and bring participants back to the here and now. Likewise, when discussing broader contexts, tune in to the vividness of the experiences participants relate. If you end up in a long or conceptual discussion, you're straying from the path to insight.

Working with the Causes of Suffering

Inquiry is a process of disentanglement—disentangling a jumble of experiences, reactions, and notions. Where is this process headed? David Kolb's experiential learning model invokes a cycle that can inform future choices, but the path of insight isn't limited to learning about implications for the future.

Insight arrives in an aha moment: awakening to wholeness instead of separation, and oneness rather than duality. This can bring the warm feeling of coming home, often accompanied by a bit of pain as we see how we've been obstructing ourselves and causing our own suffering. The path of disentanglement sometimes also produces an overarching insight: "This is what life is like. It's uncontrollable, unsatisfactory, and impermanent. I'm aware of my desire to have it otherwise. I'm aware of clinging to 'I want.' I'm aware of what I'm doing to persist with 'I want,' and I'm aware of the inevitable failure of those efforts. I'm aware of how this causes my suffering."

This overarching insight doesn't contain any new information; rather, it ensues from renewed contact with something we already knew deep down. I sometimes refer to this reconnection with deep knowing as "deep learning."

Manifestations of the Causes of Suffering

Reactivity—the root cause of suffering—contains an "I" and a "want." The basic form is "I want": "I want the nature of this experience to be different."[15] It is a way of saying no to how life presents itself to us in the present moment. "I want" can manifest in five different forms: desire ("I want"), aversion ("I don't want"), sloth and torpor ("I don't want anything"), restlessness ("I want something else"), and doubt ("I don't know what I want"). In the Buddhist tradition these forms of reactivity are represented as the five hindrances, referring to hindrances during mindfulness practice.[16] Given that inquiry explores the roots of reactivity, I'll explore these hindrances in depth in this section. But first, here's a brief overview of how each manifests:

Desire ("I want"): Clinging to what's here, longing for what isn't here, and keeping busy with these by planning or daydreaming

Aversion ("I don't want"): Resistance to what's here, tinged with anger, judgment, boredom, fear, hatred, or grief

Sloth and torpor ("I don't want anything"): Passivity, apathy, slowness, sleepiness, lack of interest, or being easily distracted

Restlessness ("I want something else"): Impatience, wanting to move, or incessant thoughts

Doubt ("I don't know what I want"): Questioning, having a sense of dissatisfaction, or tending to give up

Although I've set these five hindrances forth separately and will discuss them at length, don't get overly caught up in the exact wording of the hindrances. Every version of "I want" that can be juxtaposed with the nature of bare experience is a variation on the causes of suffering. For example, dissatisfaction can be a manifestation of aversion, restlessness, or doubt. What it boils down to is that dissatisfaction is an expression of "I want": "I want this experience to be different."

DESIRE

Desire is a fine capability that adds shine to life. It can point us in a certain direction and get us moving. It can bring pleasure and also offer refuge, a comforting place to be in difficult times. Desire isn't wrong, just like thinking isn't wrong, nor is stress—as long as it's recognized as a fleeting manifestation of the mind. To put desire to wholesome use, it is essential to first recognize a particular manifestation as a desire, to see that it is a reaction of the mind triggering a bodily response, or vice versa. This realization enables us to moderate the degree to which we identify with the desire. We can take advantage of the effects of the desire while staying aware of the mechanism at work. We can enjoy desire like we enjoy a movie, allowing ourselves to be thrilled by the excitement and suspense of the story while remaining aware of the fact that we're watching a movie.

However, we often mistake a desire for something that absolutely has to happen. We think the object of our desire is something we need to have. This transforms desires into temptations that, under the guise of pleasure, prevent us from being at ease with the here and now and therefore lead to dissatisfaction. In the words of vipassana teachers Joseph Goldstein and Jack Kornfield, "They trick us into adopting the 'if only' mentality: 'If only I could have this,' or 'If only I had the right job,' or 'If only I could find the right relationship,' or 'If only I had the right clothes,' or 'If only I had the right personality, then I would be happy'" (2001, p. 40). Unlike the other hindrances, desire tends to be close to the surface during inquiry. Participants often need no prompting to articulate it; rather, they will spontaneously express it with statements like these:

When I have all those thoughts, I think to myself, "I just want peace and quiet in my head!"

I couldn't stop thinking about the painting I'm working on. I'm in the middle of the creative phase and it's boiling inside me. I can't wait to get back to my painting.

The next time I sit down to meditate, I hope to find the same calmness again. It actually makes me laugh sometimes when I notice how hard I try to hang on to that feeling.

Likewise, they typically have little difficulty in clearly identifying a feeling as desire: "My mind often wanders to sexual fantasies as I meditate. It's as if whenever I start to meditate, the silence is immediately filled with desire."

AVERSION

Aversion works in exactly the same way as desire, except that it isn't about wanting to attain something, but instead about wanting to get rid of something. It often feels as though anything is better than the experience we're averse to. Aversion is often stronger than desire because that which we want to push away is already a reality. We are paying the price for experiencing something negative in the here and now. That stings and puts us on edge. Having the negative feels stronger than missing the positive, making aversion a powerful force.

In mindfulness training, aversion can be compounded by unmet expectations about the learning process. People often have a different idea of what the training will bring when they sign up for it. They may think, *I was supposed to feel better, not worse.* They've made the effort to come to sessions and made time for home practice, yet what they get is pain, restlessness, and pandemonium in their head. They are prepared to invest in mindfulness, but accepting these challenges, embracing them, and giving them space can feel excessive.

Aversion often presents itself as an experience with which participants fully identify—one that absorbs them:

All I felt was pain.

I was engulfed by my thoughts. I only sat there thinking. It just didn't stop. No meditation at all!

This can feel like a flawless, airtight account, rooted in the belief that the obstacle must be removed before the individual can proceed. Participants feel that surely they can't be expected to stay present to this kind of experience—that this isn't what mindfulness is about. They seek redemption, rather than acceptance. In this way, the object of aversion is seen as an obstacle to practicing mindfulness, so it must be addressed first.

As the teacher, your role here is to try to introduce some open-mindedness to loosen this belief. Is it possible to sow a seed of the realization that the object of aversion, and aversion itself, can also be the object of meditation? The first step is to open up participants' airtight accounts of their difficulties:

Was there some awareness of any other experience at all, besides the pain?

During the meditation, were there any moments when you were aware of these thoughts?

If this leads to some level of openness and awareness, you may be able to move on toward addressing the aversion as a cause of suffering. But getting there probably won't be easy, as I'll discuss later in this chapter.

SLOTH AND TORPOR

As causes of suffering, sloth and torpor include everything that frustrates attempts to achieve the level of wakefulness needed for mindfulness, such as lack of energy, scattered attention, clouded awareness, or fuzziness. Scattered attention is easy to recognize.

Teacher: What were your experiences during this meditation?

Participant: It was a mishmash.

Teacher: A mishmash?

Participant: Thoughts, feelings… I find it hard to name them. It's as if they all merge into one another.

Teacher: Were you able to be aware of the mishmash?

Participant: No, I was caught up in it.

Clouded awareness manifests in a sense of unclarity and of being passively carried along by thoughts and feelings. Clouded awareness can be hard to recognize because awareness is our faculty to see clearly. Therefore, when awareness is clouded, our ability to recognize it is limited. To make it even more complicated, scattered, clouded, or fuzzy awareness gives rise to a sense of passivity or sleepiness, which may be seen as a cause, rather than a result, of this person's state of mind. The fact is, the state of torpor is the cause, not the sleepiness or passivity that follows. During inquiry, the teacher's art is to shed light on that cause.

Participant: I always fall asleep.

Teacher: Always?

Participant: As soon as I don't have anything to do for even a minute and close my eyes, I'm gone.

Teacher: You're gone.

Participant: *(Silently cries for a moment.)* I feel like I'm constantly running on a kind of treadmill. And as soon as I stop for a second, the treadmill sweeps me off of my feet. When I think about everything I have to do, it's like I'm not in control of my own life.

Teacher: How does that make you feel?

Participant: Like I'm locked up. Like I'm stuck on a kind of hamster wheel. During the day, I'm not even aware of it. That's when I'm just running…*(Pauses.)* And what's also bad about this is that I have a kind of gray feeling all day—a feeling of never really having the energy to face the things that come up. When you're tired, all you're basically doing is surviving. Everything is an obstacle on a road that only leads to the end of the day anyway.

Teacher: It's hard, isn't it? You want it to go another way, but sleepiness is all there is. Maybe that's just what the moment is all about: sleepiness. The meditation opens your eyes to what you really need, even though you want something else. Even now, you are, in a sense, still running. You want yourself to be alert. You don't want to give in to your sleepiness. Perhaps you could use the meditation as a practice to listen to your body, instead of imposing your will on your body. What would it be like to just give your body what it's asking for, to accept that you're sleepy?

Fuzziness in regard to experiences is a bit less categorical. It doesn't necessarily suggest an absence of clear awareness. Experiences themselves may sometimes be gray, vague, or indistinct, in which case the practice becomes one of "exploring fog," as UK mindfulness teacher Trish Bartley sometimes puts it in her trainings. It's worthwhile to determine whether fuzzy attention is due to sloth and torpor or simply reflects the nature of the experience. If the latter, you need not spend a lot of time on the experience, but do take it seriously. These are valuable experiences too, and by no means inferior to any other.

RESTLESSNESS

Restlessness has a lot in common with sloth and torpor, differing primarily in that the energy level swells, rather than dwindles. During mindfulness practice, this leads to agitation, nervousness, and thinking that's quick and fierce but unfocused. Inquiry into restlessness is easier than inquiry into sloth and torpor because participants can draw on the energy of restlessness during the conversation. They are unhappy and want a solution. They are all over it:

It wasn't working at all. I was itching all over. I had ants in my pants. As soon as I begin to meditate, I start fidgeting. I don't know what it is.

I can't sit still!

My thoughts were focused on everything but my breathing. In my mind, I rode the subway several times, cleared up a misunderstanding with my partner, put a colleague in his place again, plotted the route for my drive home, and went over my tasks for the next day. I did a lot of different things during that time, but I didn't really meditate.

This agitated energy traps participants in identifying with their experiences, making it hard for them to bring an open, exploring attitude to them. As a result, inquiry into restlessness often leaves participants feeling unsatisfied. And yet, here too, the teacher's job is to invite participants to move toward awareness of the base experience.

Teacher: So you mention tense muscles, physical irritation in the belly, and an inclination to move around. Was there any noticing of all that during the meditation?

Participant: Of course! But that's not helping me. It's not what I want.

Teacher: It's not what you want. And still, this is the experience there is. Quite the challenge!

Participant: All kinds of thoughts tumbling over each other.

Teacher: And were you able to sometimes be aware of that: "all kinds of thoughts tumbling over each other"?

Participant: No. I was simply swept along on the stream of these thoughts. It took me away. It's as if I was absent the whole time.

Teacher: So your experience was being swept along, taken away, absent the whole time...Wow!

Participant: I don't have a solution to this.

Teacher: Neither do I. Perhaps this isn't something opposed to your meditation; perhaps this *is* your meditation. Thoughts are tumbling over each other and there's no solution. What would it be like to sit with that? That's what happens, and it doesn't have to be any other way—a meditation on tumbling thoughts.

DOUBT

Of all hindrances, doubt can be the most difficult to work with. Joseph Goldstein and Jack Kornfield explain this well (2001, pp. 43–44):

> When we believe it and get caught by it, our practice just stops cold. We become paralyzed. All kinds of doubt might assail us: Doubts about ourselves and our capacities, doubts about our teachers, doubts about the dharma itself—"Does it really work? I sit here and all that happens is my knees hurt and I feel restless. Maybe the Buddha really didn't know what he was talking about." We might doubt the practice or doubt that it is the right practice for us. "It's too hard. Maybe I should try Sufi dancing." Or we think it's the right practice but the wrong time. Or it's the right practice and the right time, but our body's not yet in good enough shape. It doesn't matter what the object is; when the skeptical, doubting mind catches us, we're stuck.

There are two kinds of doubt: fundamental doubt and doubt about technique. The latter form of doubt is often a manifestation of a desire for control, security, or perfection. It can present itself in practical questions about posture, technique, and purpose, and you can deal with it using common inquiry techniques. (I'll discuss this form of doubt later in the chapter.)

Fundamental doubt, which revolves around the idea of giving up, can be more challenging to address. It's generally best to distill the doubt in the words right away and put it out in the open.

Participant: That's when I say to myself, "What's the point of this? This doesn't help me either. I've made another poor choice."

Teacher: Do you recognize this in yourself—these kinds of thoughts?

Participant: I do. I start something, and after a while I begin to doubt whether it's right for me, and then I give up.

Teacher: That's how doubt works.

Participant: *(Sighs.)* It's so destructive...

Teacher: That's doubt. That's what doubt does to us. Doubt is one of the major hindrances to the practice. As soon as we give in to it, we're lost. Doubt undermines our commitment.

Confusion is a form of doubt, and during meditation it's often based on illusive beliefs promulgated by Western culture—for example, beliefs about how we should use our time. Yet these beliefs are thoughts. They have content and are therefore relatively easy to explore.

Participant: I tend to fold laundry while the body scan recording starts. Why does that introduction take so long? I've heard it enough by now...

Teacher: So you have this thought of "Why does the introduction take so long?" And then you decide to fold laundry and cut some time off from the body scan. Why do you think that introduction is there?

There's also healthy doubt: the benefit of the doubt that some participants give to the training when they start out. (I'll also discuss this in detail a bit later in the chapter.)

Going Down the Path Together

The path to illuminating the causes of suffering isn't always clear or straightforward, yet participants want to gain better insight into these causes. Approaching the causes of suffering calls for striking a respectful balance between restraint and perseverance, which in turn calls for sensitivity. As soon as suffering becomes tangible and maybe even visible, what remains is to sit with the suffering together and eventually wrap up the subject again, just as sensitively and respectfully as it was unwrapped.

OPENING THE PATHWAY

Not all causes of suffering are equally easy to work with. Desire is often fairly straightforward to recognize and acknowledge. Aversion can be a bit more difficult. It is as if the energy of aversion is turned against mindfulness, which often makes it difficult to note aversion as a cause of suffering. A remark such as "This is aversion" or "Can you see that this is aversion?" may lead nowhere: "Of course I can! But what good does that do me? It doesn't make it go away!" The emotions underlying aversion, such as anger, are often quite powerful. The question is whether participants have sufficient tolerance for frustration to be able to bring mindfulness to their aversion. However, regardless of their tolerance, you can still gently point in the direction of their experience.

Teacher: So there is pain, and you're aware of it, and you're mindful of your aversion. And there you are…doing what?

Participant: Right, doing what? I'm in a fight with myself.

Teacher: And you're seeing that. And seeing that means knowing it: that everything you're doing adds fuel to the flames. There is something unpleasant; there's fighting. Can you just be mindful of that? Be okay with it?

Participant: Yes, but when I experience pain, I have to do something about it!

Teacher: You describe that very well. That's exactly what happens in all of us: we have to do something about it, it has to change, and we won't let go of it. Does that reaction make what's difficult easier or harder?

Participant: Harder.

Teacher: Are there any other options?

Participant: Doing nothing.

Teacher: Sitting with aversion…quite a challenge: There is aversion and it doesn't need to be different. Could that be an option?

Participant: I don't know.

Teacher: Perhaps this could be a relief: "Thank god. There's no need for it to be different—nothing to do, nothing to change." It's okay. Even aversion is allowed to be there. What a relief!

Due to having an element of agitation, manifestations of doubt and restlessness are typically harder to bring home to their causes than manifestations of desire. Sloth and torpor can also be difficult to handle due to the opposite issue: their lack of energy. Yet the invitation is the same in all cases: "Can you see that there is restlessness [or doubt, or sloth and torpor]? How does that feel? What does it trigger? And can you be okay with that?"

MAKING A CONNECTION

In inquiry, moving from an experience of suffering to the cause of that suffering takes several steps. First, confirm the experience as it is:

So there is restlessness [pain, unease, worrying…].

So that's how it is. There was restlessness. That was your experience.

The second step is to confirm the reactivity:

And you don't want it and therefore fight it.

And there is judging. And then you judge the judging.

The third step is to offer an invitation to participants to soften their relationship with the nature of their experience:

You see all of that and realize, "This is it. This is what there is. This is my here and now…" Being with that and breathing with that.

When you realize that this experience is already here, maybe you can also see how you can become more at ease with it… Being comfortable with what's there simply because it's already there anyway.

These three steps are the blueprint for helping participants make a connection with the causes of their suffering. Although it's helpful to have these steps in the back of your mind, be aware that in the practice of inquiry, they often aren't clearly demarcated.

Participant: I just cannot stop looking at my watch and thinking, "Oh, another twenty minutes to go. How will I make it through those twenty minutes?" Although I do stay seated, it's like I've got ants crawling all over me inside.

Teacher:	Restlessness.
Participant:	Now, as I'm looking back, there is some distance, but when I'm in the middle of it I don't know how to deal with it.
Teacher:	This is exactly how restlessness works.
Participant:	Right…
Teacher:	What if you were to see it like this: "This is restlessness, this is how it works, and sometimes it comes over me." Realizing that, would it maybe open a way to relate to it as it happens, as best as you can?

Although the steps can be intermixed, see if you can end inquiry with the third step: softening reactivity.

EXERCISING RESTRAINT

The causes of suffering are constantly at hand. After all, they underlie all of the reactivity discussed during inquiry, although they are often covered up with layers of not-seeing and confusion.

As the teacher, you will often be able to identify a cause underlying a reaction. The degree to which you can try to peel back the layers depends on the setting: the participant, the group, the program, and so on. For example, a group of advanced participants will more readily make the connection with painful patterns and the causes of suffering than a group that has just embarked on its journey of discovery. With a group of beginners, it's probably best to touch upon the topic of underlying causes lightly, if at all.

Participant:	I was irritated throughout.
Teacher:	So there was irritation. How were you with that?

Another issue is that sometimes these major, weighty issues may arise when you're dealing with a different topic or don't have much time. In such cases, it might be best to consciously make the topic smaller again, even if it was put forward by a participant.

Participant:	My mind often wanders to sexual fantasies as I meditate. It's as if whenever I start to meditate, the silence is immediately filled with desire.

Teacher: That can happen. Fantasies are thoughts too. See whether you can, as best as you can, simply be aware of them with patience and without judging them, and then, when you're ready, return to the object of the meditation.

Alternatively, if time permits and you're working with a more advanced group, you could use this as an inroad to discussing the causes of suffering.

Teacher: So desire comes up. Perhaps you can also notice how it manifests itself—how it begins with a thought that's attractive, and how this soaks up your attention, gains momentum, and expands, perhaps also in your mood and your body. That's how desire works: it lures us away.

PRACTICING PERSEVERANCE

Participants can be conflicted about delving into the causes of suffering. On the one hand, they have the intention to explore, and on the other, they are reluctant to face up to difficult patterns. Sometimes a certain degree of perseverance on your part is necessary to help participants overcome their initial reluctance, allowing them to go further than they would have on their own. However, you should only take this route if you feel the participant in question has the courage and capacity to join you on this path and an interest in doing so. You will be venturing into precarious territory, working close to the limit of how far the person is willing to go, and this is a point you don't want to go beyond.

In the following example, the teacher is practicing perseverance. The statements that follow, in italics, are alternatives the teacher could have used to let the participant off the hook if it seemed the participant was nearing her limit.

Participant: I kept thinking about my divorce. That fills me with sadness and anger and rage. I keep coming back to that.

Teacher: And? (*So there were thoughts, and then emotions.*)

Participant: I don't want to keep rehashing it! It happened so long ago, and I've been in therapy for it for so long, yet it's dominated my life all that time. I want to be done with it. I want to move on.

Teacher: Perhaps you can never be done with it. (*See whether you can stay present with it, with that desire to be done with it.*)

Participant:	It's already been such a struggle. I thought I'd find silence here, a bit of peace and quiet.
Teacher:	Can you choose what comes up during your meditation? *(Sometimes you have to work through restlessness and unease to get to something else.)*
Participant:	No.
Teacher:	But given the way you speak now, it seems as if you have a great aversion to certain meditation experiences. *(If you have no control over it, what are your options?)*
Participant:	I suppose you're right there.
Teacher:	Then how can you find rest? *(Great. Thank you.)*
Participant:	*(Remains silent.)*
Teacher:	So there is aversion.
Participant:	That is exactly what I don't want…
Teacher:	Yes. This is the core, right? The core is the not-wanting. You can be accepting and mindful of everything except that. You have the feeling that you have to get rid of this first, before it's possible to be mindful again.

In general, when opening a path toward a cause of suffering, keep it natural. Make sure your approach fits you and fits the level of the group. Follow your intuition and interests, and preserve the flow of the process, perhaps by alternating with other forms of inquiry.

Arriving at the Root Causes of Suffering: The End of Inquiry

When inquiry arrives at awareness of how reality is, and of wanting things to be different, the disentanglement process has come to a conclusion. You can let go of inquiry and simply sit together with the group with whatever has arisen, in its clearest form. Then the group can begin to explore how they might engage with it.

An illusion has been lifted. At this point, you can simply say, "So here we are. This is what restlessness [desire, dissatisfaction...] is like."

SITTING WITH THE DIFFICULT TOGETHER

As soon as the difficulty is out in the open, you can also ask questions to further explore the participant's relationship with it:

And at those brief moments, those flashes of insight and seeing it, could you say to yourself: "So this is worrying. Now I see it"? Could you create, as it were, some room around it, if only a whisper of space?

And then there is that pain, and you notice that your attention keeps being drawn to it. Can you just say, "This is pain. Let me feel it. Even this pain is okay"?

Seeing a cause of one's suffering triggers a lot of experiences. Participants realize how they're obstructing themselves and the pain this produces, and this often makes people sad. On top of that, they see a larger context: that obstructing oneself is human, and that they have this in common with others. This confers a sense of innocence that brings relief. It also brings a sense of connection, because all of these experiences will resonate with the group.

When the patterns of our suffering are out in the open, words lose their prominence. There's nothing left to say and nothing left to do. This group is sitting together sharing common experiences. Seeing, feeling, and experiencing together creates a strong bond within the group. The word that best captures the mood or the feeling that binds the group together is "compassion." This is the natural reaction we have when we see pain and suffering in others and let it get through to us.

In those moments, the room is filled with compassion. Words are often too much and distract from the intensity of the moment. In such situations, keep your questions brief, and refer to the participant's relationship with difficult experiences.

Participant: There was only pain.

Teacher: And what was it like to be present to that?

Participant: There are thoughts. There's anger, bitterness. That's when I think, "I don't want to continue."

Teacher: And what's there now?

Participant: All kinds of things at the same time: the pain and everything I said before. It's so hard…

Teacher: It is hard. And you don't have to do anything with it. Just feel it.

Desire, aversion, restlessness—they all arise in such struggles. They are all seen, and there are no words you can add to them except perhaps something that underlines what everybody is already feeling: "We're all in this together. Staying present to this is all there is to do, and it's the only thing we can offer ourselves."

The word "compassion" means "suffering with," or "suffering together." It is an experience of shared openness to difficulty that has a healing effect. To express arrival at this space of compassion, all that may be needed is a short statement to confirm what's happening: "That's it," "This is what it's about," or simply "Yes." Sometimes silence is best. And sometimes you may need to devote a few more words to framing the supportive, holding quality of the space:

Just to feel this: what's difficult, the struggle, our best intentions—and our powerlessness in light of these things.

This is what it is. It isn't any other way, even if we so badly want it to be. And here we are.

Now we can see how it works: that we are driven by it, and that it causes suffering. Seeing this, letting it in, sitting with it…

You might want to emphasize being gentle with what's difficult and express appreciation of this approach:

There is restlessness. And you notice how it moves and touches you, shakes you around, and turns you upside down. And now the question is, could you be okay even with all of that? Instead of resisting it, could you give it all the space it needs? Surrendering to it, stepping out of the arena, and letting the restlessness do whatever it wants to do?

That's when the emotion arises and you're aware of all of these reactions that want to make it go away, to change it, and so forth. And then perhaps there's a realization: "So this is my experience of this moment. It's my practice to relate to this now. How can I relate to this with friendliness, in an open way, with kindness toward myself?"

And there is a realization: There's no need to do anything about it. It doesn't need to be more pleasant than it is. It's difficult, painful, or daunting, but it's okay for it to be difficult, painful, or daunting. And you're doing great, surfing these difficulties. The experience doesn't have to be different from what it is. Phew, what a relief!

You can also recognize and appreciate the moment by placing it in the broader context of common humanity. Generalizing creates space around the subject without distracting from it and leaves participants free to work with it as they please:

Jon Kabat-Zinn wrote a book entitled Full Catastrophe Living. *It's about living in the eye of the storm. Everyone can recognize the sensation of life sometimes being like a catastrophe, and only having ourselves, and each other, to hang on to. So here we are, sitting in the eye of the storm.*

This is hard, right? We're touching on a major issue here, a source of suffering— not only for you, but for everyone. Looking at it and simply seeing how it affects us…Wow!

This isn't about finding calmness or some brief relaxation. This is about the big themes of life. Finding peace with these themes is one of our missions in life.

Whether you remain quiet or say something, your nonverbal presence should be strong. Precisely in these moments of intensity, it's a key factor. Your sensitivity combined with your firmness provides the holding and security participants need in order to stay in contact with their vulnerability. Making eye contact is important here. You can also make your presence felt by nodding your head and through your physical posture.

In practice, such a moment will last only a few minutes, but the intensity will condense time. It will feel as if the air has become heavy, time has slowed down, and the silence has deepened. To the extent that there is healing power in mindfulness training, it lies in these moments, in which the group is sitting together with the difficult. Such moments are sacred.

At these times, the group has reached the most essential and valuable part of mindfulness training: practicing finding peace with the nature of their experience and, indeed, of life. Mindfulness training then shifts from a learning cycle with implications for the future to honing the art of being with what is. Participants experience a radical change of perspective in which frustration with uncontrollability becomes surprise, dissatisfaction becomes appreciating the perfection of what is, and a sense of instability becomes wonder at continuous change and the transient and fleeting nature of life. Looking at one's experience as it is often isn't easy, but it always has a soothing effect. What it comes down to, in the words of mindfulness teacher Trish Bartley, is "gently being with the difficult" (2012, p. 150). This calls for something you cannot bring in with techniques: compassion. Sitting together amidst our splintered patterns of suffering, there is nothing to do but experience the pain and muster a kind of mildness toward it.

COMPLETING THE EXPLORATION

After the arc of the exploration has been completed and it seems that everything has been said and felt, it's good to break up the atmosphere of intensity. After heaviness, you need lightness. Once, when my group and I were sitting with painful experiences after an intense exploration, a loudly cawing magpie landed on the edge of the roof. Someone said something about the noise, which prompted another group member to offer a bit of general information about magpies. For the next few minutes we talked about magpies, and that was actually a very nice way of wrapping up the exploration.

It can also be refreshing to resolutely move on to the next subject:

Let's move on to a sitting meditation.

Let's move to reviewing the homework. I'm curious: Did any of you struggle with the home practice last week, or simply not get around to it?

If you feel that might be too big or sudden a step, check whether the group is ready for the transition:

Does anyone else have anything to add? Shall we proceed? Is that okay?

As you move on, the heaviness will subside, but the feeling of connection can remain and bring an atmosphere of dedication, stillness, and intensity to the next part of the session.

That said, sometimes you may instead want to deepen the moment further, especially if emotions have come to the surface that still require some time to be processed. These could be difficult emotions, such as sadness or anger among participants about what they're doing to themselves. However, these emotions could also be lighter, such as delight in the absurdity of the ways in which they keep making things so difficult for themselves, or warmth as insights give participants a sense of essence and take them closer to the heart.

All of these emotions are framed by the softening glow of insight. Giving emotions room to emerge and be felt together is part of processing them and containing them. This takes time. Working through a major theme together, as a group, is key. In these moments, remember that you've arrived at the essence of mindfulness training. If need be, drop the program for it. Don't jump to a new subject too soon. You never know when the next opportunity will come along.

Another option at these times is to suggest a few moments of meditation, which can bridge the transition between staying present and moving on. You could even customize this meditation to whatever has arisen by, for example, guiding participants in staying connected to the pain that was being felt and breathing with it. Following that, you might briefly inquire about how everybody is doing, with special attention to the participant whose experience was explored.

If you notice that someone is particularly touched by the subject and needs more time for processing, check in to see how that participant is doing, perhaps by asking what he needs. Then check to see whether it's okay to proceed. If more is required, you also have the option to talk to the person individually after the session.

At some point, the group will be ready to proceed with something lighter. This is part and parcel of the waves of intensity and relaxation and the rhythm of attention. When this moment arrives and you wrap up the inquiry, be sure not to add anything new to the topic. Even just drawing a conclusion could disturb participants' processing.

Considerations in Working with the Causes of Suffering

Being skilled in working with the causes of suffering starts with the recognition that you've arrived at an opportunity for deepening what the training is all about. This is beautiful, and you may feel some excitement or eagerness. However, it's important to honestly assess whether you're willing and able to take that road at the time. Whatever you choose, there are two key considerations to keep in mind: being sensitive to the difficulties participants may experience, and acknowledging your fundamental not-knowing and noncompetence.

BEING SENSITIVE TO PARTICIPANTS

A basic rule is that the more difficult a participant's experience is, the more careful and respectful your approach should be. So after a participant shares something challenging or vulnerable, you might initially simply acknowledge the scope of the issue:

It's good that you notice this. This is one of those things people often struggle with.

This seems to exceed our meditation, doesn't it? It's as if we can't work with it within the parameters of the meditation.

That's a difficult one, right? I have a feeling that it affects you in a deep way. Does it?

This is a big issue. And it's coupled with a sense of powerlessness, a sense that there's nothing you can do with it. I can relate to that feeling. That sense of powerlessness is quite something just to hold in awareness, isn't it?

Then you can ask permission to inquire further, while also establishing a considerate tone and pace:

Let's calmly take a look at this.

Would it be okay with you if we take a bit more time for this and delve into it a little deeper?

This cautious approach, which should be reflected in your tone of voice, body language, and words, as well as in silences, shows that you respect the participant and see her as she is, in contact with something difficult. The participant is vulnerable: something that's difficult for her is now out in the open and potentially the subject of exploration. This can be uncomfortable. Is the participant able to join you in the exploration, or does she seem to want to back off? Aim to proceed openly, patiently, and without expectations regarding results.

ACKNOWLEDGING NOT-KNOWING AND YOUR OWN HUMAN LIMITATIONS

Sometimes you may find it hard to relate to a participant's suffering, or you may simply feel that your compassion falls short. If so, stay true to that. Be genuine by accepting and acknowledging your not-knowing or the limits of your competence. Staying authentic opens the door to being compassionate on another level.

And you can still always take the most important steps: paying attention to whatever participants bring up and letting them know that you see them in their powerlessness and suffering:

> *I'm just not familiar with chronic pain. My experience with pain doesn't extend beyond the experience of a bad toothache. I don't know what to say to you, except that I'm sorry to see how hard it is for you.*

> *I don't know either. I completely follow what you're saying about what's going on inside you and the feelings that are triggered, and also about how you feel unable to get in touch with it. That must be so hard.*

> *I feel your sadness and it affects me. There's nothing more I can do besides sharing my feelings with you. Words fail me.*

Pitfalls in Working with the Causes of Suffering

By now, you're probably well aware that exploring the causes of suffering is delicate work. As such, there are many potential pitfalls. In the sections that follow, I address some of the most common hazards.

PLACING YOUR OWN EMOTIONS IN THE FOREFRONT

Perhaps needless to say, the purpose of mindfulness training is not to process the teacher's emotions. Taking inquiry as an opportunity to deal with your emotions can compromise the safety and boundaries you've painstakingly established. In addition, becoming emotional will disturb your balance and cloud your ability to see what the group needs. Of course, crucial qualities of the teacher, such as embodiment and compassion, require vulnerability. However, professionalism requires that you handle this vulnerability consciously and not lose yourself in it. The guidelines for self-disclosure, set forth a bit later in this chapter, are therefore particularly relevant when you find yourself touched personally.

SIDESTEPPING SUFFERING

As mentioned previously, you don't have to take every opportunity to home in on the causes of suffering. The program, the context, and the nature of participants themselves can all offer good reasons not to. However, you might also have personal reasons that pull you away from taking advantage of a possible avenue to accessing a cause of suffering.

As a teacher, sometimes you may feel your spirits sag when you contact participants' powerlessness and suffering, especially if they express this very poignantly. Maybe you're simply at a loss as to how to deal with such a difficult experience. Perhaps the experience is too intense or becomes too much for you. Maybe it touches too acutely onto your own experience. Perhaps you think, *This might be a Pandora's box. If I were to open it, I would be overwhelmed and unable to guide whatever emerges.* As a result, you might be inclined to make light of the difficulty, perhaps by making a joke, or you may briefly express your compassion and then move on to something else. Either way, you're basically sidestepping the difficulty.

Such reactions are understandable. After all, mindfulness teachers are human too. When these kinds of reactions occur, try to reflect upon them afterward. Ask yourself whether sidestepping the issue was the best option, or whether it was driven mainly by your own fear or insecurity. Could you have handled it differently? If the way you handled it arose from an automatic reaction, that would be worthwhile to explore. This kind of reflection on your own reactions is not so much about finding a solution, but more about expanding insight in your humanity and your potential as a teacher.

BEING OVERLY EAGER

In contrast to backing off too much, you can also be too eager. You may think, *Aha, now we're getting to the heart of the matter.* If so, you may start to explain exactly how it works and how things should be…until you see participants' eyes glaze over and realize that you lost touch with what this learning moment needed. Your eagerness to explain made you miss that it was time for compassion, for feeling rather than explaining.

Another form of overeagerness is to go in guns blazing and confront the participant:

So that's when there are only thoughts and you're gone completely. That's your meditation. It is what it is. The thing is to accept that.

There's pain, and you want it to be different. This is aversion. Do you recognize it?

This kind of approach makes it abundantly clear to participants what they are doing and how they're obstructing themselves, but in a hard way. It's like rubbing it in but then leaving participants there. How will that make them feel? Will they feel supported in exploring their relationship with the difficult any further? Probably not. It's more likely that they'll give whatever answer they think they're expected to give and then withdraw.

Confrontation is a risky tactic, one you should only use when you're confident that it's the only way of making progress. You must also be confident about whether the participant and the rest of the group will be able to handle it.

RESORTING TO PLATITUDES

Dealing with the causes of suffering is a sensitive process wherein certain words can be too much or may not be taken well. Rash language can do damage. This can lead teachers to fall back on standard phrases, as can a feeling of power-lessness or a moment of mindlessness. Although standard phrases can serve as an effective invitation or eye-opener in some situations, they may come across as plati-tudes in others:

And now you see it.

So that is your pattern.

Just let it be the way it is.

I can't offer a general rule here. The right wording will vary depending on the situation and on the person. When sitting with the difficult, at a bare minimum your words should be conveyed with presence and feeling—something that often doesn't happen with overused standard phrases. If in doubt, it's better not to say anything at all than to fall back on a platitude.

When Inquiry Is Challenging

Inquiry invites participants to look inward and explore their inner being where it has not yet crystallized out, where feelings and thoughts tumble over each other uncensored—sometimes intense, sometimes superficial, sometimes in quick suc-cession, sometimes slowly, sometimes clearly, sometimes vaguely—in order to bring these experiences to the surface and report on them to a group of relative strangers, using words that may seem inadequate, with the outcome being uncer-tain. In this way, inquiry is an invitation to be vulnerable. That's why it requires a setting of calmness, spaciousness, and safety. Difficult moments especially call for careful guidance so they don't become a hindrance, preventing participants from surrendering to the sensitive process of exploration. In this section, I'll discuss a few of the most common types of challenges participants face in the context of inquiry.

The Sense of Being Consciously Incompetent

For most participants, mindfulness training will be their first experience with inquiry, a process that involves taking a fresh look at their inner experiences, which can feel both very close and very far away, and finding words to express those experiences. Initially, adopting this new way of perceiving and expressing tends to be slow and difficult. Participants may feel insecure, hesitant, uncomfortable, awkward, and sometimes even despairing. They are at the edge of their learning capacity and feel conscious of their incompetence. Guide participants through this phase in a friendly and supportive manner, giving them time to learn.

Participant: It's a feeling…I don't know how to put this into words.

Teacher: That happens sometimes, doesn't it? A clear experience, but no words to go with it.

Participant: Hard, dark…I don't know…

Teacher: I understand. We're trying to find our way in a new realm. In our culture, there aren't many words to describe inner experiences. We struggle to find words for them, and when we do, they seem inadequate. We're all fumbling in the dark together.

Also be supportive with respect to participants' sense of clumsiness, and bring the same sense of common humanity to this struggle.

Teacher: We're all clumsy together. We lack the vocabulary and tools to deal with this. It's as if we're supposed to do stone masonry with our bare hands.

Participant: It's a sense of space…That takes the edge off the feeling. That may sound silly. I don't know how to say it.

Teacher: You've said it very well. I understand what you mean.

Participant: I'm not allowed to say "good." That's judging.

Teacher: Of course you are! That's how we talk. We need words to express ourselves. And there are gradations in meanings.

It can be helpful to remind participants of how important and extraordinary their work with the group is.

Teacher: If anyone were to come in now, they would have no idea what we're talking about. Yet we're talking about the most important thing there is: how we meet ourselves and our inner experiences. We're trying to capture that in words, perhaps for the first time in our lives. That's quite extraordinary, right?

The Sense of Being Stuck

Sometimes participants may feel stuck, as though they can't get the knack of practicing mindfulness, or as though they aren't making any progress in that respect. As an example, consider a participant who keeps falling asleep during meditation and says, "I've tried everything. I feel that I'm stuck." A somewhat standard response might be along these lines: "This sense of being stuck, where do you feel it? How does it feel? What it's like to be present to that?" However, the participant would be likely to respond, "I just can't do it! Surely falling asleep isn't what's supposed to happen."

Basically, you're being asked to provide a solution. This pressure will be particularly strong when participants have become frustrated or are starting to despair. What's most important in such moments is to let participants know you see and acknowledge their difficulty, and to communicate that you are with them in being with the difficult. You might follow up with sensitive attempts to introduce some lightness or relief by inserting a bit of humor or by referring to a larger context or a moment when the practice did go well.

If this approach doesn't produce the spaciousness required for exploration, leave it at that, perhaps concluding by noting the lingering sense of dissatisfaction the participant feels. If you sense growing openness toward exploration, however, there are several angles you can take as you proceed with inquiry: challenging, explaining, questioning, or being compassionate. I'll provide an example of each, in response to the last statement in the preceding exchange: "I just can't do it! Surely falling asleep isn't what's supposed to happen":

Challenging: "What's wrong with sleeping? There are lots of things going on while we sleep. Just lie down and sleep. Your mind will still pick up what's important to you."

Explaining: "You're not supposed to fall asleep. When we decide to practice, we aren't deciding to go to sleep. And yet we still do. It sometimes simply happens on its own. That sense of doing it wrong is added later. That's basically you judging yourself. You can ask yourself whether that's helpful. Anyway, there is judgment happening. This you could note as such during the practice: 'Judgment…Judgment.'"

Questioning: "When you sleep, you cannot be aware. That's true, however, you're not aware when you're falling asleep. So how can anyone say whether it's good or not?"

Being compassionate: "You fall asleep and later feel that you aren't doing the practice right. That's quite common. How could we best take care of that feeling?"

But sometimes there simply isn't room for further exploration. That can be the case when participants are clinging to their own aspirations for a practice.

Participant: So I was sitting here and planes kept flying over.

Teacher: How did you work with that?

Participant: Looking up, it looks quite nice—such huge aircraft. That isn't something you see every day.

Teacher: And what else?

Participant: There wasn't a lot of meditating I could do, so I gave up. There was no rest.

Teacher: Ah, rest. Wonderful! But what if there is none? How about when you're sitting and planes keep flying over, can you still meditate?

Participant: What meditation gives me is that I sometimes become calm. So when I know that won't happen, there's no sense in continuing.

Participant: I couldn't stay focused at all. I was just cold.

Teacher: Where did you feel that in your body?

Participant: Well, you know, cold everywhere.

Teacher: Was there any room to explore it—where you felt it, how it felt?

Participant: I was focused only on being cold and how much longer it would be. I was inclined to get up and grab a blanket.

Teacher: So you had this experience of being cold. And then you thought about doing something about it by grabbing a blanket. Can you describe what happened next?

Participant: I decided not to get up because I didn't want to disturb the others.

Teacher: So, first the thought of getting up entered your mind, and then the consideration that it would be better not to get up so as not to disturb the others. Interesting. And then?

Participant: I stayed there, lying down until the end, but I only had "being cold" on my mind. It was no picnic.

Teacher: You only had being cold on your mind. Was there any moment of being aware of that, in the sense of "These are sensations of being cold, and these are my reactions to that"?

Participant: No. To be honest, I don't see what good that would have done me in that moment.

In these examples, the participants lacked some degree of openness to being mindful, making it hard for them to detach from their experiences and reactions. It may be different next time, or it may never be different. Can you, as the teacher, leave it at that and still give these participants the support that will help them continue? Can you trust the process in this kind of situation, just as you ask participants to trust the process?

Technique as a Distraction

During inquiry, participants will ask questions about the right posture for meditation, the difference between using a cushion versus a chair, whether they're allowed to move during the body scan, whether mental noting is the same as thinking, what exactly the foreground of awareness is, whether it's okay to do walking meditation in the woods, how an exercise relates to a certain Buddhist tradition, whether they need to sit with their hands folded or open with the palms turned upward, and on and on. These are exploratory questions with a technical slant. They can hint at things participants struggle with and experience as obstacles impeding their practice. In some cases, you can immediately eliminate the obstacle with an adequate answer. But in most cases you can't, because there simply isn't an adequate answer or you don't know it.

A technical answer is often not the best option, as it would be too detailed and distract from the participant's practice and its challenges. Besides, technical questions often conceal or cloak deeper obstacles, such as perfectionism or doubt.

The rule of thumb is that if you can answer a technical question briefly and clearly, do so. If not, don't even try, and be clear about that, then address the larger context of the issue at hand: How important is this question? What are the motives that sparked the question? Finally, if necessary, and if you can, offer the participant support in returning to the practice.

Because this issue comes up a lot, I'll provide an in-depth discussion of the preceding ways of responding: providing a technical answer to the question; addressing the relative importance of the question; and identifying and exploring the theme or motive that underlies the question.

PROVIDING TECHNICAL ANSWERS TO TECHNICAL QUESTIONS

When providing a technical answer, limit your response to the information the participant needs to be able to proceed: "Meditating on the floor is a custom that stems from Eastern tradition." Also, be practical whenever possible: "If lying on the floor hurts the back of your head, use a pillow" or "It may feel scary if your breath gets irregular or speeds up when you focus on it, but there's no real danger. You won't choke."

Be as clear as possible when explaining the purpose of a technique and defining boundaries. It's okay to be directive in such replies: "If you feel pain or are uncomfortable, change your posture. There's nothing wrong with that. This isn't a practice in asceticism. As long as it's a conscious choice, it's part of the meditation."

Also be clear about the limitations of your own competence:

I'm not a physical therapist or an expert on that. I would be careful with that.

I don't know what enlightenment is. I have an idea of what mindfulness is and how to practice it. I don't know a great deal about those other things.

Buddhism undoubtedly assigns meaning to that, but I haven't really studied it.

I'm not sure whether or not it would be good to proceed if you feel pain. Explore it for yourself, and if you have any doubt, don't do it. We are here to get better, not worse.

Sometimes a technical question will be about something you're particularly interested in or will involve one of your areas of specialty. In these cases, you can go into greater detail. If you're a physical therapist, for example, you'd answer a question about posture differently than a vipassana teacher, yoga teacher, or a psychotherapist would. You bring your specialties to the training, and participants know that. Besides, conveying your personal passions and interests adds value to the training. Just make sure you do so in a conscious, considered way. Offering too much information from your specialist background may distract participants from the core of the training: practicing mindfulness.

ADDRESSING THE RELATIVE IMPORTANCE OF QUESTIONS

Participants tend to overrate the importance of technique. When they do so, point out where the issue that's been raised fits into the broader perspective of the practice:

Many people prefer to meditate on a cushion on the floor. It's a change from your normal posture and it might give you the sense of being grounded. But you could just as well meditate while seated on a chair. It's up to you to explore which posture best supports your mental attitude for meditation.

The external form and the instructions aren't what's most important. They are merely suggestions. See for yourself how they can be helpful for you. Other than that, you don't have to think about it so much.

If you start thinking about a meditation instruction too much, it may not be the most helpful instruction for you. It probably means you don't need it. Instructions should not be obstructions.

As soon as an instruction becomes an obsession, it misses the point. That's when you start fighting and lose your mindful stance. When that happens, see how you can make it easier for yourself so that you regain some space for other experiences and for mindfulness.

EXPLORING THE UNDERLYING MOTIVE FOR POSING A TECHNICAL QUESTION

Participants' technical questions are often born from insecurity about whether they're doing the practice right. You could call this "minor doubt," meaning doubt about the content of the practice, not about quitting, which would be "major doubt."

An urge for perfection or control also sometimes underlies technical questions. In this case, participants are focusing excessively on the instructions, wondering exactly what they're supposed to do, fixating on what some word or another means, and so on, all of which lead to the pitfall of striving to *get* the practice in a cognitive way.

Try to figure out what prompted a specific technical question by asking questions along these lines:

Were you aware of this question arising during the meditation?

Was there a certain experience that preceded it?

How did you deal with that experience?

How did you deal with the question that arose?

Here's a more specific example.

Participant: Are we allowed to move during the body scan?

Teacher: Did that question occur to you during the practice?

Participant: I had restless legs. I was trying hard to keep them still.

Teacher: It sounds as if they wanted to move of their own accord.

Participant: It did feel that way.

Teacher: And that's when you had the thought that you should keep them still?

Next, you could provide information about restlessness during the body scan, but what's more important is to point out that this phenomenon can be part of the practice of mindfulness: "Being aware of what you just described, that's exactly what mindfulness is all about—that and then seeing how you can relate to this consciously. That is the practice."

A TECHNICAL QUESTION AS A WAY INTO A DIDACTIC PRESENTATION

A final consideration in regard to technical questions is that they can sometimes lead into a didactic theme. I'll address the themes of didactic presentations in chapter 5. For now, just keep in mind that inquiry sometimes offers a natural transition into didactic presentation.

Teacher: Sometimes you may find that you're spending a lot of time on the external aspects of meditation. This can easily become a "thing," as if you're doing it right when you get the form right. Guidance during meditation always includes suggestions containing specific forms and metaphors, and not without reason: experience has taught us that most people find these suggestions to be supportive. But when a specific form or metaphor doesn't suit you, you need to find your own way with it, in a conscious manner. That too is practicing mindfulness.

Expressing Doubts About the Training

Some people initially have little faith in the training. However, they give the program the benefit of the doubt, and that's a legitimate starting point. In the pretraining interview, they've hopefully resolved to postpone any judgment until after the experiment, when the course has concluded. Nevertheless, for these participants important unanswered questions may hover above the training: "Is mindfulness for me?" "What good will it do me?"

They can only draw conclusions after they've completed the training, not when they're halfway through or when they've adapted the experiment to their needs. Therefore, entertaining doubts in the interim isn't productive. The one exception would be when dealing with participants who begin to doubt for concrete reasons—for example, those who get sick, who have to tend to family matters, or whose condition starts to worsen considerably. In such cases, it's only logical—and often also necessary—to evaluate the training with the participant individually in order to determine whether it might be best to somehow adjust or even interrupt the program.

For all other participants, deal with their doubt about the training like a vehicle breakdown: See what you need to do for these participants so they can continue the journey. Patch a tire or replace it if need be, and orient them toward continuing the journey. You'll often be alerted to these doubts by participants' questions about effects:

This isn't doing anything for me. I wonder what it's like for others?

I'm still not noticing any change.

Are there any other exercises I can try if this doesn't work?

The contents of these kinds of questions vary widely, but the message is the same: "It isn't doing for me what I hoped it would do. What now?" Make sure you address the underlying doubt while still respecting the question.

Participant: Why are we actually doing this?

Teacher: That's a good question and I do want to go into that. But what's equally interesting is to look at where that question comes from. Could you say a bit more about that?

You first acknowledge the importance of the content of the question, and then move on to the underlying motive. You could also go into the content of the question first.

Teacher: We do this because walking meditation is traditionally considered an equally important practice as sitting meditation, and we present it as a variation so that participants can also get familiarized with this form. Within this brief time span, I will offer many different practices, a kind of toolbox, so that you can later compile your own set of instruments to suit your preferences. But I also have a question for you: What makes you want to know this? Why is it on your mind?

If this helps the participant gain insight into the underlying doubt, you could frame your answer with a bit of explanation.

Teacher: Listening to your critical mind is totally okay, but be aware of it when you do so. What is your reason for listening to doubt? Is this really a good moment to evaluate, or did doubt arise because you entered a state of not-knowing that felt uncomfortable, or because things weren't going your way? Perhaps taking a leap and surmounting the hurdle will bring you further than buying in to the doubt.

Confusion Caused by False Friends

In the Buddhist tradition, there are four qualities known as the powers of the heart, or the four immeasurables: loving-kindness, compassion, empathetic joy, and equanimity. These are qualities we can develop and also states of mind we can inhabit. For this reason, they are also called the *brahmaviharas*, meaning "sublime abodes."

There can be a deceptive side effect to using these states to find one's bearings. Each of these powers can be mistaken for states of mind that are similar but not desirable: selfish love, pity, selfish joy, and disinterest. These are harmful, rather than healing. Referred to as "near enemies" in the Buddhist tradition, they masquerade as the real powers of the heart. In my view the term "enemy" is a bit too severe, so I prefer to use "false friend."

Like doubt, false friends can lead participants astray. However, persevering with mindfulness practice generally clears up the confusion and eventually leads people to wholesome states of mind. Still, sometimes individuals inadvertently end up cultivating an unwholesome state of mind, which can hinder their clarity even as they think they're on the right track. This undermines the self-corrective capacity of mindfulness.

False friends can be recognized by a hidden, selfish interest. In contrast to compassion, pity involves condescending toward the other, which inflates the ego. In contrast to equanimity, disinterest is fed by egocentricity. And in contrast to loving-kindness and empathetic joy, selfish love and selfish joy basically serve the individual's ego or own interests. Examples would be love that is a cover for separation anxiety, and joy that revolves around some self-interest in the success of the other, rather than simply feeling joyful for the other person's success.

Mindfulness training often involves reference to the seven attitudinal factors that form the foundation of mindfulness (set forth at the beginning of this chapter). Each of these factors also has a corresponding false friend—a quality that, upon close scrutiny, turns out not to be helpful to mindfulness and is characteristic of the driven, doing mode of mind.

Attitude of Mindfulness	False Friend
Nonjudging	Indifference
Patience	Doggedness
Beginner's mind	Naivety
Trust	Being laissez-faire
Nonstriving	Aimlessness
Acceptance	Resignation or endurance
Letting go	Disintegration

You may wonder about indifference, aimlessness, and resignation being cast as characteristic of the doing mode of mind. The reason is that they express the other side of a dualism evoked by doing and achieving results.

Basically, with all of these false friends, words that come from the perspective of the being mode of mind are transferred to the doing mode of mind, which subverts their purpose and leads to judgment and hardening. The risk of confusing attitudinal factors with their respective false friends looms particularly large with people who are habitually quite harsh and judgmental with themselves and therefore aren't very open to an alternative to the black-and-white perspective of the doing mode of mind: trying hard on the one hand, and failure on the other.

Another example of a false friend is confusing indulgence with friendliness and gentleness. When that happens, taking care of oneself turns into indulging in something with a short-term feel-good factor to it, as evidenced by the following kinds of remarks from participants:

> *I've been taking good care of myself over the past week and didn't practice because it felt too difficult.*

> *If I were to be friendly to myself, I simply wouldn't go to work.*

If you sense this kind of confusion in participants, it's important to take some time to address it.

Teacher: There's a difference between doing what feels good and doing what's good for you. If you ask yourself what's good for you and you stop and think about it, you're likely to get an answer that's different from your first reaction. Then you can see the difference between superficial resistance or a desire for immediate gratification and what's good for you in the long run, even if the latter isn't the easiest option. Only you can figure this out, and you have to do it by connecting to a deeper knowing. Then you can see whether you can find the energy to do what's good for you, without becoming rigid or hard in the process. Learning to see what's good for you is a mindfulness practice in its own right.

Feeling Unseen

Besides the conditions of rest, space, and safety, another basic condition for readiness to learn is feeling seen. You yourself may have sometimes felt a tendency to withdraw or rebel when you feel unseen. Even in a perfectly innocent conversation this can provoke a highly emotional reaction.

Participants will feel seen when you give them personal attention. This doesn't mean you have to check in with each participant individually every thirty minutes. They key is to make sure that no one is left out and to be alert to those moments when a participant needs individual attention—something you might notice by hearing someone moving restlessly, or simply through your radar picking up tension in a group member. However, also be sure to maintain a dual focus: on both the individual and on what's happening with the rest of the group.

When you notice that someone is having a hard time during inquiry, try to briefly make eye contact, nod, or smile. If you feel that the individual's difficulties are important, you can come back to the person later or even interrupt the inquiry to address the issue:

Marlene, are you okay? I sense that there's a lot happening for you.

You were fidgeting. I wonder if there's something you want to say.

You can also use your role as moderator to give attention to participants individually: "John, what were your experiences?" In addition, be sure to seek input from participants who tend to be quiet: "Let's hear from someone who hasn't spoken yet. Petra perhaps?"

Another consideration is that it's important to attach value to less spectacular experiences.

Participant: The experiences I had weren't very special.

Teacher: Would it be okay if we looked at them anyway? The striking experiences often come first, and then we forget to make space for whatever didn't initially seem so special. Those experiences can then slip past, even though they may be interesting as well.

Other approaches that help participants feel seen are to offer compliments, say something supportive, or even challenge them:

Nicely put. You said it all, and in simple words.

That's not easy. I totally agree with you there.

Come on! You meditated too, didn't you? Let's hear it!

Showing respect is also a way of helping people feel seen. You can indicate respect by asking permission, seeking confirmation of your interpretations, or thanking participants for their efforts and openness. (I'll discuss this further later in the chapter.)

Ultimately, people will feel seen when you address them with a combination of words and gestures conveying genuine attention and openness. Being truly present for someone, if only for a moment, can do wonders. It helps people feel seen in their situation, and in their existence, for a brief moment. It also offers rest and support and can energize participants. In this way, feeling seen facilitates renewed dedication and intentions for the training.

Unexpected Events

The training doesn't unfold in a vacuum. In the same way your practice at home can be enriched by an unexpected sound, perhaps someone drilling next door, unexpected events can also influence the course of a group session. These events can take infinite forms, from concrete occurrences, such as something falling over or a participant getting sick, to more intangible events with a major emotional impact, which could come from either outside or within the group; for example, a participant may make contact with a former trauma. Particularly during inquiry, with its subtle structure, you face the question of how to work with such an event: Do you incorporate it into the process, or does it not fit in? If you do incorporate it, what will you do with it, and how can you return to the program?

Events of a Concrete Nature

Dealing with concrete unexpected events generally isn't difficult. The solution is often supplied by the facts of the circumstances. A phone ringing, a cup falling on the rug, a bird scuffling at the window, a police siren howling outside, a fire alarm going off, someone's chair collapsing—these are all events that briefly distract attention away from the practice. Go along with the group's natural reaction and then find an informal way to return to the agenda for the session, even if this diversion takes a few minutes from the program. When returning to the session, you might insert a short break to create a transition.

Events of an Emotional Nature

Handling unexpected events that are emotional in nature can be more complex. In these kinds of circumstances, it's often important to be sensitive to the needs of the participant or group. I'll illustrate this by way of an extended example. Imagine a situation where, early in a session, you're about to start an inquiry and someone says, "I'm here, but I'm not sure if it's a good thing that I came. I don't know whether or not I'll stay. Something happened yesterday that really upset me."

Although you don't have much time to assess this unexpected situation, you may be beset by numerous questions: Is it indeed good for her that she came? Should you address what she's said? If so, should you ask her about the story or the emotion? And what implications does all of this have for the program you'd planned? Be aware of your own reactions to unexpected situations and take a little time. What's best in a given situation will generally arise on its own.

Continuing with the preceding example, imagine that this participant tells you that she found out she's pregnant, and that she's very happy about that. She was so excited that she told everyone at work, and when the news reached her boss, he reacted by firing her. As she tells the story, tears well up in her eyes and she struggles to keep talking. The other participants express sympathy, and then the room goes quiet.

Meanwhile, you have yet more thoughts, questions, and considerations swirling around in your head: What can you say to be supportive without going into the story at length? How can you do justice to this event without it dominating the entire session? How, in that moment, can you work with the other participants' sympathy? How much space does this event merit? Will it dominate the session, which was supposed to have an unrelated theme?

An initial step could be to confirm the emotion: "That's great news! And that's a nasty reaction by your boss." You could also create an opening toward processing the story without going into detail: "Being fired like that isn't necessarily the end of the story."

Of course, there will be reactions from the group, which you'll also have to navigate. Some of these reactions will address the details of the story: that it's not even legal to fire someone for being pregnant, and that the participant should fight her dismissal. Some participants may affectionately make suggestions or offer to help. Others may share experiences with similar situations. All of these reactions are inspired by emotion and commitment.

Now imagine that in response to questions or comments, whether from you or the group, the participant in question goes into some of the details, but the way in which she does so makes it clear that she doesn't really feel a need to process the experience. At last, you know that you won't be abandoning her if you curtail the discussion and move the conversation to the planned theme.

Teacher: So all of that happened, and yet this evening you still decided to come to class. What made you decide to come anyway?

Participant: I thought, "Perhaps this is exactly what I need right now. If I stay at home, I'll only be thinking about what happened." And I also thought about the fact that I enrolled in this training precisely to learn better ways of dealing with stressful situations. I don't want to abandon this program. I'll see how it goes tonight. If I can't do it, I'll go home early.

Teacher: I'm glad you came. Feel free to choose for yourself what's good for you, including going home early if that feels right. I'm also glad you brought this up. By doing so, you don't have to leave it out of the room. You can relate to it now, here, within this group and the theme of this training. Thank you.

Then, before diving into the content of the day's program, consider quickly checking in with both the participant and the group at large.

Teacher: How are you doing now?

Participant: I'm actually ready to get started.

Teacher: And how about the rest of the group?

Consider whether, in situations like the previous example, you have any control over events. Can you direct what's happening? Yes and no. You had no control over the emotions and needs of the participant or the group. You were, however, present as a moderator, allowing the event to unfold within the setting of mindfulness training. It may sound paradoxical, but this sometimes means the teacher must step aside for a moment and stop guiding. And yet the teacher did offer direction at certain moments during this example.

What were the teacher's motives? Perhaps they were to ask the participant about her story, to give the group space to respond, and then to choose the right moment to return attention to the program. However, even these types of things aren't directed. Ultimately, it's a matter of seeing what arises in the flow of events, noticing any inclinations about what to do or say that arise inside of you, checking these inclinations against your pragmatic consciousness, finding the right moment to respond however you see fit, and then doing it—or not doing it, because sometimes other events have already happened. And after all of this, yet other options will present themselves.

Working with Trauma

Another type of emotional event that often comes up unexpectedly (even though it may have been addressed in the pretraining interview) occurs when participants connect with experiences or emotions associated with some sort of trauma. Trauma can feel like a firmly locked door with a huge "Danger" sign on it. However, because it is an important part of people's life experiences, it cannot be ignored in the endeavor to get to know one's reactive patterns. Therefore, in this section I'll give a bit of background on the mechanisms that cause trauma and discuss how to work with trauma (to a limited degree) as part of the training. I'll also give pointers on what kind of support to offer.

THE FALLOUT OF A HEALTHY SURVIVAL REACTION

A trauma is an experience that the individual once deemed to be so threatening that the mind-body system blocked it out. Trauma reactions are healthy because they ensure that people don't fall apart when they can't cope with reality. The experience is put aside, isolated in a locked inner room in the mind, and the person forges forward, basically ignoring the existence of this small room.

You might expect people to start processing trauma as soon as they're better equipped to do so—for example, after some time has passed and in a quiet and safe setting. However, this doesn't happen. People keep avoiding the trauma. It's as if the door to that small room has to stay locked because their learning tells them that whatever is lurking behind that door is a threat to their life. The moment they start rattling the lock or even come close to the door, the traumatic feeling is triggered, leading to a powerful aversive reaction, as if the threat were still real. As long as they steer clear of that door, they don't feel the fear. It's as though it doesn't exist, and everything's okay. But it takes energy to avoid that room and keep the door locked. That's the price of the survival reaction.

When we hear the word "trauma," we tend to think of something big, such as war experiences, a car accident, an assault, or sexual abuse. Yet the response created by a major trauma can also occur on a smaller scale, such as failing at something in front of a class or having an embarrassing experience at a meeting or party. Of course, such experiences typically don't have as great an impact on a person's well-being and general ability to function, but the mechanism is the same.

Reliving a trauma won't kill a person. However, reactivating a trauma without sufficient preparation will reignite the defensive reaction in full force. It's important to first explore the actual contents of that locked-up room; otherwise the effects of those contents will only be confirmed, leading to retraumatization. Therefore, the best approach, the one that is usually taken in trauma therapy, is to slowly, step-by-step, tune in to the defensive reaction and locked-away energy while maintaining contact with something safe that gives the person a feeling of staying in control. This safety anchor is intended to prevent the person from being overwhelmed when the door is carefully opened just a bit. In this way, the frightening message of the trauma—"Stay away from that door because the secret locked inside is one you won't survive!"—is neutralized little by little.

THE LIMITS TO ACCOMMODATING TRAUMA IN MINDFULNESS TRAINING

Processing trauma belongs in the realm of specialist therapy, not in mindfulness training. If you suspect that a candidate for the training is suffering from the effects of trauma, this may stand in the way. Mindfulness training is a revelatory approach: People are given instructions to turn their attention inward and then asked to find their own way with whatever emerges. During the practice, they are responsible for their own journey and self-care. This calls for a certain level of strength and stability of the ego. If in doubt about a certain participant, either prior to or during the training, it's best to bring your concern up directly and perhaps refer the person to some other sort of training or even therapy.

Even so, a participant may still be confronted with a past trauma during the training. If it's a major, unprocessed trauma, you simply may not be able to deal with it in the setting of the training. Handle the experience as best you can in the moment, then, after the session, engage the participant in a discussion of other treatment options and whether it's possible for her to continue participating in the group. The trauma may be something the participant has known about for some time and has been processing, or it may be a relatively minor trauma. In either of those cases, you can probably find a way to work with it in the context of mindfulness training. But even in these situations, it's best to be cautious.

The basic rule is to make sure such participants feel safe by letting them be in charge of how to deal with the locked door and how close they want to get to it. On the one hand, challenging this limit or exerting pressure can cause the fear of being overwhelmed to become too great and eventually cause participants to quit—perhaps skipping just one exercise, or perhaps dropping out of the training altogether. Or participants may respond by forcing themselves, which will definitely lead to a sense of being overwhelmed and quite possibly retraumatization.

On the other hand, being insufficiently challenged can lead such participants to continue to avoid the door altogether. So, within mindfulness training and the group process, the best approach is generally to offer subtle invitations to approach the door while allowing these participants to retain control. Leave participants free to accept or reject that invitation, and let the safety of the environment prevail over processing the trauma. After all, these participants aren't in trauma therapy.

Sometimes this may mean that you have to work around or avoid a trauma. Or it may mean that a participant avoids certain subjects or pulls out of certain practices, especially when they become emotionally intense. Participants suffering from trauma may even quit the training. If this happens after you've carefully explored ways of dealing with the trauma but found none, you'll know that you've done what you could. The trauma is simply what the training brought the person to at that point in time. Whatever amount of training the person did participate in may prove helpful. Perhaps this was the first time she approached the trauma with awareness and in a gentle way, and without being retraumatized. That could be the first step toward healing.

TAKING BABY STEPS

As for implications during inquiry, whenever participants broach the boundaries of an extremely sensitive area, there is only one thing for you to do: offer support and safety. The more support you provide, the more the participant will feel up to exploring this frightening terrain. Here are some ways you can express your support while also helping participants maintain their own safe boundaries:

You always have your solid anchor with which you maintain contact. [Specify that anchor, such as looking at something comforting.] *Don't let the waves take you so far that you can't maintain that contact. As soon as the waves are taking you out too far, turn back.*

Remember that you can always take your foot off the gas by, for example, opening your eyes, moving around a bit, or returning to a safe anchor, such as bringing attention to your breathing or the weight of your body on the seat.

Simply seeing how long you can stay present to it: that's already quite something. It may be the first time you've entered this territory without immediately turning away. Just by being there you are owning it, little by little.

Moving in very carefully, baby step by baby step. Putting your feelers out, and then retracting them, like dipping your toes into a pool to get a feel for the water temperature without leaving the safety of dry land.

What could serve as resources for you in this? Imagine you're in that difficult territory. What could you think of or what image could you invoke to use as your safe haven?

Expecting the Unexpected: Fearless Presence

After an emotional moment, including touching upon a trauma, a variety of scenarios can unfold. However, in the context of the training, there's no need to sift through all possible variations. The fact is, you can't prepare for the unexpected with a protocol or plan. When the training takes an unexpected turn, there isn't a fixed line to follow, and there are no set choices to prepare. The best way to prepare for the unexpected is to practice not preparing—in other words, to practice openness and trust.

In any case, you are only human, and you have your own sensitivity, vulnerability, and reactivity. Sometimes you'll say or do something you later regret. That's part and parcel of the teaching process. When you realize your reaction to an unexpected event wasn't in line with your intentions, in that moment you gain the opportunity to deal with it skillfully by, for example, coming back to the event later, through an intervention or response, and presenting a new learning moment for the group. What matters is having an intention to deal with every situation mindfully and genuinely, with authenticity being especially important in vulnerable emotional moments. In other words, it's not what you do that counts; it's how you do it. If you are genuine, you may make mistakes, but the way you handle unexpected moments won't be "wrong." Trust that you will always bring yourself, with all of your intuition, experience, and skills, to unexpected events. That trust will enable you to face the unexpected with what Jack Kornfield calls "fearless presence" (2008, p. 99). That is your best preparation.

In short, there are no rules for dealing with the unexpected except for one: try to get time on your side. Unexpected events trigger a need for control. The stress this provokes pushes us to regress to hasty interventions and old habits and reactions. Remember, it isn't necessary to always feel in control. Indeed, it can even be counterproductive.

So try to slow down. This will provide the space for you to become mindful of your tendencies and whether you should follow them or seek better options. And if taking time doesn't lead to clarity, there is always the very respectable response "I don't know right now."

Feedback

During inquiry, sometimes participants give feedback on the program or the teacher. Feedback takes the training to a metalevel and, in a sense, transcends the rules of the game. Therefore, strictly speaking, it isn't part of inquiry. An especially tricky aspect of feedback is that it can affect teachers personally, opening up the pitfall of reactivity.

How Feedback Interferes with Inquiry

In terms of the group's learning process, it's seldom helpful to delve into feedback during the session. Participants have already committed to the training, with all of its elements. You, as the teacher, have prepared yourself to the best of your professional ability, and the current teaching moment is what you have to offer at that point in time. Opening up to discussion what you're doing or how you're doing it can undermine participants' trust in the process and in you as a teacher. It might also serve as an invitation to other participants to start evaluating. This will interfere with the attitude needed for inquiry.

That said, feedback during inquiry isn't always negative: it can contain valuable information about your work and the process of the participant who's giving feedback. So you'll probably want to take this information about your work into consideration.

Participant: This last exercise wasn't good. I wasn't ready to be present to it. It came too quickly after the previous exercise, which had been very intense for me and was still lingering in my mind.

Teacher: Okay, so that's how it worked for you. Thanks for the feedback. I'll take it into consideration.

In that brief exchange, the teacher acknowledged that feedback was given, but you don't always have to make that explicit. Sometimes information provided in feedback can immediately be used as a starting point for inquiry. So building on the previous example, the teacher might say, "You felt that you weren't present to it. What experiences made you notice that?" However, by not making it explicit that you're taking the comment as feedback, you risk coming across as defensive. The participant, or other participants, may feel the need to reiterate the point.

Participant 1:   They were just too close together. I can't do anything with that. It comes too soon, for me anyway.

Participant 2:   Yes, I had that too. I was unable to make the switch so quickly. I thought, "Why is he doing this?" The subjects were also very different.

The discussion is now firmly and explicitly in the realm of the metalevel of feedback, and the teacher will have to respond on that level. To prevent this, always make it clear that you're acknowledging the feedback and let the group know that it isn't the time to go into it. In some cases, you can return to inquiry directly from feedback by focusing on an underlying theme the participant has expressed as long as you ensure that this doesn't come across as a defense strategy.

Positive Feedback

Both positive and negative feedback will have an effect on you. Feedback touches your ego. It's important to be aware of this process and deal with it skillfully.

When you receive positive feedback, you'll feel your ego swell. Perhaps you'll feel an urge to expand the subject or even indulge in it. But whether you highlight the compliment or downplay it with your response, it's still all about you. As a result, you may lose sight of other layers of the remark. For example, a compliment also says a lot about the person making it. Perhaps offering the compliment is done in an attempt to avoid some other feeling or get some attention from you.

Still, even if you're able to pick up these underlying layers, they would be difficult to explore. A compliment simply isn't a credible starting point for inquiry. To see why, imagine that a participant has said, "I find the sound of your voice so pleasant." If you were to say, "What is it that makes you experience it as pleasant?"

this wouldn't sound or feel natural. Positive feedback is therefore best received without going into it. A simple thank-you could be the best response.

Negative Feedback

Negative feedback is more difficult to work with than positive feedback. Not only will it affect you more, but it will also put the group on alert. Suddenly everyone is on edge: "What's wrong?" "Do I agree with that?" "How will the teacher respond?" When the feedback is of a technical nature and relates to a quality that's integral to the training, it's reasonably easy to not take it personally. An example would be "You speak so slowly. It makes me sleepy."

If you aren't sure whether a piece of feedback says something about you, about the program, or about the participant, just acknowledge it without going into the specifics.

Participant: I feel like we're going too fast sometimes. Sometimes I'm still processing a theme you just wrote on the board while we're already moving on to the next theme. Or I want to say something but haven't found the words yet, and then find that the moment has already passed.

Teacher: Thank you for your feedback. It's important for me to hear how you experience it. I'll take it into consideration.

Criticism

Sometimes feedback is worded much less technically and more personally, which can come across as criticism.

Participant 1: Can't you keep your mouth shut a bit more while we practice? I'm not getting around to my own meditation.

When feedback is worded like this, it might disturb you more, making it harder for you to find inner space around it. If you feel personally criticized, let the group know.

Teacher: All kinds of responses are occurring to me. I don't know what to say right now. I'll take some time to let it sink in and come back to it later.

With this kind of response, you express that you've received the feedback and are taking it seriously. You don't have to go into it immediately or have a ready response. When criticism touches you personally, it's best to take some time to create inner space before responding.

Sometimes other participants will help you out when you've been criticized. Their responses show that there are nuances to criticism, and they can take the edge off potential tension in the group.

> *Participant 2:* Yes, but is that irritation perhaps more a part of you? I didn't have that problem at all.

> *Participant 3:* I don't think it's that bad either.

Be careful about how you respond to such support. Leaning on these kinds of "helpful" comments will undermine your autonomy. And it could also lead into a conversation about the training and take you further away from the inquiry. When participants start exchanging opinions about you or the training, don't wait too long to take charge again. The best bet is generally to set a new course.

> *Teacher:* Shall we leave this for what it is? This training is sometimes intense, and emotions can be touched. And as a teacher, I can only present the program to the best of my abilities. Everyone, including me, can look at which parts of this feedback apply to them and which don't. Is it okay to leave it at that?

Sometimes participants may offer very personal and direct criticism. Here's an example: "What you just said to Sandra, that went too far. You keep firing questions at her while she's sad. I thought mindfulness was about kindness." Any retort on your part would cause the conversation to spiral into a war of arguments. Besides, as the teacher, as soon as you go on the defensive, you've lost:

So you think I'm not kind.

I'm only human. I try my best.

That may be your view, but the others might not share it. I'd like to know what Sandra herself thinks.

You can initially buy yourself some time by responding with a neutral remark: "Jeez, that's a sharp remark! It's taken me aback." However, the initial remark still requires a reply, and therefore a conversation at the metalevel on which feedback exists. Engage in that conversation in all openness. You don't have a role to fall back on in this context. You're sitting in the fire, and all you have left is your embodiment of mindfulness.

There are no instructions on what to do in this situation, just a guideline: What's at stake here is not winning or losing, but genuineness. Success in this situation isn't emerging triumphant from the battle, but emerging from the battle with full integrity. From that perspective, if acknowledging your limitations feels right, that may be your best move: "You're right. I might have had my focus too much on arguments, without taking the emotional side fully into account. I apologize."

Cross Talk

Cross talk is dialogue among participants. There are mindfulness teachers who give space for cross talk and even invite it. And there are arguments in favor of cross talk, commitment being chief among them. On the one hand, a group that engages in conversation among themselves unprompted by the teacher is cohesively engaged in the process. This also underscores that the teacher doesn't have a monopoly on wise words. Perhaps participants have mastered the curiosity and questions that characterize inquiry and are able to start applying this perspective and process.

On the other hand, many teachers feel that inquiry is one of the most difficult parts of mindfulness training and that it requires a great deal of practice and experience. In this view, letting participants conduct inquiry themselves is seen as generally undesirable. One consideration revolves around the participants asking the questions: Do they still have the attention and openness necessary for their own process? Or will they, perhaps without realizing it, be diverted from their own process of inquiry due to their active focus on what's happening with the other participants?

Another consideration is how cross talk affects the setting. When cross talk is allowed, the teacher withdraws, at least somewhat, and gives the floor to participants. Anyone can get involved, and perhaps in any way. Is this the best way of conducting the training, or does it implicitly say, "Your questions are as good as mine"? There's the risk that this can undermine participants' faith in your abilities to guide them in the process. In addition, when personal questions can come from all sides, participants may not feel sufficiently safe about saying whatever arises, or they may start anticipating what others will think or ask.

Some participants are motivated to support and advise fellow group members. Others may be inclined to try to get one up on others or alleviate their personal unease by focusing their attention on someone else. These kinds of motives can take the conversation in directions that aren't desirable for inquiry. Then you're faced with how to get it back on track. Often, it can be a waste of energy to let the conversation fan out in all directions in the first place, so that you have to pull the reins in again.

Clearly, there are many arguments against cross talk. It comes with many risks and has too few benefits in terms of the objectives of inquiry. That said, sometimes there's value in allowing participants to ask questions of each other. The key is to keep a close eye on how this affects the process of inquiry. Consider the following dialogue between two participants, Roberta and Alex.

Roberta: Alex, just look at what's going on. You can't find the time to meditate, and when you do, you fall asleep. You're working too hard!

Alex: My life is just very full.

Roberta: Sure, but falling asleep every time you try to meditate, that means you're too busy. Doesn't that bother you?

Alex: Things are just like that right now.

Roberta: I have a suggestion for Alex. That problem of falling asleep, I used to have that too. Now I meditate in the morning and I never fall asleep.

Alex: I'd have to get up at five thirty instead of six fifteen. That's too early for me.

Roberta: It depends on how far you're prepared to go.

Alex: I'm not a morning person.

This kind of dialogue could also take place between Alex and the teacher, but that would have a different feeling than when the questions and suggestions are coming from a fellow participant. That said, in either case Alex could end up on the defensive. As the teacher, consider whether cross talk is helpful. If it isn't, intervene.

Participant 1:   Alex, just look at what's going on. You can't find the time to meditate, and when you do, you fall asleep. You're working too hard!

Teacher: Hold on. Let me make something clear: It's okay to ask each other a question now and again, but everyone has their own circumstances and possibilities, so we aren't in a position to judge each other's choices.

If a group gets into a habit of asking each other questions, you could consider introducing a rule to limit this.

Teacher: Let me be clear: It's fine to ask each other for clarification, but try to refrain from giving advice or discussing options. Otherwise, in very short order we'll end up trying to solve each other's problems. There are other groups for that.

Auxiliary Conversation Techniques

Given that inquiry is a form of conversation, you can also make use of standard conversation techniques. As with all tools, their effectiveness depends on your skillfulness in using them well and in the right context. A sledgehammer is a handy tool, but not to put up a picture frame, and tweezers aren't an adequate tool when you need to repair an electrical outlet.

In the following sections, I'll provide a brief overview of numerous conventional conversation techniques that may prove helpful during inquiry. Some are also discussed elsewhere in the book, but for the sake of completeness in this section, I've compiled all of the conversation techniques here. I've categorized them based on their function: supporting, opening, helping, structuring, activating, and limiting, followed by a final, catchall category for other useful techniques.

Supporting

One of our tasks as teachers is to facilitate participants in the difficult endeavor of delving into their own experiences, seeing them clearly, discerning tendencies and patterns of reacting, and so on. A sure and strong way to facilitate group members in this way is by finding supportive words.

CREATING SPACE

When participants are trying hard and have tensed up, they generally fall into the doing mode of mind. You can help them create space and return to being mode of mind by saying something that exudes trust in the process:

You don't have to solve everything at once.

If you take care of the process, the process will take care of the results.

The grass grows by itself. You cannot coax the blades out of the ground.

Being aware is most important. Solutions will present themselves.

Our patterns are so strong. Mindfulness simply needs time to grow.

GIVING COMPLIMENTS

Remember that, in most cases, you're are teaching participants something entirely new: to explore inner realms they've never looked into before, to cultivate interest in experiences that formerly didn't register, to treat familiar experiences in a new way. Offering compliments is an important way of making this new field a fertile one. Giving compliments during inquiry should become second nature:

Good, good.

Well described! I exactly get what you mean.

That was well noticed.

You're right, that's what it's all about. Beautifully put!

You're doing it right. This is mindfulness: simply looking, describing, and noting. There's nothing more to it.

It's important to reinforce this at the end of a session, to give participants the take-away message that they're doing well:

We did well today.

It was wonderful to see everyone contributing with great dedication and openness. By doing that, you're also giving something to the group, and I want to thank you for that.

ACKNOWLEDGING

One way of supporting participants' commitment to practice and to engage in inquiry is to provide acknowledgment and affirm their effort. This is particularly helpful when the results may not be instantly evident to participants:

We explored a lot of experiences here. Quite a job!

Your meditation was very eventful.

CONFIRMING

Earlier in this chapter, I discussed the importance of feeling seen or confirmed as a person. In inquiry, you can convey this by confirming participants' words. A simple nod of the head or just saying "uh-huh" often suffices to let participants know that you're present and have heard what they said. Of course, you can also use words for this kind of confirmation:

Your description was right on the money.

That's right.

Yes, yes.

Okay, so that was your experience.

You can go one step further and also note the experience as you confirm it, labeling or briefly describing it. Beyond providing acknowledgment, this may help participants register their experiences, see them more clearly, and perhaps gain a bit of distance from them. For example, if a participant seems to be feeling or referring to emotions without using that label, you could say, "So you experienced emotions there." By doing so, you may be helping the participant realize that there were emotions.

ESTABLISHING COMMONALITIES

Asking whether the group at large resonates with the individual's experience offers all participants the insight that so many struggles are part of our common humanity. In addition, seeking the group's perspective on an individual's experience can provide support because it helps individuals feel that they aren't alone in struggling with their difficult experiences. Seeking this kind of input from the group is integral to inquiry:

Is that recognizable to anyone?

I wonder if you're the only one having that experience.

ASKING PERMISSION AND THANKING

During inquiry, you're asking participants for access to something very personal: the way in which they are with themselves. In Western cultures, we are often quite direct when it comes to sharing feelings that lie behind the social facade. But that doesn't mean there are no limits. Indeed, we often feel quite vulnerable when others want to take a look inside our inner being. Caution and great respect are essential when entering this very personal space.

For you as a mindfulness teacher, laying inner experiences bare and working with them is your daily bread, like sawing and working with wood are to a carpenter. But for participants, this process will usually be new and may at times feel awkward. Yet participants often bring great willingness to inquiry, sharing experiences that are laden with embarrassment, guilt, self-reproach, or grief. They may share things they've never even shared with their best friend. The more carefully you build a safe and respectful atmosphere, the more willing to share they'll be. One way of creating that kind of atmosphere is by asking permission first:

Would it be okay if we went into this in a little more depth?

Can I ask you a bit more about this?

You called it "irritation." I think it would be interesting to look at that a bit more, at how that works. Is that okay?

By sharing a personal experience, participants are giving something to the group and adding intensity and depth to the training. This merits respect and appreciation, so be sure to thank participants after they've shared:

Thank you for your contribution.

Thank you for letting us take such a close look at this. I realize that this is very personal.

Sometimes thanking participants for sharing may come across as unnatural, especially in regard to apparently mundane experiences. But you can't really know how it felt to share. There can be major emotional undertones behind a simple event, so it's always a good idea to express appreciation. Sensitivity in this area is always valued and contributes to the overall atmosphere of safety and respect.

Opening

Given that inquiry is an invitation to look at one's experiences in a new way, creating a sense of openness is quintessential. Here are some conversation techniques to support this open way of looking at things.

ASKING OPEN-ENDED QUESTIONS

The types of question you ask can have an immense impact on the direction inquiry takes. Different kinds of questions can steer the inner exploration in certain directions, shut it down, or open it further. Of course, the latter is most effective for the purposes of inquiry, so be sure to ask open-ended questions:

What occurred during this meditation?

What did you experience?

What experiences were there?

Can you tell me a bit more about it?

What did you come up against? How did that go?

Open-ended questions are also helpful for inviting participants to continue their exploration:

What is it that made you realize that?

And what happened next?

Did it stay that way, or did it change?

"How" questions may seem open-ended but they generally aren't. "How was it?" tends to lead participants to draw a conclusion or form an evaluation: "good," "nice," "not as good as at home," and so on. You can, however, use "how" questions when asking about how participants related to their experience: "What reactions are there? And how do you deal with that?"

It's almost always best to steer clear of "why" questions, as they send people into the realm of cognition and the doing mode of mind. For example, the question "Why is this meditation difficult for you?" solicits analysis. It would be better to ask "What's difficult for you?" or "Can you tell me a bit more about this experience of difficulty?" Likewise, rather than asking something like "Why did you change position during the meditation?" instead inquire, "What experiences made you change position during the meditation?"

NOT-KNOWING

By not answering questions, you can prompt participants to engage in further inner exploration. Indeed, when you don't answer a question, the question can become more important and start reverberating in participants' minds. However, do note that not answering doesn't mean not saying anything:

Good question. The questions are often more important than the answers.

I don't know.

Even if we think we know something, when we look back on it later, something that seemed bad may turn out to have led to something that seems good. So is it good or bad? We don't know.

REFLECTING PARTICIPANTS' QUESTIONS BACK TO THEM

From the perspective of inquiry, exploring where a question came from is often more interesting than concluding the discussion by answering the question. Again, this emphasizes that the question is more important than the answer:

What are your thoughts on that?

What interest of yours lies behind this question?

We can answer the question, but it may be more interesting to see where that question came from. Can you tell us how this question occurred to you?

MAINTAINING SILENCE

Silence is underestimated as a tool in inquiry. Driven by the need to do things "right," beginning teachers often speak too early and too much. This tendency can be curbed by keeping in mind that maintaining silence isn't the same as withdrawing or remaining completely speechless. Silence also has an effect on the tempo. It helps slow things down and keep everyone in the being mode of mind.

There's often a brief silence after someone has finished speaking. Wait a bit before responding. Stretch the silence, make it longer than usual in day-to-day conversation, while staying present nonverbally. One context in which it's especially appropriate to maintain silence is when a subject has more or less been wrapped up.

Participant 1: So that's what I do. I push away all these things I don't want to feel.

[Silence]

Participant 2: This reminds me of a colleague. I have to tell him that his work isn't up to par, but every time I get an opportunity to tell him that, I think, "Oh well, let's give him some more time to improve." I dread telling him and keep putting it off, and meanwhile the situation keeps getting more unbearable by the day.

Teacher: Thank you.

[Silence]

Teacher: Anyone else want to add something about this theme?

[Silence]

This technique can also be productive in the middle of a dialogue, especially when a participant is looking for direction during inquiry and exploring new territory.

Participant: So I wonder whether this is good pain or pain that tells me to stop. Can you say something about that?

[Silence]

Participant: Perhaps I could explore it some more myself.

[Silence]

Teacher: That seems like a good idea to me.

[Silence]

Participant: I'm accustomed to just using my body for whatever is needed. It never occurred to me that I can also ask what my body needs. This is new to me.

[Silence]

Teacher: Thank you for your contribution. It was interesting to hear it put that way.

Silence is also effective during moments of great intensity, when a participant is seeing and feeling a great deal, such as when the causes of suffering are perceived. In those moments, it can create space, providing an opportunity for a new, deeper insight to arise or for the inquiry to take an unexpected turn. You've probably experienced the creative effects of silence. Whenever we stop thinking, talking, and doing, we often get new insight into whatever we were so busy with. Whereas incessant talking keeps the mind on a limited associative track, silence can switch the conversation to a different track. In fact, there's an approach to interpersonal interactions based entirely on speaking from silence, as outlined in Gregory Kramer's book *Insight Dialogue* (2007).

A related technique, which is also quite effective, is to use words with little substance. In essence, such words fill time, giving earlier, more meaningful words an opportunity to register and contribute to insight:

You're right there.

That's the way it is.

Thank you for that.

Helping

Certain kinds of questions and remarks can help participants clarify their experiences and how they communicate them. Just be sure to use them only when they will actually help. Also, be aware that the following techniques often have the effect of editing participants' experiences. So as you recap, reframe, or reflect, always ask for confirmation that you've rephrased the person fairly accurately. Remember, the experience is the participant's, so only the participant can judge whether or not you've captured it well.

INVITING, ENCOURAGING, AND RAISING INTEREST

People tend to think their inner experiences are rather minor events not worth exploring. During mindfulness training, you're conveying the opposite. You're teaching participants to look at familiar experiences with beginner's mind. This requires interest, but often this interest doesn't come naturally, given that you're dealing with experiences that may seem mundane, and that looking at them differently doesn't instantly lead to a visible result.

It's up to you to set an example, valuing the "ordinary" as interesting. The teacher's exemplary role in creating an atmosphere that invites curiosity is never as important as it is here. It can lead participants to think, *Hey, if the teacher finds this so interesting, there must be something to it. I might as well take another look at it myself.*

The primary challenge with this technique is that the vocabulary available for showing interest is relatively limited. Fortunately, it's often enough to simply say, "Interesting!" Or you can devote a few more words to it:

Normally, we never look at that, even though it determines a large part of our experience. Funny, isn't it? I find that amazing.

It's beautiful, the way you phrase that. It seems very ordinary, but...

What I find so fascinating is the way you describe how this works. You can wake me up for that in the middle of night!

Be aware, however, that such expressions can lose their depth and impact if they are repeated too often. And ultimately, your effect will hinge on the genuineness of your feelings. Interest is expressed more through an attitude than through certain words.

RECAPPING AND REPEATING

During the training, and particularly during inquiry, participants are seeing their experiences in a new light. As a result, they often struggle to find words to express what they're observing. In such cases, recapping can be helpful:

What I'm hearing you say is...

If I understand you correctly,...

Can I summarize it as follows?...

So, basically you're saying...

Use the participant's words as you recap, and always be sure to seek confirmation:

Is that right?

Am I saying it correctly?

Is my summary on track?

You also have the option to repeat what the participant says, word for word. If done insensitively, this can amount to mere parroting. When done properly, however, it serves two important purposes: confirming what the person has said, and delaying continuation of the narrative. It can also help participants see that an experience is valuable, even though they might have initially expressed it somewhat nonchalantly. Then they can give it the recognition it deserves.

> *Participant:* And then that thought disappears as well, and there is silence for a second and nothing else.
>
> *Teacher:* There is silence and nothing else…
>
> *Participant:* I tried everything, and I just don't know what else to do.
>
> *Teacher:* You just don't know what else to do…

The effect is that the repeated part of the sentence is singled out and highlighted. Ideally, the repetition is followed by a brief silence that gives the participant an opportunity for deepening his exploration or his understanding of what he just said and the experience these words referred to.

As seems appropriate, you can also pose a follow-up question after the repetition:

You just don't know what else to do…Is there also an emotion with that?

REFRAMING

Reframing goes beyond recapping and repeating to add something to the person's statement. It puts the person's words in a certain light. This technique is frequently employed in cognitive behavioral therapy to neutralize irrational and often negative biases in clients' mental processing. It's also widely used in more activating approaches, such as solution-focused therapy and coaching. Here's a typical example of reframing in coaching or therapy.

> *Client:* I haven't got a clue as to what can make this conversation useful.

Coach or therapist: You're still wondering wh2at can make this conversation useful.

And here's an example of how it can be used during inquiry.

Participant: I was thinking the whole time and was barely aware of the moment.

Teacher: There were a lot of thoughts, and there were a few brief moments of mindfulness.

When using this technique, be aware that you're processing participants' words and, in a way, redefining their experience. Be sure to consider whether the way in which you're rephrasing the original statement is helpful. If it isn't, participants could withdraw because they can't relate to your alternative. In extreme cases, they may even feel manipulated. If a participant doesn't resonate with your statement, take a step back:

Do you recognize this description, or am I way off?

I see that I didn't quite describe it accurately. When you say "barely," do you maybe mean never ever?

Be sensitive to the difference between reframing and interpreting. When you're asking about a participant's current experience, beware that a somewhat subtle kind of interpretation doesn't sneak into your questions.

Participant: This meditation worked very well for me. I was present to it every moment.

Teacher: "Present to it." Can you tell me a little more about that?

Participant: As if I'm fully immersed in it…as if everything else disappears briefly, even my thoughts or what I'm supposed to think about it. I'm fully present to the practice. That's it.

Teacher: Could you call that a present-moment experience?

Participant: Yes…Um, what exactly do you mean by that?

Apparently the teacher's concept of "present-moment experience" isn't aligned with the participant's, leading the participant to think, *What does she mean? Am I missing something?* This can cause participants to shift to a conceptual level.

Structuring

Structuring techniques help illuminate an underlying cognitive framework. When using these techniques, you're making a brief foray into didactic presentation.

ESTABLISHING CONNECTIONS

By establishing connections, you help participants be more aware of the underlying structure of the training. For example, you can connect an insight with previous practices or previously discussed experiences. This makes the training, and mindfulness practice itself, a coherent whole:

This is precisely what the raisin exercise showed us.

So you're continuing to meditate anyway. That's practicing trust and patience, isn't it? Those qualities are part and parcel of practicing mindfulness. Remember the attitudinal factors I wrote on the board last time?

USING JUDGMENTS

The possibility of teaching without any kind of judgment is a myth. If, as a teacher, you could never judge anything, you'd only be able to use formulations along the lines of "on the one hand…, and on the other hand…" This generally offers participants too little direction and comes across as overly measured. Teachers need judgments in order to guide. Instructions inherently contain judgments, as do even the most neutral answers. Consider the following interchange.

Participant: Am I doing it right?

Teacher: I wouldn't think too much about whether or not you're doing it right.

This reply contains a suggestion, a preference, and eventually a judgment (that it's not right to be busy with thoughts about whether one is doing it right).

When you use judgments, be sure to steer clear of blame. Making participants feel that they're doing something wrong will only frustrate the learning process. Even ambiguous remarks with minor blaming nuances can have an immensely discouraging effect on some people. So be careful with remarks along these lines:

You don't understand it.

You're doing it wrong.

You're mistaken.

You're deviating from the instructions.

Such remarks can give participants a feeling of "I can't do this right; this isn't for me." This can cause participants to become quiet and withdrawn, and your work in creating an atmosphere that invites innocence, vulnerability, curiosity, and openness will be undone. You simply can't ask participants to explore and openly share their experiences, suggesting that there's no wrong way to do so and that you'll be on their side, and then condemn the results of this exploration.

All of that said, you can still steer participants' way of practicing by stating practice guidelines in a way that's clear but not blaming:

The method you describe is an option. You could also consider the following option…

So there's calmness during your meditation, and that's beautiful. Might it be possible to get anything more out of it, given the fact that mindfulness meditation isn't just about calmness?

Shall we take a look at what made you not follow the instructions? Something interesting might have happened there.

Activating

As discussed in chapter 2, a good learning environment is firmly grounded in the qualities of being mode of mind, with its sense of safety, but it will also sometimes encourage qualities of the doing mode of mind in order to prevent passivity and lethargy. The following activating conversational techniques can bring a sparkle and higher level of energy to inquiry.

CONFRONTING

Sometimes a group becomes drowsy or lazy and needs some rousing. When that's the case, don't hesitate to use words that might sting a bit:

"Nice," "good"—that doesn't mean anything to me.

What do you actually mean?

Did you not have any experiences?

So you start hyperventilating. Let it happen. Trust me, it won't kill you.

If the group had dozed off a little, perhaps due to an atmosphere of "everything is okay," they'll be awake again! You may be concerned that this sort of approach will create an awkward atmosphere. That's seldom the case, as long as the confrontational statement is framed within a positive context.

Sometimes it's necessary to confront a participant individually. This isn't easy, especially if you suspect that it might make the person close up. In that case, you could use an indirect approach and confront the entire group with the feedback. Alternatively, you could direct it toward another participant to whom it also applies, and whom you know can take it. The person for whom your remark is truly intended won't be confronted directly but is still likely to get the message.

For example, if a participant has a persistent pattern of interrupting, you could explain to the group as a whole that it's important to let others speak. Or if a participant doesn't do the home practices and is difficult to approach about this, you might indirectly prod that person by explaining how important home practice is to another participant who didn't do the home practice either but seems to accept such prodding more easily.

WITHDRAWING

Sometimes a group may be dominated by an inert, passive mood. If there are no clear external reasons for this, you might be the cause. You may have overdone it as a teacher, excessively taking the lead and allowing the group to comfortably lean back. After all, it's far easier to have something handed to you than to discover it for yourself.

In this situation, you need to use some sort of intervention to get the group back to work. Confronting is one possibility. Withdrawing is another. With this approach, you simply do nothing. You stop handing everything to the group. For example, say you've asked a question and received no reply. Remain silent. After a few seconds, the group will wake up as they feel that things aren't going smoothly anymore.

You can also use words. It's okay to tell them what's going on, being as wordy as you feel appropriate:

I cannot make this happen.

It's not up to me to put you to work. It's your training, not mine.

We're here to explore these experiences. To be able to do that, you have to look at your own experiences first and put them into words. I cannot present them to you.

Regarding home practice, one possible cause of a passive attitude is a problematic relationship with authority. In that case, suggestions or instructions for home exercises invoke associations with unpleasant tasks from the past (for example, in school), and the teacher is subconsciously equated with former authority figures. If you sense that this may be the case, you can withdraw from this role of authority—a role that was imposed on you:

You don't have to do this on my account.

Okay, then don't do it.

Another approach is to ask participants to revisit and clarify their initial intentions:

Ask yourself, "Why am I taking this training? For myself or someone else?" That's where you'll find your answer.

ASKING FOR ADVICE

You can always ask the group for advice on something one particular participant is struggling with. This will bolster a sense of mutual solidarity and support the emancipatory nature of the training by emphasizing that the teacher isn't the sole expert:

Noting thoughts—is that a form of thinking, or isn't it? What do you all think?

What I hear from you is impatience and the sense of urgency that goes with it—a sense of "I can't carry on." So what do we do when we get to that point? How do some of you work with that?

However, do be aware of the dangers in having participants give each other advice, as discussed in the section on cross talk. Certain subjects are better suited for group advice than others. Advice on concrete matters, such as working with pain or finding the right meditation posture or time to meditate will quickly become too solution oriented:

You should do it in the morning. That's when you're freshest.

Just set your alarm and get up. It's as simple as that.

What's helped me enormously is valerian.

However, when group input is turned to less practical matters, this can lead to fertile discussions that deepen inquiry.

Teacher:	So you find the noting part difficult. I wonder how others are working with it?
Participant 1:	I don't note. I see a thought before me, as it were. And then I see a fence and throw the thought over it.
Participant 2:	I really see it as described in the meditation: clouds that are floating past. And sometimes there will be a label on the cloud or the cloud will have the same color as the thought.
Participant 3:	I always use the same word, "thinking," and repeat it. But only when there are many thoughts and I want to create some distance.

Limiting

Limiting conversation techniques are helpful for making efficient use of the time and energy available. They are sometimes also necessary to counterbalance an invitation to openness, which may, without guidance, lead to unchecked wandering.

INTERRUPTING

You've probably been in situations where someone just keeps talking and you want to interrupt, but you can't find the right moment to do so. During mindfulness training interrupting may seem even more difficult, given that participants are sharing very personal things. Yet sometimes interrupting is necessary during inquiry. Participants may still be unskilled in keeping their attention focused on the subject of the inquiry. And some people simply have a habit of going off on a tangent and losing themselves in side issues.

If you allow individuals to digress too much, the group will be deprived of valuable inquiry time. Meanwhile, attention can start to slacken, and getting it back will take yet more time. Plus, people who get stuck in their narrative sometimes realize that this has happened but don't know how to get back on track. In such cases, interruption will not only liberate the group but also set the speaker free.

Nevertheless, many teachers find it difficult to interrupt participants because this doesn't seem to agree with their ideas about embodying mindfulness. Furthermore, therapists and coaches sometimes have a conditioned reflex to not intervene. However, it is possible to interrupt without judging and without impatience, and in a helpful way. Use inner indicators to find the right moment to interrupt—perhaps a sense of physical tension or a loss of interest in the story. Trust these indicators. Then interrupt as if you're cutting a rope using a sharp knife: quickly, clearly, and cleanly, but without excessive force. Don't raise your voice, and don't go into what the person was talking about. Simply go back to the last reference point that was relevant or of interest:

Can we go back to…?

And how about the question of whether…?

Can I interrupt you there? I follow what you're saying, but I'd like to go back to…

Sometimes you may have to go all the way back to the beginning:

Hold on there for a second. The question was…

I'd like to go back to the beginning. You started by saying…

Other times it may be best to move on to a new subject:

I want to interrupt you here and move on to the next experience. Is that okay for you?

Thank you for your contribution. Who's next?

By interrupting, you display firmness. You set boundaries and manage the conversational space. Your presence and intervention will strengthen your role as a moderator and reinforce participants' faith in your competence to guide the process. To ensure your interruption has these positive effects, don't put pressure on participants, as if you were chairing a meeting. Certain kinds of remarks will only introduce a sense of haste and stress:

Please be brief.

Could you limit your story to the essence?

INVOLVING THE BODY

When we talk, our attention is focused on the mind, especially when the conversation involves some level of tension, such as sharing with a group. In such situations, people can quickly get out of touch with their physical experience, which in most cases offers information that's far more rich than any story of the mind, especially when emotions are involved.

Interrupting a participant who's speaking excessively from the mind requires a tactful approach. There's a major risk that the participant will be frustrated or unable to resume after the interruption, as illustrated in the following dialogue.

Teacher: Hold on. You're speaking from the mind. Can you involve your body?

Participant: Um…

Teacher: What are you feeling in your body?

Participant: You know, just… What do you mean? Now I don't remember what I was saying.

The key is to use the right words: neither harsh nor overly light. Strike the right tone and tempo: shifting attention to the body generally means slowing down. It doesn't matter if such interruptions cause participants to lose their train of thought, as long as they aren't put off altogether. For example, the teacher in the previous dialogue might have facilitated inquiry with the following approach.

Teacher: Can I make a suggestion? What you're saying is very valuable, and before you continue, you could perhaps make it even more valuable by taking a bit more time and also seeing if you could involve your body in the experience…*(Pauses in silence.)* Just take it slowly…We're not used to that…*(Pauses in silence.)* Yes, like that… *(Pauses in silence.)* Just seeing what's there…and involving your body. What do you notice?

LEAVING A TOPIC OPEN

During inquiry, topics don't have to be neatly wrapped up and concluded. In fact, open-ended issues are precisely the ones that will reverberate, as their unfinished nature gives them an unsatisfactory edge. However, this unsatisfactory edge can be a double-edged sword, tempting teachers to persist too long, especially if they're driven by a need to satisfy participants. Practice ending inquiries even when you feel the issue hasn't been wrapped up:

This is a profound issue about which there's still a lot to say. Shall we leave it at that for now?

We have to cut it short here, even though it doesn't quite feel concluded yet. This subject will surely come back at some point. At this point, we're going to proceed with the next subject.

And still we're going to end this discussion here. You simply cannot finish everything in one go. Explore for yourself how this makes you feel. It might feel somewhat unsatisfactory.

Contrary to interrupting, these kinds of statements recognize the subject as relevant. You establish that you aren't ending the discussion because it lacks relevance or interest, but due to a lack of time.

NOT GOING INTO SIDE ISSUES

Not going into a topic differs from leaving a subject open or not answering a question, because it involves making it clear to the group that the subject isn't relevant. When a subject isn't relevant or interesting within the scope of the training, entertaining it would be a waste of the group's time and attention. Be clear about that. Don't waste time on an apologetic or overly diplomatic answer that you really don't want to give. A clear formulation is the most respectful option here— for the person who raised the topic, for the rest of the group, and for yourself. This keeps the process of inquiry clean and keeps the setting and focus of attention fresh:

That's an interesting subject, but it's beyond the scope of this training.

That's intriguing, but within our framework there isn't time to delve into it further.

There are other courses where you can explore that.

This training is about exploring our experiences in the moment and during our sessions, not about prior episodes in our lives. So I don't want to go into that at length.

Not going into something can establish boundaries for the inquiry and serve as a clear statement of "no." There are quite a few kinds of situations where this function can be useful:

- When someone's questions steer the inquiry into a dead-end street, splitting hairs on a version or nuance of a word or exercise: *Those are details; don't be distracted by details* or *I simply don't think that's important.*

- When someone tries to lure you into a debate on everything that's wrong in our society and how mindfulness could mend the situation: *That isn't something we can work on in this context, so I won't go into it any further.*

- When someone wants you to address things such as karma or reincarnation: *I already find it quite challenging to deal with the here and now properly, in this life. For now, let's refrain from that discussion.*

- When someone wants to go into concepts from an underlying body of thought, such as psychology, yoga, or Buddhism: *That's not my area of expertise* or *Going into that science in depth now would lead us too far from the theme of this session.*

- When someone asks you about your personal practice: *My experiences are not so important here. Everyone follows their own path. So a far more interesting question could be what it's like for you. Can you explore that for yourself?*

Other Auxiliary Conversation Techniques

Human communication is so rich that every categorization falls short. There are more conversation techniques that are important for mindfulness training but don't readily fit into any of the preceding categories. Some important ones are working with humor, using aphorisms, and using metaphors.

WORKING WITH HUMOR

The basis of humor is typically to contradict expectations. Humor is a direct means of loosening people up from their patterns. Humor can be a helpful addition to inquiry: it refreshes attention, questions beliefs by doing something unexpected with them, and puts the heaviness of the undertaking—looking at reactivity and patterns of suffering—into perspective. It also adds fun to the process and can serve as a vehicle of kindness and compassion. In this way, humor can connect people.

Although the function and power of humor cannot be overestimated, humor can also serve as a distraction or cover-up. Humor has to suit the situation, which requires a delicate touch. In addition, meditative awareness heightens people's sensitivity, making them more selective about what is deemed suitable or unsuitable.

Also bear in mind that humor needs to appeal to everyone. When people aren't in on a joke, they feel excluded. Finally, humor only works when used in moderation. Running gags are too much of a distraction, and as soon as the mood is dominated by hilarity, it will be hard to get the group back to the needed level of concentration and effort. Besides, the training isn't intended to be entertaining, light, or necessarily fun. So although participants may initially welcome a humor-filled session, they'll feel disappointed afterward because that's not what they signed up for.

Above all, don't force humor. If a humorous remark occurs to you, run it past your pragmatic awareness before sharing it. Given all of the considerations above, it's generally a good idea to exercise restraint in using humor.

USING APHORISMS

Poems and parables serve an important purpose in the training, inviting participants to transcend the cognitive framework of the mind. The same goes for aphorisms (and metaphors, the topic of the next section). Aphorisms are one-liners—simple, pithy summaries—often containing some wit or an unexpected analogy. Aphorisms speak the truth in a simple way. And due to their succinctness, aphorisms are easy to insert into the conversation, unlike poems and parables.

Well-chosen aphorisms are like court jesters: they aren't part of the rational debate but can expose the core of truth of that debate like nothing else. In addition, aphorisms generally introduce lightness and space into inquiry by adding a new dimension to the sometimes overly serious process. At the same time, an aphorism recaps a theme, making a firm statement about it that's clear but not overly forceful. Finally, an aphorism is a fine tool to use to wrap up a topic and create space for a new orientation or a new subject without the shift seeming contrived.

Aphorisms are powerful. Just think about how politicians and other people in the public eye tend to rely on them. During inquiry, sometimes the discourse won't register, while an aphorism used to recap it will. You may notice this when a participant suddenly quotes an aphorism back to you that you'd forgotten you used;

for example, "You once said, 'Discipline is a resource.' This line keeps reverberating in my head when I catch myself struggling with what I want to do. It always brings a smile to my face." In this way, aphorisms can serve as convenient reference points for learning.

By lingering in participants' minds, aphorisms can give the learning process a powerful push and trigger a breakthrough insight—a whole new way of looking at things. An aphorism may well prove to be the key to a door that someone has been trying to open for some time, as reflected in these kinds of statements from participants:

You said, "We are not here to learn something, but rather to unlearn something." For the first time, I'm not being asked to do my best, but instead to stop doing my best. This sounds so liberating to me!

What stuck with me most was when you said, "You are not your thoughts." That was a real eye-opener for me. I'd never looked at it that way.

Here are a few short aphorisms that are easy to incorporate into inquiry:

The little things are not little.

Less is more.

Staying mindful is enough.

Deep learning is slow learning.

Working with aphorisms is one form of the skillful use of words (a topic I'll discuss in chapter 6). There aren't fixed rules about using them; it's an intuitive and playful thing. However, there is one guideline: don't use aphorisms in ways that come across as contrived, mechanical, or repetitive. If you do, they'll trigger resistance and make the inquiry grind to a halt. As an example, consider this anecdote that a mindfulness student once shared with me:

My previous teacher always said, "It is what it is." With everything we talked about—"It is what it is." After three sessions, I knew exactly when he would say it. Someone would share something, and he would say, "It is what it is." Before long, whenever he said it we were all looking at each other annoyed.

Finally, stick with aphorisms that resonate for you or fit your style. These are the ones that you'll automatically remember and use when the time is right.

USING METAPHORS

Figurative speech and metaphor are parts of the mindfulness teacher's basic tool set. Something that can't be communicated by thousands of descriptive words can often be conveyed by a metaphor in a flash. The more concrete and recognizable your metaphors are, the more effective they'll be. It's best to derive them from simple, recognizable, everyday examples that have some striking parallel with the situation at hand:

It's like hitting the gas and the brakes at the same time (illustrating how we sometimes try too hard to relax, bringing the doing mode of mind to the process).

It's like a computer that, when not in use, does background tasks, such as consolidating files (explaining how mind wandering is a default activity of the brain).

It's like a GPS navigation system that tells you the way again and again, always patiently, even if you lose track a thousand times (talking about the patience and friendliness needed to bring attention back, again and again, during meditation).

CHAPTER 5

Didactic Presentations

Learn your theories as well as you can, but put them aside when you touch the miracle of the living soul.

—Carl J. Jung

The emergence and blossoming of understanding, love, and intelligence has nothing to do with any tradition, no matter how ancient or impressive—it has nothing to do with time. It happens on its own when a human being questions, wonders, inquires, listens, and looks without getting stuck in fear, pleasure, and pain. When self-concern is quiet, in abeyance, heaven and earth are open.

—Toni Packer

Complementing practice and inquiry, didactic presentation is the third teaching format in mindfulness training. It is the furthest removed from experiential learning and is similar to the rote learning so typical in conventional education settings. Because didactic presentation is straightforward and basically involves simply offering information—and also because it isn't specific to mindfulness—I've chosen to keep this chapter quite short and instead devote more time and words to aspects of the teaching that are more challenging or unique to mindfulness training.

Didactic presentation shifts the focus from the specific, current personal or group experience to the broader human context, addressing how things work in general. Didactic presentation is akin to explanation, setting forth the why and how of mindfulness. This promotes learning by boosting the development of insight, and also by strengthening commitment to and trust in the process.

Didactic presentation involves offering information that may be supportive for the learning process, helping participants interpret their experiences and insights so they can understand them in a more general context. In contrast to inquiry, this isn't an inductive movement, from a unique experience to a more general insight; rather, it is deductive, bringing general knowledge to a unique experience. Hence, the teacher assumes a different role: instead of being a coach who facilitates exploration, in didactic presentations the teacher is an authority on the matter, somebody who knows.

Although didactic presentation requires that you shift out of the role of guiding exploration, this doesn't mean you become a traditional teacher who tells students how things are or how things are done. Given that you're addressing a vivid and currently relevant theme, and that you're bringing your own lively, personal interest in it, the theme will remain connected to the group's experience. In this way, it's a more interactive form of teaching.

Mindfulness training includes teaching about a number of subjects that have a fixed place in the curriculum, such as education about the doing mode and being mode of mind, the tendency to take our thoughts for facts, or how obstacles can function as learning opportunities. Other, "floating" subjects don't have a fixed place in the training but are still important for supporting the learning process. At the end of this chapter, you'll find a list of these topics with references to sources that provide further explanation of the subject material.

Functions of Didactic Presentations

Didactic presentations solidify present-moment learning in many ways. Here are some of the functions that allow them to do so, with an example of the effects of each function:

Explanation: *Now I see how it works. I hadn't looked at it that way yet.*

Recognition: *I'm not the only one to stumble upon this; it's a well-known theme.*

Support: *The suffering I experience is part of a broader suffering, of common humanity. We're all in the same boat.*

Connection: *I can now see a broader context in the patterns in my life and how I'm not alone in my struggles.*

Registering: *The theoretic context makes it easier for me to remember this pattern so I can recognize it next time.*

Alignment with the Course Materials

The subjects to be covered in didactic presentations revolve around the themes of the training. For most of the topics, it's a good idea to provide handouts that participants can read and review at home. As mentioned in the introduction, one element of the teaching setting in many mindfulness-based approaches is a workbook that includes informational handouts, along with poems and other inspirational readings, and occasionally other materials. In such programs, the workbook is the written counterpart of the didactic presentations you'll offer. Therefore, it's a good idea to align the two sources of information: didactic presentations covered in class and topics covered in the workbook.

Alignment with Inquiry

In a sense, inquiry is imbued with didactic presentation. Every confirmation or acknowledgment by the teacher contains a message:

That's how the mind works.

Now we see how persistent our patterns are.

Such a statement about how things are provides a potential segue into further explanation, if the time is right for that:

The mind is always busy, with the best of intentions, trying to avoid the unpleasant and cling to the pleasant. Its workings cause us to develop scenarios that even stretch out into the future. But...

Our habitual patterns are like the grooves in a vinyl record...

However, as soon as you start explaining, you've left the process of inquiry. It's a good idea to highlight this transition, perhaps with a statement like "Good question. Let's go into this a bit deeper because there's more to say about that..." As you wrap up a didactic explanation interwoven into inquiry, see if you can mark this ending to prepare for the transition back into inquiry: "So that's the difference between concentration and mindfulness meditation. Is this information helpful for your practice?"

You can then return to inquiry with just a brief sentence or two:

Does this link up with your experience?

Is that recognizable? We so often think we're alone in struggling with this, but there you have it: it's a common struggle. Thank you for bringing it up. Shall we move on now?

Now let's get back to our review of the practice. Does anyone else want to say something about their experiences?

When to Offer Didactic Presentations

Didactic presentations are pertinent when the program is addressing a fixed theme, such as living on autopilot (session 1 in MBSR) or how stress works (session 4 in MBSR). These presentations are part of the core teaching to be conveyed through the training, and they are addressed as such both in sessions and in handouts.

Themes such as stress and being on autopilot are so central that they're addressed in every program, as are themes such as attention and working with the body, even though the latter themes don't have a fixed place in the curriculum. Other themes are more pertinent for some groups than they are for others, such as physical posture during meditation, the difference between concentration meditation and mindfulness meditation, and acceptance versus enduring or even indulging in difficulties. Didactic presentations on these kinds of topics can be used to supplement or deepen the learning process.

You can plan to include floating themes—those that don't have a fixed place in the curriculum—in particular sessions, or you can include them as seems appropriate as a session unfolds. In either case, make sure the theme is aligned with the group's experience. For example, an eating meditation may provide an occasion to provide didactic information on the felt sense of experiences or working with the body. Likewise, the beginning of a sitting meditation can offer a good opportunity to address the specifics of physical posture and the role of posture in meditation. In this way, didactic information, or cognitive understanding, is interwoven with lived experience.

Didactic Presentation by Request

You might also choose to provide didactic information in response to specific questions or stated interests. For a training or practice sometimes you simply need to explain what the objective is, what the guidelines for the practice are, or what the idea behind it is. This may seem to contradict the basic principle that mindfulness practice is a form of exploring and open questioning, and not being influenced or filled by information from the teacher. However, explanations can sometimes help people continue with their exploration. Furthermore, some participants have a more reflective or abstract learning style and therefore tend to need a theoretic framework in order to surrender to a practice. For these participants, when an obstacle to practice arises, it can be helpful if the teacher frames the obstacle in a more general way, through a brief foray into didactic information, rather than continuing to inquire into the participant's experience.

Participant: When I stay settled on my breathing for a long time, my breathing tenses up. Then I feel like I don't know how to breathe anymore.

Teacher: This is a fairly common phenomenon. The moment too much tension develops around an anchor for your attention, just drop it. Then the anchor isn't helpful anymore. Just sit without an anchor or shift your attention to another part of your body, such as to the sense of contact of the body with the seat, or of your feet with the floor. Later, when you're ready, you can carefully see whether you can bring your attention back to your breathing in a light manner.

Meditation instructions are merely intended to teach you how to respond smoothly to the movements of your attention. If you get tense, you can't practice this. Remember that when you're meditating.

Participant: I'd been sitting uncomfortably for a while, so I changed my posture, and then I started thinking about whether that was okay or not.

Teacher: It's just fine. You may have heard it in the instructions: you are free to change your posture, but when you do, make sure you do it consciously. Sensing our physical posture is also an object of mindfulness practice, not something to keep at the outskirts of our awareness. See whether you can make the way you're sitting be a part of the meditation. It need not be fixed; just be aware of it and find an external posture that supports your inner attitude.

Didactic presentations can also be used to make the structure of the training process explicit: "This is what we are doing, and for the following reason…" or "This is necessary for it to work, and these are the boundaries." When you explain the process, you're inviting the group to become mutually responsible for its implementation.

List of Teaching Subjects

Earlier in this chapter, I identified stress, being on automatic pilot, being mode of mind, and doing mode of mind as some of the core themes of the training. Of course, there are many others. The following topics are also important teaching points that are often the subject of didactic presentations in mindfulness training:

Acceptance: How this is an active process and differs from submission

Attention: How it drives our experience and that it can only be controlled to a limited degree

Automatic reactions: Being aware of them and choosing to respond consciously instead

Boundaries: Being aware of them and respecting them

Breathing: Its value as an anchor

The felt sense of physical experiences: Why tuning in to this is valuable

Here-and-now experience: Understanding the value of the present moment and its fleeting nature

How the mind works: That it's always trying to help us but isn't always equipped to do so

Meditation: Its objectives, the process, and obstacles

Obstacles and hindrances: How these are generally difficult and useful at the same time

Pain and suffering: Distinguishing between the two

Physical meditation posture: Its value for attitude—the "how" of meditation—and for balancing the attitudes of mindfulness with physical and emotional needs

Practice: How it helps us develop, understand the importance of commitment and being disciplined, distinguish a result-driven orientation from one that's process driven, and distinguish between formal and informal

The primary benefit of mindful awareness: How it opens up a path out of automatic patterns and reactivity

Reactivity: How it exerts a grip on us and can cause us to hold on to experiences or push them away

Slowing down: Why this is valuable

Taking care of oneself: What this means, why it's necessary for balance, and why it isn't egocentric

Thoughts: That thoughts are not facts, and that our mental state influences how we perceive our experience

Using what is learned: The art of anchoring insights

Mindfulness teachers must be able to offer clear didactic presentations on each of these subjects. For more information on these topics, you can consult Jon Kabat-Zinn's books *Full Catastrophe Living* (1990) and *Wherever You Go, There You Are* (1994), which revolve around these themes. Handouts from *Mindfulness-Based Cognitive Therapy for Depression* (Segal, Williams, & Teasdale, 2013) also provide didactic presentations about some of the subjects in this list. You might also consult the growing number of self-help workbooks centered on mindfulness-based applications, which contain handy, participant-friendly language you can use to present these themes to the group. Examples include *A Mindfulness-Based Stress Reduction Workbook* (Stahl & Goldstein, 2010) and *The Mindful Way Workbook* (Teasdale, Williams, & Segal, 2014).

CHAPTER 6

What the Teacher Brings to the Training

If I speak in the tongues of men and of angels, but have not love, I am a noisy gong or a clanging cymbal.

And if I have prophetic powers, and understand all mysteries and all knowledge, and if I have all faith, so as to remove mountains, but have not love, I am nothing.

If I give away all I have, and if I deliver up my body to be burned, but have not love, I gain nothing.

—I Corinthians 13:1–3

This work is not about being perfect, whatever that might mean. It is very much about being human.

—Jon Kabat-Zinn

In the previous chapters, I discussed structures, techniques, and principles. Does that mean being a teacher is a purely technical affair? To a certain point, it is; you need to know what happens or can happen during the training process, what choices you can make in different situations, and what the implications of your choices may be. Educational courses are designed for this. To become a teacher, you need teacher training. Research findings show that the level of teacher training is the factor most significantly related to the results of an MBSR course in terms of well-being, lower perceived stress, and satisfaction with the course (Ruijgrok-Lupton, Crane, & Dorjee, 2015).

This is akin to mastering music, which is purely technical at first. Musicians practice over and over again, absorbing all of their experiences from earlier practices and everything their teachers share. They've practiced all of the basic skills endlessly, along with the specific technical challenges of particular pieces of music. They've studied the score and know each note, and each silence. But when it's time to perform, this knowledge isn't at the forefront of the mind. They leave it behind and let the music come out, through them, as it were. In this way, musicians themselves are the main instrument and operate from a sense of trust that all of their preparation will enable them to do what the moment asks of them.

And just as a musical performance doesn't equal reproducing the score, mindfulness training doesn't equal reproducing a protocol. For mindfulness teachers, like musicians, the performance is mainly about being something, rather than doing something. All of your preparations, personal passion, practice, and ups and downs are reflected in the training you provide. The training will continuously raise the question "What does the process ask of me at this moment?" You'll never have the answer to that question in advance. You can never know what will happen. But you do know that you will always bring yourself to those moments, and from all of your background, answers to this question will emerge.

One of the challenges of being a teacher is how to deal with paradoxes: being both results oriented and process oriented, utilizing both doing mode of mind and being mode of mind, following your program and working with whatever comes up, embodying both knowing and not-knowing, doing your best and working without effort. To be able to hold these paradoxes and keep them alive, you need space—a kind of space that can only be created through trust. You must trust that what you bring to the training is sufficient, and that the responses emerging from your experience merit being heard and honored. Being a good teacher is therefore about adequately managing your own inner territory, meaning all of the elements of your inner life: your perceptions, ideas, thoughts, and pragmatic consciousness, and even your tendencies in reacting and responding. In the words of American education expert Parker Palmer, "The most practical thing we can achieve in any kind of work is insight into what is happening inside us as we do it. The more familiar we are with our inner terrain, the more surefooted our teaching—and living—becomes" (1998, p. 6).

This chapter is about everything you bring to the training, as a teacher and as a human being. I'll start with passion—the flame that burns in your heart, supplying you with commitment and intention. Of course, passion alone isn't enough; embodiment of the qualities of mindfulness is equally if not more important, so I will also discuss embodiment. Then I'll address the personal strengths and limitations teachers bring to the training, as well as the importance of practicing what you preach. In the context of mindfulness training, one implication of the latter is that you have to take good care of yourself. Next, I'll discuss skillful use of a teacher's most important resource—language—and then how you can keep learning as a teacher. I conclude this chapter with a description of the competencies crucial for teachers and also emphasize the importance of verifiable criteria to evaluate these competencies. In short, this chapter is about everything you can rely on when faced with the question "What does the learning process ask of me at this moment?"

Passion

In the words of Jon Kabat-Zinn, "The early years of MBSR and the development of other mindfulness-based clinical interventions were the province of a small group of people who gave themselves over to practicing and teaching mindfulness basically out of love, out of passion for the practice, knowingly and happily putting their careers and economic well-being at risk because of that love, usually stemming from deep first-person encounters with the dharma and its meditative practices, often through the mediation of Buddhist teachers and acknowledged masters within a number of well-defined traditions and lineages" (2010, pp. xi–xii). Such passion is fed by the heart's deep natural need to give and to do good. Passion is love. The heart overflows with the need to express what the individual personally experiences as liberating and valuable in the practice. For teachers, it brings our work to life. A passion for awakening is the foundation of teaching mindfulness. The training is the vehicle that enables us to let our heart pour out its tide.

"One teaches out of one's passion for the practice," confirms Belgian mindfulness teacher Edel Maex (2011, pp. 167–168). So cherish this passion. There will be times when teaching mindfulness will feel like working a "regular" job, perhaps because you meet with resistance, because turnout is disappointing, because you're tired, or because there's a lot of administrative work involved. At those times, try to reconnect with what drives you. Passion is also what makes you shine, which is contagious and will encourage participants to take their practice further.

Cherish your passion by maintaining a connection with your commitment. Regularly remind yourself why you're doing what you're doing. It's likely that many of these reasons originated in key moments in your life, starting with early childhood but particularly arising from within your own practice, from your first retreat to your most recent morning meditation. Passion is what adds sparkle to your training, and it's a prerequisite for teaching mindfulness.

But it isn't the only prerequisite. If you're driven purely by passion, it may end up blinding you. When your motivations for teaching mindfulness are overly grounded in your personal experience, you may assume that others must discover the same things that were true and valuable for you. To prevent passion from blinding you, it must be balanced with the fruit of the practice: embodied mindfulness.

Embodiment

When I say "embodiment," I'm referring to the embodiment of mindfulness. As pointed out in chapter 4, guiding inquiry is challenging for teachers because it can create a feeling that you have to do something right, without having any tools to steer or control the process. The situation is similar for embodiment, wherein the belief that the teacher must personally serve as an ideal can cause teachers to become tense and unnatural. People tend to think that a mindfulness teacher should provide a perfect example of being in the moment, acceptance, and so on. This is based on a conventional image of mindfulness: that it means always being present, with a serene mind. This is a misconception. Embodiment is not the same as being calm, imperturbable, wise, thoughtful, or still. Embodiment is not about perfection, but about imperfection. What determines teachers' degree of embodiment is not their perfection, but the ways in which they deal with their imperfections. You cannot offer your group a greater learning moment than letting them sense that, at times, you are also struggling with maintaining a mindful attitude, that you're aware of this, and that it's okay.

To embody mindfulness is to live an invitation: the invitation to be mindful of the dance between sleeping and being awake, between reacting automatically and responding wisely, between the doing mode and being mode of mind. Embodiment of this invitation is perhaps the most important thing you can offer a group. In the words of Segal, Williams, and Teasdale, "The MBCT instructor's own basic understanding and orientation will be one of the most powerful influences affecting this process" (2002, pp. 65–66). Crane and colleagues (2010) specify that embodiment is an "overarching principle" of the foundations of the learning process, and "that the central mechanism through which mindfulness-based approaches have their effect is through enabling participants to be able to choose to shift from a 'doing' to a 'being' mode of mind, that this learning is communicated in the class through the teacher's direct personal experience of 'being,' and that this experience is gained through mindfulness meditation practice" (p. 78). In regard to living mindfully, the poet Rumi said, "If you remember everything else and forget this, then you will have done nothing in your life" (1997, p. 17). This is also true for teaching mindfulness: if you forget about embodiment, then you will have done nothing in your teaching.

Think back to a particular teacher from your youth who inspired you—a teacher who had a special place in your life, who taught you a lot, and for whom you were willing to do almost anything, even when it had nothing to do with school. Or think back to an uncle, aunt, or neighbor who inspired you. What were the qualities in this person that appealed to you? When you think about it, you'll probably find that the appeal didn't revolve around the person's expertise or skills, or even the person's wisdom. People who inspire you embody something that resonates with you. It's often said that the efficacy of interventions in fields such as education, therapy, and leadership depends more on attitude and charisma than on actual words and techniques.

According to Crane and colleagues (2012, p. 17), the teacher embodies mindfulness in the training through the following:

- Present-moment focus—expressed through behavior and verbal and non-verbal communication

- Present-moment responsiveness—to internal and external experience

- Calm and vitality—simultaneously conveying steadiness, ease, nonreactivity, and alertness

- Attitudinal foundations—conveying mindfulness practice through the teacher's way of being

- Person of the teacher—the learning is conveyed through the teacher's way of being

This list once again confirms embodiment as a highly abstract concept; for example, what does "way of being" really mean? And once again, we are confronted with the contradiction between doing and being. Embodiment isn't something you can "do," making it hard to capture it in words. But I will try anyway.

Relating in a Conscious Way

Embodiment of mindfulness is about how you express and relate to the seven attitudinal factors mentioned in chapter 4: nonjudging, patience, beginner's mind, trust, nonstriving, acceptance, and letting go. Again, you don't have to perfectly capture these factors, but they must be central to your orientation, and you must be mindful of how you relate to them. In this way, embodiment means maintaining a conscious and authentic relationship with the attitudinal factors that are the foundation of mindfulness practice.

Like all relationships, this one is dynamic. It is not a result, but a process. If mindfulness teachers are impatient, judgmental, mistrustful, and so on, this isn't a problem as long as they approach their impatience, judgment, or mistrust in a mindful way. Mindful awareness defines the difference between being impatient and experiencing impatience.

Your relationship to the key attitudinal qualities will be challenged in class. Here are some examples of how to respond to them mindfully:

I want to prevent being pressed for time, because I know that will make me tense.

What just happened surprises me. I have all kinds of thoughts, and I don't know how to proceed.

This affects me. I'm at a loss for words and don't have a response either. I feel powerless. I feel that, perhaps for this moment, it will be enough to simply be present to it.

I'm inclined to respond to this, but I also have a feeling of insecurity because it's not my area of expertise.

I feel honored by your words. I'm glowing with pride! My ego says, "more, more!"

Beyond words, attitudes are expressed in actions, both big and small: the way you close the door or sound the meditation bells, your response to an everyday question, or the care you devote to explaining a home practice. Embodiment often lies in these kinds of details.

Embodiment and Being Tense

Embodiment is about who you are. However, this doesn't mean "just being yourself" in the sense of simply externalizing everything you feel—that wouldn't be a very professional approach! As the teacher, you're responsible for the learning process and offer direction (with the understanding that you can't always control everything). One factor in this direction is consciously choosing how to deal with your personal experiences. The key criterion is that you should do so in a way that's beneficial to the group's learning process. As an example, during the first session, when participants are still nervous and somewhat uncertain, it probably won't be helpful if you, as the teacher, show your own nervousness.

So how do you deal with your nerves at that moment? You have three options: change, stay present, or cope. Changing would mean doing something to break the tension. Staying present to it requires that you do something to allay your nerves (something I'll discuss in detail a bit later in the chapter, in the section on limitations). The third option is to cope with your nervousness, which can often be achieved by focusing your attention on your role as best as you can. When the first two options (changing and staying present to your nervousness) aren't helpful to the group's learning process, coping with it is the best option.

Consciously coping means keeping the feeling to yourself, containing it, and choosing to work with it later, at a more suitable time. This last aspect, doing something with it later (for example, by sharing it with a colleague), is essential. If you don't, you'll keep it inside and it will grow. By taking good care of yourself in this way, you're also taking care of your relationship to the attitudinal factors and thereby your embodiment. To see this process in motion, let's turn to an example: As a new group enters the room for session 1, you notice that you're nervous. To put mindfulness into action, you notice this hindrance, recognize it, explore it, and then consciously choose a response:

1. "Can I change this feeling at this moment by doing something for myself in such a way that the group's learning process is not affected?" In the event that the answer is no, you proceed to the next question.

2. "Can I allay my nerves by doing something for myself in such a way that the group's learning process isn't affected?" In the event that the answer is no, you go with the third choice.

3. "I'll opt for containment. I'll cope with this nervousness and deal with it later."

The Human Teacher: Strengths

The strengths you bring to the training are resources you can draw on, time and time again, to find a response to what the moment asks of you. Among the many potential strengths mindfulness teachers may bring to the training, those I'll cover here are deep knowing, spirituality, integrity, life experience and personality, and professional qualities.

Deep Knowing

Your most important source of strength is your own deep knowing—your deep understanding of the practice of mindfulness and how it benefits quality of life. You nourish your relationship with deep knowing through practice: meditation, everyday informal mindfulness, retreats, and having a dynamic and personal connection with some of your own teachers. You also nourish it through how you deal with obstacles and challenges; with your work; with your relationships with others; with your free time; and with what you eat, drink, see, and breathe. In a sense, all of these are practices, and all nourish your deep knowing, including the awareness that you can always reawaken to your experience or awaken to it even more. Your deep knowing is the most solid foundation you have when entering the session room. Without it, the message of this book will be no more than dry knowledge.

Spirituality

In the context of mindfulness training, spirituality is the trust you derive from a sense that there is more to our human existence than science and secular culture acknowledge. Almost everyone—religious or not, Buddhist or not—has some sort of relationship to higher principles. Even the most rational scientists wonder at the mysteries of the universe, including the tremendous vigor and irrepressibility of life. In this context, we might speak of the intelligence of life and of self-healing powers. Or we might call it the intelligence of evolution, existence, god, dhamma, or consciousness. Many people feel that there is a power at work that's focused on making life good. If you foster a sense that the core principles of the training are aligned with this self-healing intelligence, it may provide participants with a spiritual grounding that can be a powerful resource whenever doubts arise about how the training process is unfolding.

Integrity

You know that you make mistakes; that's part and parcel of being human. However, you can act with the best intentions and to the best of your knowledge. Integrity involves having pure intentions. Succeeding or failing in various actions determines our day-to-day success. Integrity transcends that. People are sensitive to integrity and inspired by it. Nelson Mandela inspires not because he was imprisoned, but because he walked out unbroken. The Dalai Lama inspires not because he has been exiled, but because it hasn't diminished his spirit and his smile.

You could formulate a mindfulness teacher's integrity as follows: "In every situation, I have the intention to choose, to the best of my ability, the most effective response available to me." If you make integrity your criterion for success, success will no longer hinge on everyday successes and failures but on whether you consciously choose the best options available to you. This is what business consultant Fred Kofman refers to as "success beyond success" (2006, p. 65).

No matter what a situation presents, nothing can take away your intention to handle the situation with integrity. If that is your criterion, success is guaranteed.

Life Experience and Personality

Crises, successes, hopelessness, euphoria—the things you've been through in life provide vivid learning experiences that can give you the strength to trust that new solutions will always arise, as will new twists or challenges. This knowledge that new solutions, obstacles, and surprising turns of events will present themselves is further strengthened by your daily personal practice.

In that sense, your practice is not only a source of nourishment and regeneration (as I'll discuss in the section on taking good care of yourself), but also a source of strength. Furthermore, your practice will reinforce your passion and embodiment—the strength of your heart and of your resilience. You will be more nimble minded, have more stillness inside you, be better able to focus your attention, and find it easier to open up to the present moment.

Of course, you also bring your personality and the strong points of your character to the training. Although not to the same degree, everyone possesses certain strengthening traits, including creativity, assertiveness, spontaneity, intelligence, energy, sensitivity, and empathy.

Professional Qualities

Aside from your life experience as a human being, you also bring your knowledge, skills, and experience as a professional to the training. Most mindfulness teachers have worked professionally with people in settings that revolve around personal development. As a teacher, you draw on the qualities you've acquired in these or other fields along the way. Whether you are a psychiatrist, yoga instructor, or coach, the qualities you've developed in your profession provide a solid footing for teaching mindfulness. However, as discussed in the following section, it's possible to go too far in drawing on one's professional qualities, which will transform them into potential obstructions in participants' development of mindfulness.

The Human Teacher: Limitations

As a teacher, you need to remain oriented toward your professional role: facilitating participants' learning process. Part of this is preparing yourself with a structure and form for the training. Adhering to this form will make the training feel smooth and give you a sense of control. That said, having too tight a focus on the structure of the program will put you at risk of getting out of tune with what's happening inside of you. This can result in tension in the background.

It's important not to sweep feelings of powerlessness, stress, or incompetence under the rug. That just puts them underground and turns them into enemies. Instead, seize the opportunity to engage in a conscious relationship with these feelings. Put them to service in deepening your teaching; they may be transformed in the process. In this section, I'll focus on a few broad behavioral patterns that may be limiting you: a sense of inadequacy, nervousness, or a tendency to exaggerate your strengths. If any of these limitations resonate with you, try to approach them not so much with a critical, judgmental perspective, but with a sense that they offer opportunities for personal development.

Sense of Inadequacy

You may often feel utterly inadequate as a teacher. For example, when you witness the depths of human suffering, you may think to yourself, *What can I say? I don't have an answer to that…*or *This is too big; I'm not equipped to handle it* or even *Who am I to guide this person through this?*

The way in which participants process their experiences in the training hinges on their sensitivity, level of understanding, learning style, development, and personality. For you as a teacher, this may trigger a sense of inadequacy as you realize that no matter how hard you try, you can't make it possible for every participant to receive the full benefit of every practice or exercise. In those moments, realize that participants' learning path isn't something you can control.[17] This is one of the times when you need to draw on your own acceptance, patience, trust, and other qualities that shape your embodiment of mindfulness.

Also consider the possibility that you may not need to do as much as you think you have to. It could be that you're able to achieve a great deal through embodiment alone, particularly through your ability to be present to the imperfections and suffering in the world. So once the training has started, remember that you have only one job: to create the best learning environment possible within a given context. And if you can trust the training process, you can also trust that each participant's individual learning pathway will lead to insights that heal, one way or another. From this broader perspective, you can't fall short.

Tension

You're allowed to be nervous, insecure, or stressed, even as a mindfulness teacher. After all, you're only human. As pointed out earlier, it's important for mindfulness teachers to consciously engage with their experiences. This is particularly salient in regard to nervousness, which often leads to efforts to use strength or power to overcome it. Those reactions will lead to narrowing, causing your performance to come across as contrived. Here are some techniques that can be helpful in dealing with nerves:

- Allow yourself more time to prepare and to arrive. Knowing that you're well prepared for the practical aspects of the session will provide important reassurance. For example, if you have an evening session with a new group, you might consider taking the afternoon off to give yourself some extra time.

- Meditate before a session.

- Talk about your nervousness with a colleague or friend. If it's a recurring issue, discuss this with a teacher or supervisor.

- Note your sense of nervousness to the group. Doing so may help you remember that participants are with you, not against you. Just be sure to do so in a well-considered manner that will be helpful to the group's learning process (as discussed in the section on self-disclosure a bit later in this chapter).

- Adapt the program to your needs. For example, you can insert a few moments of silence, extend a meditation, or have the group exchange experiences in pairs instead of through group inquiry.

Give yourself permission to be imperfect. Also draw reassurance from the fact that participants cannot see inside you. You can feel nervous or as though you're still finding your feet and nevertheless come across as self-confident, calm, and collected.

Exaggerating Strengths

Insight is something that can't be directly evoked, whether by participants' efforts to seek it or by steering from the teacher. Therefore, insight resides in the tradition often referred to as grace—it descends upon you like a gift from heaven.

This element of intangibility isn't easy to accept, and teachers often find it hard to concede that they have limited control over it. After all, you want to teach participants the mindfulness practices. You want to show them, if not convince them of, the core insights. You may often think, *Don't you get it? Do you still not see how it works?* Sometimes you may even want to cram insight into them! However good your intentions, such tendencies often make teachers overshoot the mark during inquiry. When that happens, we tend to fall back on our personal vision of the matter at hand, taking it upon ourselves to supplement participants' exploration with our own knowledge.

This illuminates the flip side to being good at something and knowing a lot about it: it can color your interpretation of what a participant needs. Sometimes this may arise from a personal affinity, perhaps with a certain school of Buddhism. Sometimes it may be informed by a belief you've derived from your own practice.

It's also common for teachers' views of what someone needs to be colored by their professional background. For example, a psychologist may interpret a participants' obstacles on the path to insight as psychological disorders, whereas a physical therapist may see them as physical blocks, and a life coach may consider them to be lack of vision and decisiveness. In this way, the strength of professional expertise can become a hindrance, when it serves as a filter and is used to interpret and direct.

Because professional guidance style can have such profound effects on the training, I'll close this section with brief descriptions of a number of styles that, when exaggerated, can hinder participants' process. You may identify with one or more of these styles, even if you don't hold the related profession. (Also, please note that I've chosen professions that tend to typify a given quality and its related exaggeration. Not all of them are common vocations for mindfulness teachers.)

Professional Qualities and their Exaggerations

Profession	Vision	Strategy	Quality	Exaggeration
Social worker	"Your problems are my concern."	Solving people's problems	Providing support and care	Depriving people of their own path and strength
Therapist	"Let's track down the cause first."	Interpreting and analyzing	Broadening the context	Overanalyzing
Teacher	"If you understand it, you can do it."	Conveying knowledge	Explaining, clarifying	Overexplaining and clarifying excessively
Judge	"Let's get to the bottom of things."	Seeking clarity and identifying differences	Elucidating	Lacking a dynamic quality due to excessive preciseness
Life coach	"Having attained insight, you must take steps right away."	Immediately doing something with insights	Being pragmatic	Pushing excessively for action and solutions

Profession	Vision	Strategy	Quality	Exaggeration
Consultant	"You need good advice."	Giving good advice	Orienting	Steering
Sports coach	"You can do it!"	Always going further	Stimulating	Pushing
Salesperson	"I have what you're looking for."	Promoting	Focusing on the positive and on potential	Having a misleading, one-sided view
Priest	"I'll help you forgive yourself for your mistakes."	Casting everything as good	Accepting	Lacking a sense of reality and sharpness
Missionary	"Follow me. I've seen the light."	Conveying inspiration	Activating	Preaching
Guru	"I am the light."	Exuding charisma	Inspiring	Paralyzing
Antiteacher	"I know nothing."	Letting everyone find their own way	Empowering	Abdicating

The Human Teacher: Challenges

The role of being a teacher brings along certain challenges inherent in the human condition, including personal vulnerabilities and uneasiness or a sense of threat in regard to one's pride, ego, or vanity. Participants might project their ideals onto you, even as certain situations provoke you (or call on you) to reveal characteristics that are less than ideal. At times, you may need to acknowledge that you aren't in charge of the situation or admit that you're personally touched by something and feel limited in your capacity to respond to it. In this section, I'll discuss issues surrounding idealization and self-disclosure—challenges you'll certainly meet while teaching.

Idealization

You can probably remember a situation where you wanted to learn something from someone you looked up to or idealized. Some participants will, quite understandably, have a similar experience in regard to you. Imagine the following situation: You've never meditated before. You've read something about mindfulness and picked up a few laudatory and scintillating terms that appeal to you, but you find mindfulness difficult to put into practice yourself. Then you attend a mindfulness training course with a teacher who seems to have answers to everything and appears to be highly mindful. This would probably make you think, *The teacher has something I don't have. I have to listen closely to what she has to say and pay close attention to everything she does because she has mastered something that I want to learn.*

Idealization is a double-edged sword. It can be both helpful and obstructive in the learning process. On the positive side, it stimulates imitation-based learning, the avenue for a great deal of learning. That's how a toddler learns from his parents, a child from her teachers, and an adolescent from role models: "I want to be able to do what they do."

Unfortunately, people of all ages are often blind to the fact that their role model is, in many respects, just as imperfect as they are. Idealization colors their view. The learning process then gets obstructed if the role model's skills or qualities seem unattainable: when the thought *I want that too* is immediately followed by *I can never get there*. Placing emphasis on what they can't achieve is discouraging. It can even break people's faith in their own strength.

Another downside is that imitation can take the form of rigid copying—aping the role model's motions without benefiting from the inner experiences that go with them. In addition, fixating on an ideal can go too far, eliminating personal reference points and the ability to think critically. This sometimes happens when people have focused on one specific role model, such as a guru, for a long time. Then, if the relationship is broken, they tend to feel lost and disoriented for quite a while. They might have learned a lot, but the foundations for internalizing what they've learned may be lacking.

A final consideration is that idealization strokes the teacher's ego. This isn't inherently problematic, but it does pose the danger of the teacher bathing in this glory and starting to buy into the idealization. For this reason alone, it's a good idea to be alert to idealization and its effects. One way of breaking through idealization is to disclose a bit of your own vulnerability—the topic of the next section.

Self-Disclosure

Self-disclosure means showing your own imperfections, feelings, and experiences, including those related to failure, with the group. Showing your human imperfections can reinforce the positive effects of idealization by highlighting that you have both admirable and less than stellar qualities—that you're only human and aren't afraid to show it. You still function as an ideal, but without the aura of having unattainable skills or qualities. In this way, you become a healthy role model; you aren't hiding that you also struggle, fail, and have doubts. However, do be aware that there's a point where self-disclosure leads to impotence, which will undermine your position as a teacher. With all of that in mind, let's take a look at some techniques for engaging in self-disclosure, along with some limits you should observe.

SPEAKING IN THE FIRST PERSON

Self-disclosure starts with "I," so be sure to speak in the first person when engaging in self-disclosure. People sometimes talk about themselves in the second person. Consider this example:

> *You've worked hard. You're tired and hungry, and you still have to shop for groceries. Then you get to the checkout line, and just when it's your turn, this mom cuts in front of you with an overloaded shopping cart and a bunch of screaming kids… You curse, your heart's pounding, and you tense up. It all seems to take ages. It's like everyone is against you.*

Now compare it to this version:

> *I've worked hard. I'm tired and hungry, and I still have to shop for groceries. Then I get to the checkout line, and just when it's my turn, this mom cuts in front of me with an overloaded shopping cart and a bunch of screaming kids…I curse, my heart's pounding, and I tense up. It all seems to take ages. It's like everyone is against me!*

Although the first example is a broader way of speaking that suggests our common humanity, it's also more indefinite. In the second version, the speaker is really disclosing something about himself. When you talk about yourself in the second person, you're basically putting a screen between yourself and the story.

ADMITTING TO MAKING MISTAKES

Self-disclosure is about sharing your human nature, often by acknowledging your own imperfections and fallibility. Simply admitting to a mistake can make this apparent:

Oops! I just noticed that I've skipped something. I'm sorry. Let's go back.

Last week we talked about dealing with pain. Afterward I felt that my comments were somewhat one-sided. So I'd like to come back to that topic for a moment to correct myself on that.

Identifying your slips and redressing them wherever possible, instead of attempting to cover them up in an effort to preserve a semblance of perfection, can break any tension and bring an easy atmosphere to the group. By implication, you're conveying that it's okay to make mistakes, which creates a favorable climate for mindfulness practice.

However, showing your fallibility doesn't mean emphasizing your failures, as that can be a distraction and undermine confidence in your skills, so be careful not to overdo it. For example, you wouldn't want to say, "Oh jeez, I forgot how to do this exercise. I'm such a dope." If nothing else, self-disclosure isn't intended to invoke pity for your mistakes or limitations.

SHARING THAT YOU ALSO STRUGGLE, FAIL, AND HAVE DOUBTS

Participants who see that their teacher is limited, just as they themselves are, learn two things. One is that it's natural to have limitations. The other is that if this role model has limitations yet can still embody ideal qualities, the participant might also be able to achieve these ideals. So don't hesitate to share that there are limitations to your expertise: "I don't actually know exactly how that works. I can only tell you what my own personal experience is."

Another avenue to this type of self-disclosure is to say something that conveys "I have that too."

Participant:	Sometimes when I hear my kids playing, all happy and noisy, all I can think is "Should I ask them to tone it down so I can meditate?" But kids should be allowed to play, right?
Teacher:	I know that feeling. Last week my son was watching TV in the living room when I was trying to meditate. I couldn't concentrate

and felt my irritation growing. In the end, I didn't meditate, and I didn't ask him to turn off the TV either.

This has the benefit of showing participants that you also struggle with circumstances when you want to practice mindfulness, just as they do. This communicates "I'm not there yet either. I also lose it a lot, have doubts, and fall into traps." When you share how you deal with those doubts and pitfalls—stumbling, getting back up again, and eventually moving past them—you convey the implicit message "This is all part of it."

In fact, your examples may be most powerful when solutions are less attractive or are even absent altogether—in other words, when they aren't success stories.

Participant: Last week, I had three days where I was just too busy to meditate.

Teacher: Did you really have no time at all?

Participant: Well, sure, you always have some time. It's more a feeling of being busy.

Teacher: Oh, okay. That's what I refer to as a "not now" day. That's when I feel that there are a lot of other and more important things that require my attention. Then I don't give myself a moment of rest to sit down and meditate.

Participant: I think the ultimate goal is to keep your mindfulness in all circumstances.

Teacher: Well, when there's an almighty racket coming from the neighbors across the street, you should hear my reaction. It's not until later that I ask myself whether I could have handled that a little more calmly. But when I'm in it, I just don't stop and question my reaction. Very little mindfulness there…

LIMITS ON PERSONAL REVELATIONS

How far can you go in talking about your private life? There are teachers who are very open in that respect. Others feel that overly personal revelations aren't appropriate and tend to be too much of a distraction—especially in light of the fact that any information originating from the teacher can take on great weight. Consider the following example.

224

Participant: I glanced at my partner from the side, and then I felt so guilty over my inability to be open and reach out to him. In hindsight, I regret that I wasn't able to show affection then and there. But at that moment, I simply couldn't do it. That makes me sad…

Teacher: That's hard, isn't it—the sadness of not being able to reach out to someone? My aunt has entered the final stage of her life. We take turns visiting her, and I sometimes see my sister bend over her, holding her hand and kissing her cheek. I'm somehow unable to do the same, and then I go home and feel so inadequate.

In this case, the teacher may come across as so vulnerable that participants feel inclined to start looking after him. Or the weightiness of his revelation may subdue the participant's experience. Always remember your professional responsibility: you're there for the group, not the other way around. You are in a professional role; they aren't. Self-disclosure must serve the purposes of the group's process. So carefully weigh the appropriateness of a personal disclosure before sharing it. What's your reason for sharing it? Is it intended to stimulate participants' learning process, or is it prompted by a personal need? That's where you must draw the line.

When used carefully, self-disclosure is a gift you give to the group. You offer your vulnerability as a human being to support your teaching practice. Now that's embodiment.

Taking Good Care of Yourself

In mindfulness training, we teach participants to take good care of themselves, presenting this as a birthright and explaining that taking care of themselves first enables them to take care of others optimally. But how about teachers? Can we also embody this message, or do many of us quietly believe that the situation is a bit different for us? After all, we have to take care of the group and facilitate others. We have a task. We're doing a job. Can we give ourselves the same permission to take care of ourselves? And if we can, what would that look like?

Making Time for Regeneration

As a teacher, you put a lot into the training: You prepare thoroughly, you use your skills and talents, you make yourself fully available to the group, and you're open and vulnerable. In short, you give a lot. Therefore, it only makes sense to take time to regenerate yourself. So be sure to engage in nourishing activities: take minisabbaticals between conducting group trainings; go on retreats; take a few hours off prior to a session; and make room in your schedule for sports, hobbies, and going out. Allow yourself to make use of sources of support that not only deepen your work but also make it more pleasant, such as including a helper or coteacher in the training or calling a colleague or friend afterward to debrief. Give yourself time to study, take workshops, and consult with others when these kinds of activities are restorative, even if they aren't immediately necessary. Also make room for fun and humor by, for example, having a beer after a session or letting off steam with a colleague.

Making the Setting Suit You

Teachers can sometimes get so wrapped up in creating a good setting for participants that they forget to ask themselves whether the setting suits them as a teacher. Do you give yourself the time you need to be able to prepare in peace? Do you use a tempo that suits you? Does the venue give you a good feeling? Does the time of year in which you offer the training suit you? Do you allow yourself to do things that are meaningful for you (rituals, hobbies, and so on) before or after sessions?

Also consider whether you like working with the kinds of groups that come your way, with their particular background or nature. Don't be tempted to work with people you don't have much affinity with, even if they appeal to your caring nature, vanity, or wallet. I've noticed that when peers look back on a group that they found jarring, one of the reasons is often a lack of affinity with specific characteristics of the participants. So work in a field in which you're likely to find groups you have a natural affinity with. In all probability, these will be groups that evoke your personal interests or call for your vocational skills. This will make it easy for you to bond with the group, and you'll already have skills in that area. It will also make it easier for you to attract participants, as mutual affinities tend to seek and find each other, like magnets. So by staying close to your own affinities, you increase the chances that participants will tune in to you with their affinities.

Also, be aware that choosing something because it fits you isn't solely an act of self-interest. Given that embodiment and passion are the soul of teaching, it should go without saying that you'll have a greater ability to bring these qualities to the teaching with some kinds of groups more than with others. After all, not every group will make your heart beat faster.

Claiming Your Rights

Taking good care of yourself also means recognizing that you have certain rights, and claiming those rights:

- As the leader of the process, you decide what to do. You don't have to defend your choices. People signed up to be guided by you.

- You aren't responsible for participants' effort, experiences, or results. As mindfulness teacher Florence Meleo-Meyer once said at a teacher training, "As a mindfulness teacher, you have no attachment to the outcome."

- Make use of your personal style, preferences, and affinities. There's no need to stick to a colorless, impersonal model. Use whatever drives, shapes, and nourishes you. Offer the training in your own way.

Inviting Your Monsters to Tea

Every teacher has bugaboos: that a participant will know better; that participants will start bickering amongst themselves; that no one will show up; that you won't know what to say when everyone is staring at you glassy-eyed; that you'll have a blackout, get sick, forget your keys, or get the dates wrong in your head… Other fears are even worse: that a participant will accuse you of something, or that a participant will harm himself while taking your training. We tend to suppress these kinds of fears, hoping that if we don't look them in the eye, they won't trouble us. But they do—precisely when we avoid them.

So can you dare to invite your monsters to tea and face up to your fears? Are you willing to get to the bottom of them—sitting with them, giving them space, and exploring how they touch you and how you can coexist with them?

Along with facing your fears, it's a good idea to ask yourself, "What could I fall back on if one of these things I fear so much were to actually happen? And would it really be the end of the world?" Consider your capacity and options for responding, with all of your deep knowing, integrity, experience, and skills. Can you trust that everything you bring to that moment will somehow create an answer to the situation? Even if your answer to that question isn't a wholehearted yes, you can still know that you'll bring all of your skills, qualities, and experience as a teacher to the situation. Perhaps you can at least have some trust in that.

Respecting Your Limitations

Mindfulness teachers are like all humans: stressed, insecure, vain, and subject to neurotic streaks, blind spots, and pet subjects. If you recognize any of these attributes in yourself, you probably sometimes have thoughts along these lines:

Surely I'm not competent to give this training.

They'll be able to see through me. I'll fail.

I will lose my way and won't know what to do anymore. What then?

If only they knew what's going on inside me.

As if I myself am any good at dealing with stress.

If you succumb to these thoughts, you're forgetting that you're human, limited, and imperfect. You're forgetting that you, like everyone else, muddle along and plod away, and that some of your limitations mean you'll always muddle along and plod away in certain areas, and that this is okay.

At such moments, see whether you can balance your sense of imperfection by focusing on things that are going well, or whether you can view it from the perspective that everyone else is also imperfect, living in an imperfect world. Also try to access your own sources of nourishment.

It's good for mindfulness teachers to be aware of their flaws, to contemplate them, and try to improve or handle them better. But it's also good for mindfulness teachers to be aware of any tendency to overly focus on their flaws, as this generally leads to nervousness, reduces enjoyment, and eventually drives teachers to try to be someone they are not.

Finding the Right Words

Offering participants the information they need, in a form in which they can receive it, is a true art form. It requires an ability to sense participants' level of understanding, switch to that wavelength, and then offer the message in an adjusted form while keeping it the same at its core.[18]

In this section, I'll discuss the importance of finding the appropriate words to meet individual participants and their learning capacity. Then I'll set forth how to apply this skill in the group context, with particular emphasis on aspects of the teaching process for which it's especially important to find the appropriate words, or sometimes silence.

Tying in with Zone of Proximal Development

One of the basic facts of learning is that there are limits to everyone's learning capacity. These limits fall into a couple of key categories. One is our existing knowledge or experience. As soon as we label something "known," it's moved to the attic of our knowledge for storage, where it remains closed off. Only in very exceptional cases do we open established knowledge back up for new insights or exploration. Sometimes it takes a substantial shock to wake us up and foster the willingness to revisit our truth.

A second category of limitation is the extreme difficulty of opening up to something that lies well beyond our existing structure of knowledge. Learning is basically accommodating new information within that framework, so whenever information doesn't tie in well with the existing framework, we generally aren't able to accommodate it, in which case it simply isn't stored. An example would be the members of primitive and isolated tribes, who were allegedly unable to observe the first aircraft they saw flying over them. They lacked any kind of framework they could fit that observation into and were therefore unable to process the information.

Thus, our capacity for processing new information is limited to a specific area that lies between the known and the boundaries of our existing structure of knowledge. Russian learning psychologist Lev Vygotsky refers to this as *zo-ped*, "the zone of proximal development" (1986, p. xxxv). Everyone's zone of proximal development is different, in part because it depends on previous learning experiences. And even for individuals, this zone is flexible because we constantly take in new information and adjust our existing framework of knowledge to accommodate it. Indeed, for all of us our zone of proximal development is changing in form and boundaries all the time.

This zone reflects participants' level of understanding, if you will. Note that one level isn't better than another. In fact, one level is often indispensable for another, as seen in children's development. Therefore, terms such as "higher" or "deeper" levels of understanding don't constitute a moral judgment; they merely suggest a gradation.

When offering a learning moment, a big part of the art of teaching is to ensure that the information is aligned with the individual's existing level of understanding. If your aim is too low, it will be discarded as "know it already," and if it's too high, the person won't be able to accommodate it. Therefore, you need to offer information differently from one person to the next, and to offer the same information differently during the first session than you will in later sessions.

Also, be aware that information is processed not just by our cognitive system, but by our entire mind-body system. (Perhaps more accurately speaking, our entire mind-body system *is* our cognitive system.) Therefore, you speak not just to a person's mind, but also to that person's heart, deep knowing, and, indeed, every single cell of the body. Each part of this system has the capacity to absorb information and to know. Sometimes people don't understand information (with the mind) but do get it (with the body).

In my opinion, the term that best captures whether information registers is "resonance." This brings in another aspect of offering of information: the time factor. Although body and mind sometimes resonate instantly, there are also occasions when they need time to resonate with information or learning before it can sink in.

The Words of Mindfulness Training

In mindfulness training, words are not used solely to give information. We also use them to convey less concrete things, such as moods or qualities. Of course, they often convey both, as in an instruction such as "Take your time."

A key consideration is that most Westerners who seek mindfulness training aren't interested in underlying psychological principles or contemplative considerations. Like Jon Kabat-Zinn said in a televised interview,[19] "They're suffering. And they are coming because they want to find some relief from their suffering" (Moyers, 1993). Participants want to get rid of their headaches, to reduce work-related stress, to deal with the loss of a loved one, and so on. What would happen if you were to begin by formulating the foundations of mindfulness training in traditional Buddhist terms? Most participants would probably think, *This doesn't relate to my suffering. This isn't going to help me.* The practices might then evoke a lot of resistance, which could cause participants to drop out of the training.

In establishing MBSR, Kabat-Zinn didn't refer to the practice he offered as meditation, nor did he refer to Buddhism or the dhamma. Instead, he described it as a stress reduction and relaxation program: "Stress is something everybody intuitively understands in our society. So calling our program 'stress reduction' might give us direct entry into the realm of working with *dukkha*. It had universal appeal…. The universal response to seeing the signs up in the hospital, among patients, physicians, surgeons, hospital administrators, everybody, is that they invariably think or say "Oh, I could use that'" (Kabat-Zinn, 1999, pp. 228–229).[20] For that same reason, the Dutch mindfulness community adopted the term *aandachttraining* (attention training): more attention—that's what we all want, and there's nothing flaky about it.

One implication of the skillful use of words is that you, as the teacher, can't elucidate mindfulness by simply using the words, descriptions, and information that spontaneously arise for you based on your years of training and practice. You must adjust your language to the level of understanding of the group and confine your explanations to the zone of proximal development of individual participants. This is perfectly legitimate if you bear in mind that this "limited version" of the practices and goals of mindfulness training is also true, or part of the truth, and that you're offering it to participants so they can become familiar with the parts of the practice that are accessible to them—and that you're giving them an opportunity to explore for themselves what's of value to them in the practice.

As an example, it's pointless to talk about the being mode of mind, the value of insight, or awakening with people who haven't personally experienced these things. However, once they've had these experiences, new levels of learning become possible. For instance, participants who only wanted to attain a degree of calmness may discover that there are deeper levels of relaxation. Following that, they may start to distinguish between doing mode and being mode of mind and find a better balance between them. And in time, they may gain insight into their reactivity and patterns in their reactivity, and subsequently become more skillful at seeing these patterns earlier, and in increasingly subtle forms.

These levels of understanding in mindfulness training are depicted in figure 8. The lower levels provide answers to concrete needs, such as temporary stress reduction and relaxation, and the higher levels reflect deep insight into how reactivity works. This figure reflects descriptions of the stages of becoming more conscious or awakened, as gleaned from various contemplative traditions. However, it should be stressed that in the framework of mindfulness training, this figure refers to the levels at which information can be understood, and not to a state of awakening or enlightenment of consciousness, whether permanent or impermanent.

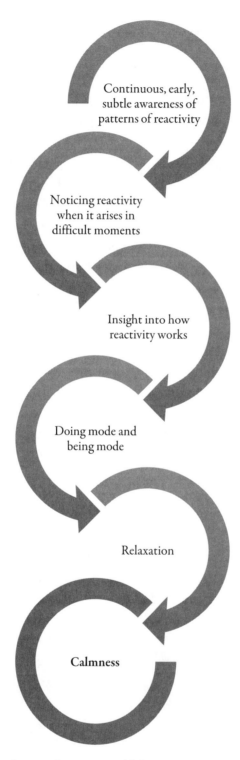

Figure 8. Levels of understanding in mindfulness training.

The Limitations of Words

Mindfulness training involves a lot of language. Through language, we seek to touch upon and illuminate the many dimensions of mindfulness. And beyond speaking to cognitive understanding, we attempt to find words to get through to the body, the heart, deep knowing, and even silence. We also look for words to capture direct experiences, but such words will always fall short. After all, words are merely concepts that cannot fully encapsulate experiences. It's like tasting wine: the experience is always more than what you can describe, even if you were to describe it in one hundred hefty tomes. In the words of scientist-philosopher Michael Polanyi, "We know more than we can tell" (2009, p. 4).

Skillful use of language depends on far more than being clear about one's meaning. It involves a degree of intuition, which, by definition, evades technical description. Although this can make the path obscure, we mindfulness teachers must continue to apply words to the training. This requires what author and meditation teacher Stephen Batchelor describes as taking a plunge "into the treacherous sea of words" (1997, p. 4)—a description that also speaks to the challenges and limitations of using words to teach mindfulness.

That said, the best approach is often to start by putting a toe in to test the water. Start by speaking to participants' initial level of understanding. As they gain more personal experience with practicing mindfulness, you can start broadening your vocabulary and the information you offer. For example, you wouldn't want to start talking about levels of reactivity during session 1, whereas this could be quite appropriate and fruitful during a later session.

The more participants' trust is grounded in their personal experience with mindfulness, the more you can use language to challenge them, push their boundaries, or even intentionally frustrate them. As trust deepens, their receptivity to what you offer will increase. They're likely to have thoughts along the lines of *I don't get this right now, but other instructions and practices in this training have been helpful, so there must be something to this as well.* During follow-up trainings and refresher days, you can crank up the vocabulary and level of discussion even further.

Skillful use of words is also important even before the training begins: in preliminary interviews, your advertising material, and even what you tell people about mindfulness training at social events. Can you explain mindfulness training in such a way as to give novices an idea of what it is, or at least replace initial skepticism with curiousness? It may be helpful to look at these kinds of explanations as a form of "elevator pitch": a marketing tool that challenges you to come up with three brief sentences to use to elicit interest in your service or product. (Three sentences, or approximately thirty seconds, is about all you can fit into the duration of an average elevator ride.) To hone your elevator pitch skills, you can practice on people in your immediate environment, such as family members or neighbors. You can also work on this alone by coming up with concise answers to questions novices commonly ask, like "What does 'mindfulness' mean?" or "How can mindfulness help me with my pain issue?" or "What good will sitting still do when what I want is change?"

Developing Your Vocabulary

Another language skill that benefits from practice is finding the right words. All learning begins with interest and attention, so when teaching, be alert to which words seem to resonate with participants. After sessions, you might even list particular words that were especially effective. This will help you develop more sensitivity to words. As you develop an interest in vocabulary, the most appropriate wordings will tend to arise for you, sometimes even in a visual way. Given that you'll be speaking slowly while guiding meditations, you may have a sense of "tasting" words before you actually pronounce them.

Professional exchanges can also be helpful, as they are in any job environment, especially if you work with coteachers. If you do, give each other feedback on wording after sessions. For example, you might ask which words registered, what they invoked, what reactions they provoked, and whether there were any alternatives.

All of that said, having a flair for language is largely tied to personality, so people simply differ in this regard. If you find the skillful use of words to be a bit challenging, you may be able to compensate with other powerful communication techniques, such as using the right gesture or using silence at the right time and in the right way.

Finding Balance

The right word for one person won't be the right one for another. Skillful language for a scientist will be different from that for a carpenter. Likewise, the right words for an experienced meditator may differ from those for a novice, and those for an impatient person are likely to differ from those for an easygoing person.

While it's good to keep all of this in mind, during inquiry you speak to one person and the entire group simultaneously. On the one hand, if you excessively tailor your words to an individual's learning style or level of understanding, they may not resonate with the group overall. On the other hand, taking an overly general approach may lead to lack of precision in finding the right word that an individual needs in order to learn.

You must also find the right balance in terms of how much information you offer. On the other hand, if you provide too little information or information that's overly tailored to participants' current understanding, they may get bored due to a lack of challenge. After all, learning is about new experiences, new contexts, and pushing beyond boundaries. But on the other hand, providing too much new information can result in the message not getting across. Consider driving instructors: they tend to say as little as possible during the first driving lesson because new drivers are unable to simultaneously perform a number of newly learned actions, watch the road, and also listen to instructions. When people are flooded with new information, they tend to shut down.[21]

Still, it's okay to offer a lot of information and challenge participants' learning ability. This kind of intensity can be good, given the limited duration of the training. Efficiency is, therefore, a necessity.

Also bear in mind that the right words won't always be the most comforting ones. So be it. Again, the trick is to strike a balance, being sufficiently challenging but not going so far that you risk alienating participants. Aim for a presentation that is optimally rich in meaning but not so challenging that it will be off-putting. In this way, you can guide participants through the realm of being consciously aware of their incompetence, offering support where needed and withdrawing it when appropriate.

Another quality to attend to in the skillful use of words is playfulness. Learning requires a context of lightness, variation, and spaciousness. But again, balance is key. Your presentation should be loose enough to invite participants to discover things for themselves and integrate what they learn in the process, but not so loose that the message becomes diffuse and participants get lost.

Utilizing Silence

Insight arises when we are silent. Encompassing, resonating, feeling, processing—it is silence, not talking, that nourishes these experiences. Sometimes it seems as if the quality of inquiry is inversely proportional to the number of words used, and more generally, many teachers notice that the amount of time they spend talking decreases as their competence level rises. When teachers start trusting the process more, their urge to explain diminishes. Plus, the more precise your words become, the fewer of them you'll need. What you say will be exactly what you mean, no more and no less. And as your inner silence increases, your outer silence will also increase. Until this happens, it's good to tune in to and ask yourself about your use of words: Would it be better to say nothing? Can you convey your message with fewer words?

Trusting Whatever Emerges

As a mindfulness teacher, you will be engaged in a continuous process of asking what the moment asks of you. The answer to that question usually doesn't arise from thinking about it. Stay open to other sources of information: intuition, your heart, the silence. It's wise to check the input from these sources against your pragmatic awareness ("Am I holding back?" "Am I going too far?" "Is it fitting for this moment?"), but don't think about it too much. Words from these sources sometimes have a one-sided emphasis, but they are never wrong. After all, they stem from a domain that's beyond correct and incorrect. So trust whatever emerges. There's no need to be overly careful. You'll find out soon enough whether your input was too strict, emotional, intuitive, or profound, and if it was, you can rebalance what you said and learn from the experience. The unacceptable alternative would be to silence authentic sources of knowing for the sake of formal perfection.

Avoiding Unnecessary Resistance

Of course, to facilitate openness in participants, it's generally best to avoid provoking unnecessary resistance. One prime way to engender resistance is to offer opinions or contexts that are unfamiliar to participants. For example, if you were to say, "There's no difference between you and me; we are all one," participants may think, *Not in my view!* Or if you were to say, "I think your soul is processing old karma," a participant may think, *That's bogus. My mother died, and that just hurts.*

Also beware of referring to practices or experiences that lie well outside of participants' frame of reference. For example, if you were to say, "Indians practice yoga close together, in fully packed halls," participants may think, *So? We're in the West, and I want some space.*

Or if you were to say, "During a meditation retreat, you won't get to the stage where you can really align with the practice before the fourth day," participants may think, *Four days?! I have trouble sticking with meditation for thirty minutes.*

Of course, authoritarian statements that disqualify participants' experience will almost always raise their resistance. For example, if you were to say, "First there's a thought, and then comes the emotion; that's how it works," participants may think, *That's not how I'm experiencing it. Am I different, or is this teacher talking nonsense?* Along the same lines, steer clear of expressing your personal beliefs in absolute terms. For example, if you were to say, "Therapy will never give you what you're learning here, participants may think, *Well, therapy actually did me a lot of good, and so far, I think I learned more from therapy than I'm learning here.* The bottom line is that putting forth strong personal opinions can result in participants feeling that their experience is devalued. Fortunately, such remarks aren't required in mindfulness training. So attend to the words you're offering and try to avoid remarks that may provoke resistance.

Making the Most of Technical Language

Mindfulness training involves discussing inner processes. Given that this material isn't very concrete, there's a fairly big risk of getting bogged down in vague language. You can help prevent this by letting technical aspects prevail over emotional content as you formulate your words. For example, instead of asking, "How have you been with that experience?" you might ask, "How did you work with that experience?" The phrase "working with" comes from the domain of labor, and participants will pick up on the connotation: work is something serious, and it entails taking responsibility and making choices. Here are a few other examples of how you might employ more technical language, with the salient word choices appearing in bold font:

The practices from this training give you a **toolbox** *filled with* **tools** *you can use when they suit you or the situation.*

Zoom out *with the attention and cover the full* **radar screen** *of awareness.*

Noting is a **technique** *that allows you to* **label** *your experiences.*

Technical formulations add weight and a quality of concreteness to the topic at hand. However, do be aware that this kind of technical language is metaphorical, and metaphors lose their effectiveness when you take them too far. If you do, your descriptions of mindfulness processes could become mechanical.

Of course, sometimes you'll need or want to discuss emotions. This often entails using vague language. Unlike thoughts, emotions are difficult to capture in words. So be sure that other elements of your language are as precise as possible. When talking about emotions, steer clear of words like "some," "a bit," or "somewhat." And when asking about emotions, try to be as concrete and technical as possible. For example, instead of asking, "What does that do to you?" ask, "What emotion does that invoke?" Or instead of asking, "How do you feel?" ask, "Can you describe what feeling is in the foreground?"

Steering Clear of Veiled Language

Dutch writer and linguist Paulien Cornelisse is convinced that we create more confusion than clarity through the language we use. That may sound like a bold statement, but the fact of the matter is that we often express ourselves unclearly, especially when we try to use words to mask something, such as difficult emotions, insecurity, or a sense of incompetence. This kind of veiled language may be useful in politics or diplomacy, but in the training it undermines authenticity and isn't helpful for practicing mindfulness. Yet we aren't always aware of our evasive maneuvers, so in the sections that follow, I'll outline several types of veiled language, in some cases drawing a bit on Cornelisse's work (2009, 2012).

PUTTING THINGS INTO PERSPECTIVE TOO MUCH

Objectivity is important. However, if you typically use phrases such as "On the one hand X, but on the other hand Y" or "There are different sides to the story," you'll leave participants hanging in a disoriented state between the different perspectives. True, this kind of language is accurate in many situations, but do try to create clarity whenever you can. It's okay to state a preference or emphasize a perspective that's salient in the moment. Plus, not everything in this world is relative. In short, dare to give clear answers. Too much nuance leads to ambiguity.

STANDARD ANSWERS

Needless to say, you will develop a sizable arsenal of standard answers, and sometimes they may be helpful for preventing the kind of ambiguity just discussed.

Do be careful, however, that you don't overly rely on them. For example, as teachers leading inquiry, we almost always find participants' answers interesting; we're even interested in comments about something being boring. But if you reply to every shared experience with "Interesting," you'll soon cease to be credible. Plus, that kind of the repetition can have a sleep-inducing effect.

Another potential danger of relying excessively on standard answers is that they can become fillers that you turn to when nothing else occurs to you. Here are some examples:

Good question [said when it's crystal clear that the question is inappropriate in the situation].

Funny you should say that [said in response to something that's not at all funny or timely].

Okay [said while you're experiencing a negative reaction to what the person has just said].

The bottom line is that it's better to say nothing at all than to say something that doesn't resonate with the situation.

PLATITUDES

Platitudes often block the dynamic of a conversation. So while you may feel that you're expressing empathy with "I hear what you're saying," if you use that statement automatically, it serves as a platitude. Then it's likely that nobody, you included, will know what to say next.

RHETORICAL QUESTIONS

Using rhetorical questions has the drawback of departing from an unspoken consensus or shared insight. If participants don't identify with what the question casts as a common truth, they'll feel shut out or may put up some resistance. For example, if you ask the rhetorical question, "We don't like to be stressed, do we?" a participant may think, *Well, I like the adrenaline rush when I have a deadline.* Another danger of using rhetorical questions is that they can create distance. To paraphrase Cornelisse (2009), a question to which an answer is not wanted implies that the speaker always knows best.

Emphasizing Common Humanity by Using "We"

Do you tend to address groups as "you," or do you use "we"? Although the roles of teacher and participant are distinct, the most important element of the training is shared: we are all seeking insight into our unwholesome patterns. Referring to that common denominator with "we" creates a sense of solidarity, whereas using "you" creates dualism: I, the teacher, and you, the group. By using "you," you place yourself outside the group, perhaps even suggesting, *I am the one who knows, and you are the ones who don't.* This isn't helpful in fostering participants' sense that they are each the expert on their own experience. It also undermines the key message that we are all in the same boat. So, whenever it sounds natural, use "we." This pronoun is inclusive, establishing that everyone is in this together and on a journey as group. Here are a couple of examples:

Last week, we practiced the body scan at home.

It seems as if we find it harder to settle on our breathing when there's a sense of insecurity.

That said, using "we" won't always be natural or logical when working with groups with a specific focus. For example, if you're working with a group of cancer patients and don't have cancer yourself, it wouldn't make sense to use "we" when talking about cancer-related subjects. The same goes for groups who share a certain characteristic, such as profession or age, that you don't have. But even in those cases, you can often avoid using "you" by offering more neutral language. For example, instead of saying, "Because you're just starting chemo treatment, you're finding it hard to focus your attention," you could simply say, "At the start of chemo, it can be hard to focus attention."

Continuous Learning

It's not hard to get some satisfaction from mindfulness training. Doing a bit of meditation, receiving some attention from the teacher, gaining some understanding of current challenges—these are experiences that give participants a sense of well-being. When you've developed some ease in guiding participants through the practices and they seem to be satisfied, you may say to yourself, *I've got the hang of this.* This could lead you to be satisfied too and adopt a stance of "steady as she goes."

But is such satisfaction your ultimate goal, or do you aim higher? Do you want to offer participants insights that might lead to permanent changes—indeed, to transformation? And when could you say you have achieved *that* ambition? In other words, what are the limits of the potential learning, change, and transformation among participants? And how about the limits in developing your own potential as a teacher? Ideally, this work will offer you a continuous invitation to develop your competencies, and to further your own mindfulness practice, allowing you to avoid routine, blind spots, and other pitfalls.

The thought *I've got the hang of this* is dangerous. If you believe it, you've fallen asleep. In the sections that follow, I'll outline some of the avenues to continuous learning, which will naturally lead to the ongoing development of competency.

The Systematic Development of the Smart Subconscious

Like skills, competencies are developed systematically. American Zen teacher Cheri Huber has captured this well in a passage I've translated from the Dutch edition of her book *The Key*: "Someone who wants to call themselves a tennis player will borrow a racket and a couple of balls and hit some balls somewhere. Someone who really wants to play tennis will buy a racket, take lessons, and play whenever they have time. Someone who wants to play tennis well will find a teacher, take lessons, practice, and play regularly. Someone who wants to be a professional tennis player will find a teacher, soak up every kind of advice they can get, practice all the time, and devote their life to training" (2000, p. 136).

When you see tennis players in a major tournament, their game is likely to seem effortless, apart from the physical exertion. The same goes for an actor's performance. Experts make their trade seem simple—until we try it ourselves and end up looking like fools. Frustrated, people often conclude that the master has been gifted with an exceptional talent that they don't possess. It's hard to do what experts do, and it is especially difficult to do so effortlessly.

American investigative journalist Malcolm Gladwell addressed this in his book on expertise, *Blink* (2005). In it, he provides numerous examples of professionals with weird, wonderful, and highly developed skills. To stick with the tennis metaphor, the subject of one vignette is Vic Braden, a top coach who spent his life coaching and training tennis players. Simply by observing a player's serve—or more precisely, the player's movements prior to hitting the ball—he could tell whether the serve would be good. Another expert could tell with the same level of certainty and in the blink of an eye whether a supposedly ancient statue was a fake, even though he wasn't able to substantiate his intuition with a rational explanation. In both cases, these experts' information processing was so complex, fast, and subtle that they couldn't consciously track it. They were unable to explain their intuition and were even inclined not to trust it, even though their intuitions were ultimately proven correct in most cases.

So sometimes experts simply don't know why they do what they do; they "just know." It's almost as if a higher force takes over. We often refer to this type of elusive knowing as talent. Neuroscientists, however, point to a different explanation.

In his highly acclaimed book *Het slimme onbewuste* (The smart subconscious), Dutch psychologist Ap Dijksterhuis (2008) points out that the majority of our mental processes, including the processing and association of information, happen subconsciously at times when the brain isn't consciously engaged in a task. Furthermore, he states that the processing capacity of the subconscious mind is about two hundred times greater than that of the conscious mind. You've probably experienced this yourself. Perhaps a creative solution to a problem suddenly popped into your mind, or a name you thought you had forgotten surfaced later, when you weren't actively thinking about it.

Due to their vast experience, experts have a subconscious source of wisdom regarding their profession, and they are able to draw on that source. Their huge experience gives experts a smart subconscious—and the confidence to let themselves be led by that subconscious, even when their conscious mind can't keep up. Therefore, their performance or brilliance has qualities of playfulness, simplicity, and elegance, both for observers and for themselves.

This is particularly salient in mindfulness training, given the importance of embodiment and teaching from the moment. Mindfulness training sets great store by intuitive teaching. Whatever emerges in the moment does, however, depend on the expertise the teacher brings to that moment. In the absence of expertise, teaching from the moment doesn't amount to much more than doing whatever pops into your head, with the attendant risks of personal pitfalls, blind spots, or automaticity.

The Ten-Thousand-Hour Rule

Dutch neuroscientist Margriet Sitskoorn (2008) says that excellence, the stage beyond expertise, requires, apart from a teaspoon of talent and a pinch of intelligence, hours upon hours of practice. To reach the highest level in any field of expertise, a person needs to train for four hours per day, five days per week, for ten years. This is sometimes referred to as the ten-thousand-hour rule, as popularized in Malcom Gladwell's book *Outliers* (2008), based on research by Anders Ericsson (Ericsson, Krampe, & Tesch-Römer, 1990). This level of practice establishes sufficiently precise and reliable neural patterns to confer mastery. That said, it's important to note that Ericsson himself has emphasized that "you don't get benefits from mechanical repetition, but by adjusting your execution over and over to get closer to your goal" (Goleman, 2013, p. 163).

Ultimately, developing this level of expertise depends on many forms of practice: Tennis players don't hone their skills only through fitness training and playing matches. They also watch others play, train by hitting a ball against a wall, talk about tennis with coaches and peers, and generally practice and immerse themselves in tennis so intensively that they even dream about it at night. As a mindfulness teacher, you can also supplement the practice provided by teaching and day-to-day meditation with various kinds of learning experiences: going on a retreat, working with different groups and coteachers, trying out new practices, attending workshops, recording guided meditation audio tracks, writing scripts for practices, sharing experiences with colleagues, reading the literature, and so on.

As you become more experienced, your competency will grow and you'll reap the benefits of your own smart subconscious. You will develop a kind of intelligence that feeds into your work. It may manifest as a voice in the background, a response that just pops into your head, or a feeling of just knowing what people feel or need.

Navigating Based on Intuitive Knowing

As discussed, you can't explain the smart subconscious. It's a feeling of just knowing. Because you probably can't capture it in words, you may simply "see" it, as though it's almost tangible. It's common for intuitive knowing to be experienced through the senses, like musicians who can hear the music when reading the score. Navigating based on intuitive knowing feels like working in perfect harmony with the situation, as if you've become one with the situation. You've entered a flow state. It's not that your knowledge and skills have disappeared; rather, they're directed by a knowing that emerges from a deeper source. UK mindfulness teacher and researcher Rebecca Crane describes advanced teaching (at the level of excellence) in terms of "deep tacit understanding" (Crane et al., 2011, p. 81). In her view, as set forth in a PowerPoint presentation, at this level "teaching skill is part of the person—fluidity/immersion in process" (2010).

Another reason to work with intuitive knowing is that it requires trust in whatever emerges, and therefore an open mind to one's experience in the present moment. Gladwell (2005) draws a parallel with improvisational theater: it often comes across as very smooth, as though it were rehearsed. Improvisational actors develop their expertise by putting themselves in such situations frequently. As they come to trust their expertise, they can open themselves up to their here-and-now experience. Then, no matter what the audience or other actors offer up, they can instantly accept and work with it, listening to whatever their smart subconscious produces in response and acting upon it. In a similar way, as a mindfulness teacher you can work with whatever arises (without expectations) rather than what you think should happen (according to expectations).

However, there are certain dangers inherent in navigating based on intuitive knowing. Although such knowing originates from a source of wisdom, it's possible to follow intuitions arising from other sources. Time is one crucial factor in determining which source we choose. According to Gladwell (2005), it takes several seconds for intuitive knowing to surface from the source of expertise; therefore, it's likely that immediate reactions emerging from impulsiveness (an entirely different source) will show up first.

Calibrating Your Intuitive Compass

Another issue is that the source of intuitive knowing isn't always available. For example, stress may block access to wisdom because it favors habitual and trusted survival-oriented reactions. Conversely, being too relaxed is also less than ideal as, in this case, we may tend to fall back on our usual repertoire because we're insufficiently alert to be tuned in to the whispering voice of intuitive knowing. In contrast, operating from the being mode of mind allows us to strike the right balance between being sufficiently relaxed yet still present and clear.

When accessing intuitive knowing, check in with your pragmatic consciousness: Is whatever emerges indeed wise and appropriate for the moment? Yet even this check-in should be done instinctively, not analytically. Otherwise, you run the risk of what Gladwell refers to as "paralysis through analysis" (2005, p. 119). Also check in again afterward to determine whether your response suited the situation. When intuition is your compass, this kind of checking in constitutes calibration of that compass, ensuring that you express your smart subconscious with the right voice and at the right time and place.

When first starting to offer mindfulness training, teachers will necessarily rely mainly on knowledge and rehearsal. With time and the gradual development of skills, it becomes less necessary to think, and offering the training becomes easier and easier, even automatic. Yet this too is an intermediate stage. Only by opening yourself up to continuous learning can you develop the intuitive knowing that allows you to see what the situation requires you to do—which may be quite different from what your well-honed skills might drive you to do. You may feel as though you have access to a higher level of creativity and wisdom than you inherently possess. At this stage, you are truly teaching from the moment.

Resources for Continuous Learning

Your development as a teacher is closely linked to the effort and intention you invest in mindfulness training—not just the number of hours you spend teaching, but also the time you invest in deepening your own practice and engaging in ongoing learning. In the following sections, I'll outline many avenues for pursuing such learning.

Practice

Your qualities and proficiency as a teacher all begin with your own personal mindfulness practice. This means meditating on a daily basis. Some teachers do the same practices as their participants during a training, an approach that's particularly advisable for beginning and intermediate teachers. Participating in at least one retreat per year is also a good idea. It's best to plan ahead and make reservations. That way, you'll always know when your next retreat will be, whether next week or next year.

Personal practice and retreats are crucial in order to embody the teaching, but everyday mindful awareness is also important in this regard. Even if you meditate for an hour every day, what about the other twenty-three hours? Do you practice mindfulness in your daily life, or do you use your daily meditation session in an attempt to compensate for spending the rest of your time running around mindlessly? Kabat-Zinn underscores how important it is for trainers to make mindfulness part of their everyday life: "While participating in periodic long retreats may be necessary and extremely important for one's own development and understanding, by itself it is not sufficient. Mindfulness in everyday life is the ultimate challenge and practice" (2011, p. 296).

Reflection

Clearly, simply racking up hours of practice is not enough. When a group session is over and you move on to the next task, the meaningful occurrences that inevitably arise during sessions will soon fade into the background and eventually disappear from your memory. No one will be inconvenienced if you forget these experiences, yourself included. You probably won't feel that anything is missing during the next session. However, if you don't reflect on these experiences, after a while you're likely to notice that you aren't developing. You can still be a very productive teacher, but without reflection you won't be learning and growing. Your teaching will remain stuck at a certain level as you continue to reel off your program in essentially the same way time and time again.

There are a number of simple resources that can support you in engaging in reflection. One is taking the time to look back on sessions and also to look ahead to upcoming sessions. There are many ways of doing this. Some teachers find it helpful to quickly review their sessions immediately afterward, whereas others prefer to do so later at home. Some reflect on their own, and others engage in dialogue with a colleague or friend afterward. You can also keep a log of meaningful occurrences or make audio or video recordings of sessions and review them later.

Bear in mind that *reflection* means contemplating meaningful occurrences, not solving problems. The process of reflecting on such moments and considering their various facets is enough to feed the learning process. Reflection will nourish the smart subconscious so that, with time, you'll notice that your teaching is developing on its own.

Teacher Training

Being a mindfulness teacher is a serious professional commitment and challenge, so it calls for serious training and development. Presenting the themes of the training and engaging in the techniques described in this book (guiding practices, conducting inquiry, and offering didactic presentations) require a number of special competencies and skills that are specific to the context of mindfulness and therefore can't truly be learned via any other professional or educational route.

My observations indicate that most experts recommend at least 150 to 200 hours of specific mindfulness teacher training before teaching independently. These days, mindfulness teacher training courses are available in most Western countries. They generally require live attendance, although a few programs do make use of online or electronic media.

Peer Consultation

Peer consultation can deepen your practice experience; in fact, some people view it as necessary to development. It allows you to put the spotlight on something and then briefly stop the clock to engage in a detailed exploration. It also gives you access to colleagues' expertise, which can help you bring insights into better focus.

Appropriate subjects for peer consultation include situations where you feel that things didn't go as your senses or reason suggested they should—situations that seemed grating in some way. During peer consultation, you can reinvoke the situation, vividly and in detail, preferably by watching a video recording of it. Then your peers can look at what may have led to that grating feeling or unexpected turn of events. This can illuminate which parts of the situation you may have overlooked and what other options you might have had. I recommend setting an agenda prior to launching into peer consultation, establishing topics and speaking times. This will prevent the process from turning into a collegial chat, which could be pleasant but won't satisfy your needs in terms of learning. On the Internet, you'll find a great deal of accessible information on peer-to-peer learning, as well as basic rules for providing productive feedback to peers.

Peer consultation isn't always comfortable, given that it focuses on your learning gaps, limitations, and blind spots. But the same principles apply here as in the mindfulness training you offer: the less comfortable the situation, the greater the learning opportunity.

Supervision

Supervisors can bring their experience and expertise to bear on helping you reflect on aspects of your teaching that you're working on. Compared to peer consultation, supervision generally puts work experiences in a larger framework, focusing less on techniques and skills and more on how personal qualities color your teaching. As a result, supervision can also be uncomfortable. Whereas you may want to solve a specific problem, your supervisor could point to an underlying pattern, putting you in the thick of it, with the solution you were seeking seeming to be even further away.

Choose a supervisor who's skilled in both supervision and mindfulness training, who you trust, and who you click with. The frequency of your meetings need not be high, but do try to maintain some continuity. This includes sticking with the same supervisor for a while so that certain themes develop over a longer period

THE MINDFULNESS TEACHING GUIDE

of time. Also, always be well prepared for supervision sessions. Your supervisor is making time for you, and it's up to you to make the most of that time by zeroing in on the issues that are currently most relevant to your teaching.

Creating Experimental Teaching Settings

An experimental teaching setting can be as instructive as an actual session. During teacher training, people often practice in groups of three or four peers, with a five-minute practice often offering enough material for up to thirty minutes of evaluation. Each person offers reflections and insights based in personal experience. To create these kinds of learning opportunities, you need nothing more than the discipline to organize the setting—getting together, choosing an exercise, and assigning roles.

Another option is to create a more informal experimental practice setting, such as with friends, with your partner or children, or with supportive acquaintances or work colleagues. For that matter, even just practicing guiding a meditation out loud on your own provides practical experience and will help you with articulation and finding the right tone of voice.

Coteaching

Like experimental settings, coteaching creates a learning environment for teachers and is a highly effective way of deepening your skills. In addition, working with a coteacher provides support and can allow you to experiment more freely, since you'll know that your coteacher can provide some balance when necessary. And when your coteacher is conducting the training, you can take a step back and observe the process from a metalevel. Perhaps the most important benefit of coteaching is that, after a session, the two of you can reflect on the session as professionals. This makes feedback from a coteacher uniquely valuable.

All of that said, there are also downsides to coteaching. It isn't conducive to your own development, or that of participants, to always work with a coteacher, particularly with the same coteacher time and again. I've devoted the rest of this section to setting forth the pros and cons of working with a coteacher—both for participants and for the teacher. As you'll see, most pros are counterbalanced by a related con, or downside, whereas others stand alone. Also, be aware that despite the downsides, the bottom line is that it's advisable to regularly team up with another teacher, especially those who are just beginning to offer mindfulness training.

Pros and Cons of Coteaching for Participants

Pro: Coteaching offers participants more opportunities to model themselves after or be inspired by a teacher.

Con: Because coteachers will have different styles, group members may be tempted to turn away from a teacher who isn't so easy to relate to, even though that teacher may offer a very instructive and valuable model.

Pro: Coteachers' distinct teaching styles can appeal to a broader range of learning styles.

Con: Coteachers' differences in style or vision may not always harmonize, leading to unrest and confusion in the group. Alternatively, as coteachers navigate the differences between their teaching styles, they may settle on an average that's mediocre and less distinct and compelling.

Pro: Coteachers can present a united front, establishing a clear (and therefore safe) division between themselves and the participants.

Con: This sense of a united front creates distance between participants on one side and teachers on the other side, making it harder for participants to be inspired by a teacher's human side and embodiment of mindfulness.

Pro: Coteachers have more knowledge and experience to draw on, spread over more fields of expertise.

Con: There is no downside to this!

Pro: In the event that one of the teachers experiences a difficulty that interferes with the schedule, such as an illness, participants are guaranteed continuity of the program.

Con: There is no downside to this!

Pros and Cons of Coteaching for Teachers

Pro: You have backup to compensate for your weak spots.

Con: Having a coteacher cover your weak spots can stifle your development in those areas.

Pro: Preparing together allows coteachers to be more effective in devising the curriculum and anticipating the needs of participants.

Con: Preparing by yourself allows you to use your own approach (for example, meditating in advance), making it easier to be more in tune with yourself when you start the session.

Pro: You may be more aware and alert due to the presence of a coteacher.

Con: You may be less spontaneous due to the presence of a coteacher.

Pro: It can be more fun to teach together.

Con: It can be more fun to teach on your own.

Pro: You can get immediate feedback and evaluation due to your shared experience. This direct evaluation can illuminate patterns in your work that may otherwise go unnoticed.

Con: There is no downside to this!

Pro: Your blind spots can be illuminated by your coteacher.

Con: There is no downside to this!

Pro: You can learn from watching the other teach the same program with a different style.

Con: There is no downside to this!

Pro: You have backup in case of emergencies, such as illness or a participant suddenly leaving the class.

Con: There is no downside to this!

Pro: Giving the training with two teachers means less workload.

Con: Giving the training with two teachers means more work hours in total, which means less income per hour.

Study

Although experiential learning comes first, just as it does in mindfulness training, study can also play an important role in your development as a teacher. In fact, this has long been recognized in the East, where contemplative studies are as highly esteemed as contemplative practice. Keeping up with the literature in the field of mindfulness is also crucial, given that this field is currently in an ongoing state of flux.

Beyond the professional literature, you can find a host of other resources that approach mindfulness from a more spiritual angle. These can provide inspiration and other important input, along with poems, metaphors, and other materials that you can weave into your training.

Depending on the program through which you received your teacher training, it may offer opportunities for further study, such as refresher days, seminars with experts in the field, conferences, and workshops. You can also seek out study opportunities in related fields, such as Buddhist psychology, and take advantage of any courses that might deepen your understanding of mindfulness. In short, there is no excuse to stop learning. Plus, taking a course offers you the opportunity to open up to new perspectives, including that of being a student again, rather than a teacher. This reminds you that you're still learning, just like everybody else.

Acknowledgments

The great, exalted, boundless thought of amity that is free of hate or malice.

—Buddha

It may be that when we no longer know what to do we have come to our real work and that when we no longer know which way to go we have begun our real journey.

—Wendell Berry

MBSR mindfulness training was developed by one man, Jon Kabat-Zinn, who chose as his life's work to make it available to anyone who showed an interest. There are few contemporary individuals who have made such a huge difference in how we view our health and well-being as Jon has. I am enormously grateful to him for his dedication. My gratitude also goes out to Mark Williams because he is (apart from being an eminent social scientist) a true teacher who has tirelessly spread his expertise. Jotika Hermsen, Frits Koster, and Joost van den Heuvel-Rijnders taught me vipassana meditation and how to bring its fruits to daily life. The students of Ramana Sri Maharshi and H. W. L. Poonja enlightened me on the perspective of a life and a world without dualism.

Closer to home, I am grateful to Joke Hellemans, Johan Tinge, and Johan's team of teachers. They set up the first mindfulness teacher training in the Netherlands, which was so significant in shaping me in my early years as a mindfulness teacher.

I'm grateful to my fellow cofounders of the Centrum voor Mindfulness in Amsterdam, Wibo Koole and George Langenberg, for the adventure of contributing to the creation of an organization that has a mission of spreading mindfulness to all parts of society. And finally, still closer to home, I am grateful for Erna, my muse. Thank you for finding me.

Buddhists take refuge in the three jewels: dhamma, Buddha, and sangha. These are basically one: Dhamma stands for the development of self-awareness, with its healing power; it is a potential that we receive by the grace of our existence (more prosaically, via evolution), and it's been discovered and rediscovered for thousands of years. Buddha stands for the transmission of the dhamma through teachers, starting with the historic Gautama. Sangha stands for the group any of us share the journey with—in my case the people with whom I took my training, went on retreats, sat down for meditation, or studied with; every single mindfulness training group I participated in turned out to be a sangha in its own right. To the extent that there is lived wisdom to be found in this book, I owe it to all of them.

It took me quite some time to compose this book. What was it that kept pushing me to my computer time and time again throughout the process, drawing the words from me? It may sound odd, but it feels as if this "I" had very little to do with it; rather, it felt more like a creative force was flowing through me, moving my hands, thinking, and mind, and that all "I" had to do was to stay out of its way. It often seemed as though, at the right moment, the appropriate example from practice popped into my head. I always seemed to run into the right person at the right moment, and to stumble on the right resources exactly when I needed them. Even a bout of flu seemed to be preprogrammed, coming at a time when I really needed to take a step back from writing. Slowly but surely, I learned to trust this self-creating force, to enjoy its grace, and even to marvel at it as if it were a flower bud bursting into bloom.

Writing this book was a lot of fun. It also gave me something far greater than fun: a sense of connection with a creative intelligence that took charge of the process. I don't know who to thank for that.

> This is love: to fly toward a secret sky,
> to cause a hundred veils to fall each moment.
>
> First, to let go of life.
>
> In the end, to take a step without feet.
>
> —Rumi

Criteria for Professional Mindfulness Teachers

As discussed at the end of chapter 6, being a professional teacher requires continuous learning and ongoing development of one's expertise, a process that's enhanced by communicating with peers and exchanging feedback. In addition, certain competencies are essential, and it would be good if these were both standardized and verifiable. A profession needs professional criteria, along with professional networks or associations. This appendix takes a brief look at the current debate on criteria for expertise and competencies and how to measure and certify these. Given that teaching mindfulness as a profession is under development, so too is this debate.

Expertise and Competencies

In the development of any new field, including mindfulness training, the supporting science goes through a number of phases, from a descriptive phase to the measurement of effects and then to understanding the mechanisms behind these effects. Following this trajectory, early Western mindfulness teachers learned mainly by observing and listening to their teachers and then just diving in (see, for example, chapter 4 in Segal, Williams, & Teasdale, 2002). However, formal teacher training courses soon arose, taking root at the University of Massachusetts Medical Center in the 1990s, and completing a formal training soon became a requirement for teaching many programs. Starting in 2008, Rebecca Crane and others worked toward developing an instrument to assess teachers' competencies, and in 2012, after intensive collaboration between mindfulness experts in the United States, the United Kingdom, and the Netherlands, this culminated in publication of *The Bangor, Exeter, and Oxford Mindfulness-Based Interventions Teaching Assessment Criteria* (MBI-TAC; Crane et al., 2012), a document describing mindfulness teaching competencies in six domains (p. 3):

- Coverage, pacing, and organization of the session-by-session curriculum

- Relational skills

- Embodiment of mindfulness

- Guiding mindfulness practices

- Conveying course themes through interactive inquiry and didactic teaching

- Facilitating the group learning environment

These domains have been parsed into key behavioral features. For example, domain 1, coverage, pacing, and organization of the session-by-session curriculum, is defined in terms of sticking to the form, schedule, and themes of the program; offering the curriculum in a responsive and flexible way; adapting the curriculum to the group's learning ability; being organized as a teacher, including organizing the space and materials; and offering sessions that flow naturally and are appropriately paced. Mindfulness teachers can then be assessed based on the degree to which these features are present in their training and rated on a six-point scale, ranging from incompetent to advanced.

Together, assessments in each of the six domains paint an overall picture. Importantly, in this view, one competency cannot compensate for another. In other words, inability to properly organize a session will always be a problem, even if a teacher excels in the embodiment of mindfulness, for example. Likewise, proceeding sequentially through a perfect curriculum can't make up for a lack of embodiment.

Development of this competency assessment tool has helped mindfulness teaching reach a new level, with teachers being assessed based on their observable behavior. This tool allows our profession to communicate about expertise and competencies, to give and receive somewhat standardized feedback, and to gain insight about areas where individual teachers could benefit from further development. Such assessment is important for ensuring the integrity of the training and comparing trainings for research purposes. However, it is even more important for the development of teachers' skills, allowing for an overview of both strengths and weak points.

Assessment requires teachers to submit their trainings for review, typically through video recordings. Showing one's work to peers is usually somewhat daunting, but it's a standard means of obtaining professional feedback. Also bear in mind that, ideally, feedback is not about judging, but about promoting learning.

The Certification Debate

In the field of mindfulness teaching, there's an ongoing debate regarding whether certification for mindfulness teachers is appropriate. Of the two sides in this debate, one (the "inclusives") maintains that mindfulness is transmitted through intention and commitment, and that this cannot be captured in rules, so no one can be excluded. In other words, mindfulness training that is rooted in rules becomes heartless. The other side (the "exclusives") argues that mindfulness teaching is a profession that, like any other, requires skills and competencies that don't just arise out of the blue. In general, it's possible to verify competencies, or at least the effort devoted to acquiring them. Basically, the latter group maintains that not just anyone can be a mindfulness teacher.

As teachers, we follow our vocation to teach people mindfulness, which essentially means facilitating people in examining how they relate to themselves and how this translates to the way in which they live their lives. Yet we teachers are ourselves restricted by our blind spots and conditioning. So at a minimum, we need to be aware of our own reactivity and work with it skillfully. Good intentions and a full heart alone are necessary, but they aren't necessarily enough.

One implication of the inclusive viewpoint is that participants who want to take mindfulness training will have to find their own way within a more expansive and therefore more confusing market. In the absence of objective criteria, potential participants have nothing to go by in choosing among the many options. Can we realistically expect this of people who don't yet have a well-developed understanding of mindfulness?

In contrast, the exclusive viewpoint maintains that potential participants can benefit from appraising teachers based on their educational background and experience. So why not set forth specific requirements and competencies? As a teacher, surely you will have taken mindfulness training yourself, gone on a retreat, devoted a considerable number of hours to personal practice, and enjoyed numerous days of teacher training. These could serve as the basics of competence; after all, this isn't rocket science.

Yet this is also the Achilles' heel of the exclusive argument, because in reality mindfulness teachers come from many different backgrounds in terms of both experience and education. What provides enough training for one person may prove a poor basis for someone coming from a different background. Furthermore, documenting and providing details on qualifications requires an organization, with its attendant employees, rules, and membership fees, which could become an institutional power that people turn to for protection, including certified teachers who want to make their position even more exclusive. This could lead to dualism between certified and noncertified trainings, giving rise to politics and power plays.

Ultimately, certification tends to become much more than a pragmatic indicator of quality; it opens up a gap between the certified and the noncertified—a gap that can seem so wide that well-intentioned aspiring teachers lose heart and give up, or perhaps start developing their own niche style without interacting with peers. Meanwhile, others may get fixated on obtaining a certificate and lose their heart in another way. In both cases, the gap between the certified and noncertified could lead to inertia, rather than elevating the level of mindfulness teaching.

Finally, certification suggests attaining an ultimate goal, rather than engaging in continuous learning. In all of these ways (and more), certification could lead to stagnation and polarization. It could shift the focus to rules, paperwork, and protocols and set specific techniques, moving teachers away from some of the primary qualities of being a good teacher, including openness.

The difficulty, and at the same time the beauty, of this conundrum is that both the inclusive and exclusive viewpoints are right—and the problems associated with both approaches are also undeniable. The dilemma of dilution (watering down standards so that almost anyone can be a mindfulness teacher) versus polarization (casting certified versus uncertified) is undeniable.

And all of that said, the drive toward certification seems unstoppable, simply because every professional group that takes itself seriously has criteria for their profession. This is reasonable; people are entitled to the somewhat objective overview that certification provides in any field—not just potential clients, but also peers in related fields, companies, institutions, and policymakers who want to work with mindfulness trainers.

In addition, the need for professional ethical standards is growing in tandem with the expansion and increasing position of mindfulness training. For many teachers, mindfulness training is supplemental to another profession, an added specialization. If this is the case for you, your professional code can serve as the primary code governing your work as a mindfulness teacher. For others, however, teaching mindfulness has become a primary occupation. For these teachers especially, a professional ethical code specific to offering mindfulness training is needed. This supports the arguments for identifying good practices and certifying providers.

The ultimate question is how you, as an individual teacher, can find your way through this dilemma. I recommend that you use your heart as your compass. Letting rules and form dominate could cause you to lose your passion about the training and enjoyment of it. If that happens, teaching mindfulness will be your occupation, rather than your vocation. Teaching mindfulness requires that you trust the passion that drives you while also keeping an eye on what's needed to maintain the quality of your work.

Endnotes

1. One exception is *Teaching Mindfulness: A Practical Guide for Clinicians and Educators* (McCown, Reibel, & Micozzi, 2010). In some of his books and articles, Jon Kabat-Zinn, who has written prolifically on mindfulness, has devoted sections to certain aspects of teaching mindfulness (2003, 2005, 2010, 2011). The people who developed mindfulness-based cognitive therapy also focused on the subject in their book *Mindfulness-Based Cognitive Therapy for Depression* (Segal, Williams, & Teasdale, 2002). What's remarkable is that there are far more publications about teaching mindfulness skills in settings such as schools than in classic eight-week mindfulness-based stress reduction courses.

2. Like most major insights, this vision appeared in a flash and in full, albeit not out of the blue. For Kabat-Zinn, it was preceded by "pondering for years 'what is my job with a capital J,' my 'karmic assignment' on the planet" (2011, p. 286), and thirteen years of intensive practice of hatha yoga, vipassana meditation, and Zen.

3. In this book, the spellings of Buddhist terms are based on Pali, the language used in the earliest Buddhist writings. So, for example, I use "dhamma" rather than the more familiar "dharma," which is derived from Sanskrit, the lingua franca shortly after the age of the Buddha. The word "dhamma" has several meanings in Buddhist teachings; in this book, it refers to practicing the teachings of the Buddha.

4. Buddhism does have a term for training: *sikkha*. Buddhist teachings distinguish three kinds of *sikkha*: *sila* (moral discipline), *samadhi* (concentration), and *panna* (wisdom). And the Buddha himself is often referred to as the great (or true) teacher of humanity.

5. The Western training model is used for pragmatic reasons, not because it is thought to be the best way of developing insight and practicing dhamma. In

fact, many people believe that traditional forms of practicing vipassana or Zen are superior. However, these approaches require a considerable amount of time and devotion, along with a teacher steeped in the tradition. Ultimately, it's difficult to offer such approaches in a Western environment, in part because doing so requires a degree of surrender to the teacher.

6. The model of the forces at play in the learning moment—the dynamic interaction between personal attributes, setting, and methods—is based on Timothy Leary's research into the effects psychoactive substances have on humans (1966). Leary discovered that a drug's effect is determined not only by its chemical composition (the substance, analogous to the method in this model of learning), but also by personal attributes (which he referred to as "set") and the context within which the drug was taken (setting). While lecturing at Harvard University, Leary ran his controversial Harvard Psilocybin Project. Leary worked closely together with Richard Alpert, who would later change his name to Ram Dass and become a trailblazer for bringing interest in Eastern practices to the United States.

7. At the Center for Mindfulness in Medicine, Health Care, and Society, in 2001 individual preprogram interviews were replaced by two-hour group orientation sessions. However, individual interviews are still conducted via telephone conversations between the teacher and prospective candidates: one prior to the orientation, and another after the group orientation for candidates who choose to enroll (Santorelli, 2014, p. 5).

8. Psychodrama is a form of group-based and active psychodynamic therapy developed by Jacob Moreno (1953; see also Sternberg & Garcia, 2000). In sociodrama, these techniques are used in professional development processes, such as in teams or organizations. Here, they focus not only on mapping relationships and establishing connections, but also on achieving more insight into relationships, including their obstacles and opportunities, in order to explore possibilities for alternative solutions. These methods derive their efficacy from the fact that their use of physical space (described in the next paragraph) allows for an alternative and often deeper exploration of a subject than would be possible within the verbal or mental dimension. Refer to, among other sources, http://www.psychodrama.org.uk/what_is_sociodrama.php and http://www.sociodrama.co.uk.

In the context of mindfulness training, action methods work best when they are applied to subjects that aren't emotionally charged. You could, for example, start by asking group members to arrange themselves according to height, the distance they had to travel to get to the class, or where everybody is from. These tasks create a context for participants to make contact and physically move in relation to each other. They also arrange the group, creating a spatial expression of relationships among group members and giving them a sense of belonging. Arranging themselves in these ways involves lots of nonverbal information about individual participants and group dynamics. Such tasks need not take long. After you give the instruction, participants will take a few moments to move through the space. Then you can move on to exchanging information about why everyone is standing where they are and then proceed to whatever is next on the agenda.

9. In *Teach Us to Sit Still* (2011, p. 235), Tim Parks offers a telling observation about attitude during the body scan (referring to a body scan from a vipassana tradition):

    And this is not the movement of the schoolboy's eye over diagrams of anatomy. It is not the movement of looking. Rather it is like a man wandering through the rooms of a house, in the dark, knocking on this door and that, perhaps after a long absence, checking if anyone is home, if anyone wants to talk, or gripe, or rejoice, or simply turn on a light for him

    For a while perhaps, there will be no response. The doors are closed, perhaps locked. You must be patient. Nobody has passed this way for some time, and it would be impolite of you to start rattling the handles. This is not a police raid.

10. There is a natural aspect to being interested. An interest is something people just pick up. It can't be cultivated through willpower; it presents itself. This is one of the reasons why mindfulness isn't for everyone. Not everyone will have an interest in exploring the being mode of mind. According to Wilson (2004), thousands of impulses reach our brain every second, several dozens of which will actually enter our awareness, and we are only able to focus our attention on one of them per moment. The choice about which impulse to attend to is driven by our personal interests. Threat and stress do, of course, have a major influence on our interests, and therefore on what we choose to attend to.

11. I got the idea of using Kolb's learning model from Mark Williams, who also sometimes works with a model in which he presents inquiry as three

concentric circles around the experience (Williams, *Aims of MBCT*, unpublished handout, 2006, cited in Williams, Crane, & Soulsby, 2007, p. 57). The innermost circle is "noticing:" it's directly experiential. The next one is "dialogue" and involves exploring the effects of bringing awareness to direct experience. The outer circle is "linking" and entails exploring how this learning relates to ways of being with inner and outer experiences in daily life. As you read on, you'll see that Kolb's steps are reflected in this model. (In Segal, Williams, & Teasdale, 2013, in the chapter on inquiry, Williams revisits this model and adds to it.)

12. The psychological literature on learning distinguishes between learning through observation (in which mirror neurons play a role) and learning through play. In addition, learning through play is currently distinguished from learning through exploration (see, among others, Gray, 2011, p. 93ff.). Exploration is less informal than play and has an element of tension to it because it explores the boundaries of what is known, and also the boundaries of what's considered safe.

    Both play and exploration are authentic motives for most mammals. For example, even when rats have found the most efficient route to food, they regularly veer off this route to explore when they're not hungry. And most young mammals learn by playing. Still, play and exploration could be considered to be activities that differ only in degree, with play being naive exploration, and exploration being play for adults.

    In an evolutionary sense, learning supplements the slow, genetically defined process of natural adaptation. Plants, which don't have the same abilities to learn, can only adapt genetically, a slow process that makes them vulnerable.

    Humans have a strong drive to learn, and thus to explore and imitate. This drive, coupled with the rapid development of the human brain's processing capacity, has given humans an extreme ability to adapt, enabling us to spread out to virtually all possible climates and continents in a relatively short time span (see, for example, Harari, 2012, and McNeill & McNeill, 2003).

13. There are also educational theorists who emphasize the adventurous aspect of learning: facing unknown challenges. In this view, learning happens in an undirected way, through "chance" discoveries followed by repetition. This is how children learn—in a way that's far less structured and more intuitive and playful. The distinguishing feature of this type of learning is that it doesn't

involve consciously choosing a challenge or cognitive evaluation of the challenge. This could be called inductive learning.

Based on this premise, psychologist Jerome Bruner developed an educational format that he referred to as learning by self-discovery, with the intention to better align education with children's natural way of learning (Wood, Bruner, & Ross, 1976). To ensure that the playful aspect didn't get out of hand, he introduced the concept of scaffolding: equipping the learning environment with structured processes that would initially support and steer learning and could later be removed as learning spontaneously acquired more structure in the child. This principle is employed in mindfulness training when we initially give participants structure and direction, then gradually fade out these sources of support.

14. According to Kolb (1984), he based his own theory on a theory of learning developed by Kurt Lewin, which distinguished the following stages: (1) concrete experience; (2) observations and reflections; (3) formations of abstract concepts and generalizations; and (4) testing the implications of these concepts in new situations.

When Kolb was developing his theory, he was a professor of management studies at the University of Massachusetts, and his model was intended to be applied in the field of social change processes and leadership development. Accordingly, he transformed stage 2 into active experimentation, and stage 3 into reflective observation (Hendriksen, 2007, pp. 19–23). Kolb's model would later be applied to learning and change processes on a much broader scale. (Kolb's theory also drew on the work of educational theorists John Dewey and Jean Piaget.)

Kolb gained prominence through his personality-based model of learning styles, described in chapter 1, which is closely related to his experiential learning model. Both of these models, either jointly or separately, have been incorporated into numerous other models of learning and change. Kolb has also shown an interest in mindfulness.

15. Buddhist tradition emphasizes wanting (or desiring). The five hindrances detailed in this chapter are versions of wanting. Still, the problem lies in the realm of the "I," rather than the realm of wanting: the illusion of an autonomous self is the ultimate cause of suffering. We can't have "I want" without self.

Nevertheless, inquiry generally doesn't lead to exploration of the illusion of self. Mindfulness training would overshoot its objective if it did, since the idea that the self doesn't actually exist would be so alien and scary to most participants that it would lead to major resistance. Perhaps the idea of a "self" is so ingrained, and exploration of it is therefore so alien, that the possibility that there is no self simply doesn't occur to people. So it's rare for an exploration of how we are not our thoughts, our pain, and so on to lead to questions like "If I'm not all of that, what am I?" even though this would be a logical follow-up question.

People are generally focused on easing the symptoms of suffering, not on letting go of the self—even though attachment to the self is the ultimate cause of symptoms. So tread with care if you want to put the subject of not-self on the agenda. Participants will already be quite extended when inquiry leads them to the basic projections of the self: manifestations of wanting this moment to be different.

Finally, to be clear, the "wanting" that leads to suffering cannot be equated with the desires of the heart. Both are forms of guiding energy and could be called "wanting," but they come from different sources (reactivity versus saying yes, or embracing) and are therefore completely different in nature. In Buddhist traditions, desires of the heart are referred to as wholesome desires.

16. Of the five hindrances, the Buddha identified three as root causes of suffering: desire, aversion, and doubt, the latter in the sense of disorientation or being in the dark. So, is it five hindrances or three? As with many similar sets of Buddhist concepts, it is more about an elaboration of nuances than about the essential differences. In this case, the hindrances are all flowers growing in the soil of the human condition. And, to be clear, difficult emotions aren't hindrances. Emotions, including fear, grief, and anger, are part of life and can come and go without triggering judgments or reactions. It is our resistance to emotions or clinging to them—in short, our reactivity to emotions—that creates the hindrances, not emotions themselves.

17. The only thing you can control somewhat is a preassessment of whether your profile (e.g., gender, professional background, and training mode) will attune with a given participant. Sometimes you can tell in advance that a specific participant would probably be better served by a different setting that's a better fit for that participant's learning style or level of understanding. That said,

participants generally adapt to the setting, including to the teacher's style. In fact, if your style initially clashes somewhat with a participant's personal preferences, in the long run this may very well strengthen the learning process, rather than undermine it. A bit of discomfort can sometimes trigger people to leave their comfort zone and allow new experiences in.

18. In the Buddhist tradition, adjusting the teaching style to meet trainees' needs is referred to as *upaya*, meaning "skillful use of means." *Upaya* calls for offering the appropriate path for developing insight. The Buddha recognized the value of *upaya*, applied himself to it, and was a true master in it, as revealed in his discourses found in the Pali Canon. When propagating the dhamma, the Buddha zoomed in to the level of understanding of the individual listener, used metaphors appropriate to the listener's perception, and left out anything that fell outside of the listener's level of understanding. He also adjusted the topic to suit the audience, teaching farmers the value of generosity (*dana*), monarchs the value of moral discipline (*sila*), and renunciates, who had already exchanged worldly life for contemplation, the value of meditation (*bhavana*). Although the apparent form and even the topic of the teaching differed dramatically depending on the audience, the core always remained true to his message. This is *upaya*.

19. This quotation is from *Healing from Within*, an episode in the series Healing and the Mind. That episode offers a fine example of skillful use of words. Moyers (1993) expresses the reservations many viewers may have in his questions: "A friend of mine who read your book said, "You know, he says that we should relax into…into physical discomfort. I don't want to relax into physical discomfort. I don't want any discomfort." Kabat-Zinn replies, "Well, lots of luck…. Maybe medicine has some magic pill which will make his discomfort go away…. But the people we see in the clinic have been that route and they haven't gotten satisfaction."

20. In that same vein, Kabat-Zinn avoids the word widely used for Buddhist practice, "dhamma:" "I should stress that I do not use the word 'Dharma' with our patients, or when I am talking to a group of mainstream professionals…. But paying attention, and what it means to be truly human, and mindfulness, and states of mind such as wakefulness: people understand such concepts without any resistance, and without having to appeal to an ideological or cultural shift in perspective" (1999, pp. 230–231).

21. Of course, in some contexts an excess of information can be used to break through people's resistance. Examples include during dynamic group therapy or when breaking down anxiety and avoidance patterns. However, even in these contexts this technique must always be employed with great care, as there's a chance of traumatization or retraumatization. When that happens, the cure is worse than the disease, despite any initial appearance of success. In any case, forcing a breakthrough isn't part of a mindfulness teacher's toolbox, if only because it requires taking the role of a therapist, which isn't compatible with the role of a teacher. Ultimately, mindfulness is about exploring for oneself, not about being directed toward a certain goal.

References

Bartley, T. (2012). *Mindfulness-based cognitive therapy for cancer: Gently turning towards.* Chichester, UK: John Wiley and Sons.

Batchelor, S. (1997). *Buddhism without beliefs: A contemporary guide to awakening.* New York: Riverhead Books.

Cornelisse, P. (2009). *Taal is zeg maar helemaal mijn ding* [You could say language is my kind of thing]. Amsterdam: Uitgeverij Contact.

Cornelisse, P. (2012). *En dan nog iets* [One more thing]. Amsterdam: Uitgeverij Contact.

Crane, R. (2010). Mindfulness-based professional practice and teacher competency in the UK—Past, present, and future (PowerPoint presentation). Bangor, Wales: Bangor University. Retrieved February 11, 2016, from https://www.bangor.ac.uk/mindfulness/documents/rcranekeynoteapr2011.pdf.

Crane, R. S., Kuyken, W., Hastings, R. P., Rothwell, N., & Williams, M. G. (2010). Training teachers to deliver mindfulness-based interventions: Learning from the UK experience. *Mindfulness, 1*(2), 74–86.

Crane, R. S., Kuyken, W., Williams, J. M., Hastings, R. P., Cooper, L., & Fennell, M. J. V. (2011). Competence in teaching mindfulness-based courses: Concepts, development, and assessment. *Mindfulness, 3*(1), 76–84.

Crane, R., Soulsby, J., Kuyken, W., Williams, M., & Eames, C., et al. (2012, March). *The Bangor, Exeter & Oxford Mindfulness-Based Interventions Teaching Assessment Criteria (MBI-TAC) for assessing the competence and adherence of mindfulness-based class-based teaching.* Retrieved January 26, 2016, from https://www.bangor.ac.uk/mindfulness/documents/MBI-TACMay2012.pdf.

Dijksterhuis, A. (2008). *Het slimme onbewuste* [The smart subconscious]. Amsterdam: Uitgeverij Bert Bakker.

Ericsson, K. A., Krampe, R. T., & Tesch-Römer, C. (1990). The role of deliberate practice in the acquisition of expert performance. *Psychological Review, 100*(3), 363–406.

Germer, C. (2009). *The mindful path to self-compassion: Freeing yourself from destructive thoughts and emotions.* New York: Guilford.

Gladwell, M. (2005). *Blink: The power of thinking without thinking.* New York: Back Bay Books.

Gladwell, M. (2008). *Outliers: The story of success.* New York: Little, Brown.

Goldstein, J., & Kornfield, J. (2001). *Seeking the heart of wisdom: The path of insight meditation.* Boston: Shambhala.

Goleman, D. (2002). *Primal leadership: Realizing the power of emotional intelligence.* Boston: Harvard Business Press.

Goleman, D. (2013). *Focus: The hidden driver of excellence.* New York: HarperCollins.

Gray, P. (2011). *Psychology,* 6th edition. New York: Worth Publishers.

Harari, Y. N. (2012). *From animals into gods: A brief history of humankind.* Charleston, SC: CreateSpace.

Hayes, S. C., Strosahl, K. D., & Wilson, K. G. (1999). *Acceptance and commitment therapy: An experiential approach to behavior change.* New York: Guilford.

Hendriksen, H. (2007). *Cirkelen rond Kolb, het begeleiden van leerprocessen* [Circling around Kolb, facilitating learning processes]. Houten, the Netherlands: Nelissen.

Honey, P., & Mumford, A. (1982). *The manual of learning styles.* Maidenhead, UK: Honey Press.

Howe, G. L. (Ed.). (1885). *The golden key to prosperity and happiness: A complete educator embracing thorough instruction in every branch of knowledge.* Chicago: Metropolitan Publishing.

Huber, C. (2000). *Zijn wie je bent. Eerste stappen op het pad van Zen* [The key: And the name of the key is willingness]. Utrecht, the Netherlands: Kosmos.

Iacoboni, M. (2008). *Mirroring people: The new science of how we connect with others.* New York: Farrar, Straus, and Giroux.

Kabat-Zinn, J. (1990). *Full catastrophe living: Using the wisdom of your body and mind to face stress, pain, and illness.* New York: Delta.

Kabat-Zinn, J. (1994). *Wherever you go, there you are: Mindfulness meditation in everyday life.* New York: Hyperion.

Kabat-Zinn, J. (1996). Mindfulness and meditation: What it is, what it isn't, and its role in health care and medicine. In Y. Haruki & M. Suzuki (Eds.), *Comparative and psychological study on meditation.* Delft, the Netherlands: Eburon.

Kabat-Zinn, J. (1999). Indra's net at work: The mainstreaming of dharma practice in society. In G. Watson, S. Batchelor, & G. Claxton (Eds.), *The psychology of awakening: Buddhism, science and our day-to-day lives.* London: Rider.

Kabat-Zinn, J. (2003). Mindfulness-based interventions in context: Past, present, and future. *Clinical Psychology: Science and Practice, 10*(2), 144–156.

Kabat-Zinn, J. (2005). *Coming to our senses: Healing ourselves and the world through mindfulness.* New York: Hyperion.

Kabat-Zinn, J. (2010). Foreword. In D. McCown, D. Reibel, & M. S. Micozzi (Eds.), *Teaching mindfulness. A practical guide for clinicians and educators.* New York: Springer.

Kabat-Zinn, J. (2011). Some reflections on the origins of MBSR, skillful means, and the trouble with maps. *Contemporary Buddhism 12*(1), 281–306.

Kofman, F. (2006). *Conscious business: How to build value through values.* Boulder, CO: Sounds True.

Kolb, D. (1984). *Experiential learning: Experience as the source of learning and development.* Upper Saddle River, NJ: Prentice Hall.

Kornfield, J. (2008). *The wise heart: A guide to the universal teachings of Buddhist psychology.* New York: Bantam.

Koster, F. (2010). Retraite anekdotes en (over)concentratie [Retreat anecdotes and (over)concentration]. *Simsara, 12*(2), 4–5.

Kramer, G. (2007). *Insight dialogue: The interpersonal path to freedom.* Boston: Shambhala.

Leary, T. (1966). Programmed communication during experiences with DMT. *Psychedelic Review 8*, 83–95.

Linehan, M. M. (1993). *Cognitive-behavioral treatment of borderline personality disorder.* New York: Guilford.

Maex, E. (2011). The Buddhist roots of mindfulness training: A practitioner's view. *Contemporary Buddhism, 12*(1), 165–175.

McCown, D., Reibel, D., & Micozzi, M. S. (2010). *Teaching mindfulness: A practical guide for clinicians and educators.* New York: Springer.

McNeill, J., & McNeill, W. (2003). *The human web: A bird's-eye view of world history.* New York: W. W. Norton.

Moreno, J. L. (1953). *Who shall survive? Foundations of sociometry, group psychotherapy, and socio-drama.* Beacon, NY: Beacon House. Available at http://www .asgpp.org/docs/wss/wss.html.

Moyers, B. (1993). Healing from within. Episode 3 of *Healing and the mind.* New York: Ambrose Video. Transcript retrieved January 26, 2016, from http://bill moyers.com/content/healing-from-within.

Neff, K. (2011). *Self-compassion: Stop beating yourself up and leave insecurity behind.* New York: HarperCollins.

Nhat Hanh, T. (1987). *Interbeing: Commentaries on the Tiep Hien precepts.* Berkeley, CA: Parallax Press.

Palmer, P. (1998). *The courage to teach: Exploring the inner landscape of a teacher's life.* San Francisco: Jossey-Bass.

Parks, T. (2011). *Teach us to sit still: A skeptic's search for health and healing.* New York: Rodale.

Polanyi, M. (2009). *The tacit dimension.* Chicago: University of Chicago Press.

Ruijgrok-Lupton, P. E., Crane, R. S., & Dorjee, D. (2015). *Impact of mindfulness teacher training on MBSR participant wellbeing outcomes and course satisfaction.* Poster presented at the Mind and Life European Summer Research Institute, August–September 2015, Chiemsee, Germany. Retrieved on January 25, 2016, from https://www.bangor.ac.uk/mindfulness/documents/EvaRuijgrok-Lupton ImpactTeacherTrainingonMBSRwellbeing.pdf.

Rumi. (1997). *The illuminated Rumi,* trans. C. Barks. New York: Broadway Books.

Rumi. (2005). *The essential Rumi,* trans. C. Barks. New York: HarperCollins.

Santorelli, S. F. (Ed.). (2014). *Mindfulness-based stress reduction (MBSR): Standards of practice.* Massachusetts: Center for Mindfulness in Medicine, Health Care, and Society, University of Massachusetts Medical School.

Segal, Z. W., Williams, M. G., & Teasdale, J. D. (2002). *Mindfulness-based cognitive therapy for depression: A new approach to preventing relapse.* New York: Guilford.

Segal, Z. W., Williams, M. G., & Teasdale, J. D. (2013). *Mindfulness-based cognitive therapy for depression,* 2nd edition. New York: Guilford.

Siegel, D. (2007). *The mindful brain: Reflection and attunement in the cultivation of well-being.* New York: W. W. Norton.

Sitskoorn, M. (2008). *Het maakbare brein* [The malleable brain]. Amsterdam: Bert Bakker.

Stahl, B., & Goldstein, E. (2010). *A mindfulness-based stress reduction workbook.* Oakland, CA: New Harbinger.

Sternberg, P., & Garcia, A. (2000). *Sociodrama: Who's in your shoes?* Westport, CT: Praeger.

Teasdale, J. D., Williams, M. G., & Segal, Z. W. (2014). *The mindful way workbook: An eight-week program to free yourself from depression and emotional distress.* New York: Guilford.

Tolle, E. (2003). *Stillness speaks.* Novato, CA: New World Library.

Vygotsky, L. S. (1986). *Thought and language.* Cambridge, MA: MIT Press.

Whitman, W. (1855). *Leaves of grass.* Brooklyn, NY: Eakins Press.

Williams, M., Crane, R., & Soulsby, J. (2007). *The mindfulness-based curriculum in practice: Summary outline, intentions, and rationale for practices.* Bangor and Oxford University, unpublished manuscript.

Williams, M., Teasdale, J., Segal, Z., & Kabat-Zinn, J. (2007). *The mindful way through depression: Freeing yourself from chronic unhappiness.* New York: Guilford.

Wilson, T. (2004). *Strangers to ourselves: Discovering the adaptive unconscious.* Cambridge, MA: Belknap Press.

Wood, D., Bruner, J. S., & Ross, G. (1976). The role of tutoring in problem solving. *Journal of Child Psychology and Psychiatry, 17*(2), 89–100.

Rob Brandsma is a licensed health psychologist, pedagogue, and author. He is cofounder and codirector of the Amsterdam *Centrum voor Mindfulness* (Netherlands) and head of its teacher training programs. As a mindfulness teacher, he has long-standing experience in teaching mindfulness-based applications, such as mindfulness-based stress reduction (MBSR) and mindfulness-based cognitive therapy (MBCT), as well as compassion-based programs.

Index

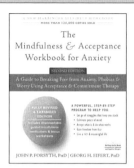
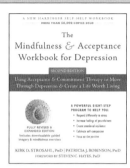

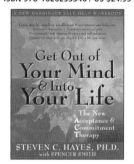
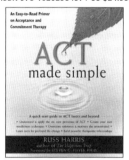